Helion & Company Limited
Unit 8 Amherst Business Centre
Budbrooke Road
Warwick
CV34 5WE
England
Tel. 01926 499 619
Email: info@helion.co.uk
Website: www.helion.co.uk
Twitter: @helionbooks
Visit our blog http://blog.helion.co.uk/

Text © John Rodgaard 2023
Photographs © as individually credited
Colour artwork © Anderson Subtil 2023
Maps © Paul Hewitt and Tom Cooper 2023

Designed and typeset by Farr out
    Publications, Wokingham, Berkshire
Cover design Paul Hewitt, Battlefield Design
    (www.battlefield-design.co.uk)

ISBN 978-1-914377-09-9

British Library Cataloguing-in-Publication
    Data
A catalogue record for this book is available
    from the British Library

We always welcome receiving book
proposals from prospective authors.

CONTENTS

Note: In order to simplify the use of this book, all names, locations and geographic designations are as provided in *The Times World Atlas*, or other traditionally accepted major sources of reference, as of the time of described events.

Dedication

to

Claire and Erin

who waited on the Neapolitan shore for my return.

ABBREVIATIONS

AFSOUTH	Allied Forces Southern Europe (NATO)		NM	Nautical mile (2,000 yards)
AGI	Auxiliary General Intelligence		NSA	Naval Support Activity
AGS	Survey ship		ONR	Office of Naval Research
ASW	Anti-Submarine Warfare		OOB	order of battle
CDR	Commander		OOD	Officer of the Deck
CIC	Combat Information Center		OPINTEL	operational intelligence
COMCORTRON 8	Commander, Escort Squadron 8		OT	Oceanographic System Technician
COMSIXTHFLT	Commander Sixth Fleet		PD	periscope depth
CORTRON	Escort Squadron		REFTRA	refresher training
CVBG	Aircraft carrier battle group		SIGINT	signals intelligence
CVS	Anti-submarine aircraft carrier		SLOC	sea lines of communication
DASH	Drone Anti-Submarine Helicopter		SOFAR	Sound Fixing and Ranging
DE	Destroyer Escort		SOSUS	Sound Surveillance System
DIW	Dead in the Water		SS	conventionally powered attack submarine
DoD	Department of Defense		SSBN	nuclear-armed and -powered fleet ballistic
FOSIF	Fleet Ocean Surveillance			missile submarine
	Information Facility		SSG	conventionally powered cruise
FRAM	Fleet Rehabilitation and Modernization			missile submarine
GITMO	US Naval Station, Guantanamo Bay		SSGN	nuclear-powered cruise missile submarine
I&W	indications and warning		SSM	surface-to-surface missile
ITASS	Interim Towed Array Surveillance System		SS-N-x	NATO designation for Soviet surface-to-
LCDR	Lieutenant Commander			surface naval missile (followed by number)
LOFAR	Low Frequency Analysis and Recording		SURTASS	Surveillance Towed Array Sonar System
MAD	Magnetic Anomaly Detection		TASS	Towed Array Surveillance System
MPA	maritime patrol aircraft		USN	United States Navy
NAS	Naval Air Station		USS	United States Ship
NATO	North Atlantic Treaty Organization		VADM	Vice Admiral
NAVSTA	US Naval Station			

AUTHOR'S INTRODUCTION

The story of three US Navy destroyer escorts (DEs) and their crews, comprising Escort Squadron 8, is a tale that took place at the height of the Cold War – specifically the Cold War below, on and above the Mediterranean Sea. Obsolete, except for the experimental anti-submarine warfare (ASW) sensor that each ship carried, the USS *Hammerberg* (DE-1015), USS *Courtney* (DE-1021) and USS *Lester* (DE-1022) were ordered to the Mediterranean Sea to demonstrate the potential of a sensor – a technology relying on a passive towed array detection sensor system of microphones or hydrophones that the Navy officially designated as the Interim Towed Array Surveillance System, or ITASS. However, the crews of the ships simply called them 'Noodles' or 'Tails'.

These 'tailships' entered *Mare Nostrum* in the autumn of 1970, and it was during this period in the long maritime history of the inland sea that the US and North Atlantic Treaty Organization (NATO) navies saw a naval operational environment characterised by the most intense concentration of Soviet submarines and surface ships outside of Soviet home waters. In fact, the years between 1970 and 1973 saw the tailships and the ships of the Sixth Fleet operating against the largest Soviet naval presence outside of its home waters in the history of the Soviet Navy or its tsarist predecessor, whose navy periodically operated in the Mediterranean during the eighteenth and nineteenth centuries. The Mediterranean became the focal point in the great naval rivalry of the United States and its NATO allies against the Soviet Union's *Voyenno-morskoi flot*.

From the standpoint of modernity, the tailships, built in the 1950s, were already considered obsolete by the time they deployed to the Mediterranean. Configured as convoy escorts for warfare at sea in the 1950s, these ships were not competitive with their Soviet counterparts, or with many of their contemporaries in the NATO navies. The Dealey/Courtney-class DEs did not have the electronic sensors, speed or weapons of their antagonists in the Mediterranean, such as the Soviet Navy's Mirka and Petya-class light frigates, or what the Soviet Navy classified as *Storezhevoy Korabl* (SKR) types – escort ships.

Nevertheless, the tailships of Escort Squadron 8 would often go head-to-head with these frigates or other superior classes of Soviet warships while conducting 'bystander' or shadowing operations against them. When Sixth Fleet destroyers and DEs routinely conducted these intelligence-gathering operations, the *Courtney*, *Hammerberg* and *Lester* were frequently taken from their primary ASW mission and directed to conduct these operations, with all three reporting numerous near collisions, while their Soviet antagonists would attempt to block or 'shoulder' them away from larger Soviet warships or surfaced submarines. Indeed, the *Courtney* was involved in a violation of the 'Incident at Sea Agreement' shortly after that agreement was signed between the US and Soviet Union.[1]

These tailships proved so successful in detecting, classifying and identifying Soviet submarines that the US Navy committed resources to refining the capability of passive towed array sensors. The navy developed and sent to sea the AN/SQR-15 Towed Array Surveillance System (TASS) and the AN/SQR-18 Surveillance Towed Array Sonar System (SURTASS).

The tailships also ushered in two new designs of ocean surveillance ships. The mono-hulled Stalwart-class and the twin-hulled (catamaran) Victorious-class were built specifically to operate SURTASS.[2] Also, in the 1980s, the AN/SQR-19 TACTAS (Tactical Towed Array System) was developed and carried aboard US Navy cruisers, destroyers and frigates as well as Canadian, Japanese and Spanish destroyers and frigates.[3] The legacy that the three tailships left continues through the twenty-first century.

Additionally, the squadron operated in a sea surrounded by increasing tensions in the Middle East. Along the North African shore, the revolutionary governments of Algeria, Tunisia, Libya and Egypt were hostile to US and NATO ships operating off their coasts. Libya and Egypt hosted elements of the Soviet Naval Air Force and provided 'fair weather anchorages' and logistic support for the ships and submarines of the Soviet Navy's 5th *Eskadra* (Squadron). Syria provided port and yard facilities for the *Eskadra*, as well as airfields for its supporting naval air arm. Arab-Israeli tensions were still running extremely high as a result of the 1967 Arab-Israeli War and the Jordanian Crisis of 1970; a crisis that greeted the tailships when they entered the Mediterranean.[4] The effects of these crises would ripple across the waters of the Mediterranean and through Europe in general.

While the squadron was stationed in the southern Italian port of Naples, the Palestinian Black September Organization created terror across Europe during the summer of 1972, including the massacre of the Israeli Olympic athletes in Munich, West Germany. That summer would see sailors of the squadron spending many a night in their Neapolitan homeport standing anti-terrorist watches with loaded weapons, whilst the pinging of an active sonar system from one of the ships would echo throughout the hulls of the moored ships, which, it was hoped, would discourage would-be swimmers wanting to plant explosive devices on ship hulls.

For many of the junior sailors aboard the three ships of Escort Squadron 8, it was their first time overseas. However, the more senior enlisted and officer personnel had made at least one six-month deployment to the Mediterranean. A few were even Vietnam veterans. For all, it was the first time to call a foreign port their own homeport. Many of the married officers and mid-level and senior petty officers took advantage of US Navy policy, the Forward Deployment Programme (FDP), and brought their families to set up house in Naples.[5] The FDP also allowed the many bachelor sailors, both officers and enlisted, to rent apartments in the city or out in Naples' suburbs.

The objective of this book is simply to tell the story of these three ships and their men within the context of the greater events of the Cold War at Sea in the Mediterranean; the successes and failures of operating the first generation of passive towed array sonar – hunting the Soviets with a microphone.

As a young sailor aboard the USS *Courtney*, DE-1021, I wasn't thinking of anything more than trying to improve my professional skills as a Radarman/Operations Specialist and apply what I learned whilst aboard to be a better sailor.

Being a husband and father, I took advantage of the Navy's Forward Deployment Programme, and arranged to have my wife and baby daughter accompany me on this tour of duty. As there was no government housing, we rented an apartment from a local landlord through the Naval Support Activity (NSA) Naples housing office. We could only afford an apartment in a rundown northern suburb of Naples, which was conveniently adjacent to the Navy's commissary and exchange. It was our first time overseas together. Looking back after 50 years, I think we had a great adventure. Therefore, the story that unfolds in the ensuing pages is not only a story about tailships' operations, it is about the men – many with families – who set up home life, living among the population in one of the great cities of Europe.

I knew that my ship and its sisters, the *Hammerberg* and the *Lester*, were doing important work. The reason that three engineeringly challenged, obsolescent DEs were brought back into commission was to conduct an extensive operational test of a state-of-the-art passive underwater sensor system – ITASS. As a Radarman Third Class working as one of two watch supervisors within *Courtney*'s Combat Information Center (CIC), I had a front-row seat for viewing the system's operational and tactical capabilities during the time when the Soviet Union had nearly a dozen submarines operating in the Mediterranean on any given day.

Courtney and its sisters would often sortie out of Naples to operate their tails in the Ionian or Tyrrhenian Seas. At times, they would operate between Crete and Colonel Mu'ammar Al-Quadhdhāfi's Libya, or west into the Balearic Sea toward the dictatorship of Franco's Spain.

The length of time away from port depended upon the operational intelligence provided by the Fleet Ocean Surveillance Information Facility (FOSIF) Rota, Spain and Sixth Fleet tactical assets. Working with Sixth Fleet's ASW planning staff at Naples, Escort Squadron 8 staff would determine the best areas in which to stream the ITASS arrays against Soviet submarines.

Additionally, the little tailships were tasked to conduct 'special hydrographic' missions; one conducted in August 1972 would see them operating in the Atlantic off the Iberian Peninsula. They collected acoustic data that would support the installation of a fixed underwater passive sonar system array, Sound Surveillance System (SOSUS) and its land-based facility in the Eastern Atlantic.[6]

Sixth Fleet would also have a say as to where the ships would operate during the many exercises it conducted throughout the year. Sixth Fleet would send them ahead to an area in the Mediterranean prior to the arrival of its carrier battle groups (CVBGs). Their mission was to detect and track US submarines playing the role of Soviet submarines during the course of the exercise. In these exercises, as well as when directly operating against Soviet submarines, my ship, *Courtney*, would operate with one of its sisters and with P-3 Orion ASW aircraft.

As a small part of the Cold War at Sea, Escort Squadron 8, its men and their tailships participated in an unseen underwater struggle between superpowers. This struggle evolved technologically in response to the maturation of the submarine as the primary threat at sea. It is my hope that you, the reader, will come away after reading this story with a greater appreciation of the day-to-day service of the men who served on three little ships on a sea that saw daily encounters between naval forces of the world's two superpowers; encounters that could threaten to turn the Cold War at Sea into a hot one.

1

THE COLD WAR AT SEA

The Cold War that dominated world political, economic, and military activities for almost half of the 20th century was, in many respects, 'fought' at sea.[1]

The first five decades of the post-Second World War world were dominated by the Cold War, pitching the Soviet Union and its client states against the US and its allies. There were many facets to this Cold War. Economically, it was free market capitalism versus centralised government control of the economy. Another aspect was that two large military/political alliance blocs of countries were created. One was NATO, which the US and its Second World War Western allies created to counter Soviet expansionism. The second was the Warsaw Pact, which the Soviet Union formed in response to West Germany becoming a member of NATO.

Each alliance waged massive propaganda and psychological campaigns against one another. Each bloc conducted extensive espionage and intelligence-gathering operations to determine each other's strengths and weaknesses. The competition even went into space. The 'space race', as it was known, would lead to the orbiting of astronauts and cosmonauts, communication, reconnaissance and scientific research satellites, and to the US landing men on the moon. The competition between the two blocs even extended to sports – the Olympic Games come to mind. However, the most prominent facet of the Cold War was the colossal military buildup of nuclear and conventional forces wielding weapons of mass destruction previously unknown in human history.

The Cold War propelled former wartime allies, who had fought against Fascism/Nazism, into a relationship characterised by intense distrust and hostility; hostility that saw outright regional conflicts, or proxy wars, across the globe. One facet of this Cold War was the Cold War at Sea.

The Cold War at Sea constituted part of the United States' grand strategic vision and its corresponding military strategy, which was encapsulated in what became known as the Containment Strategy. The renowned US diplomat and Russian expert, George Kennan, first articulated this strategic approach toward the Soviet Union. Believing there could not be a way of working with each other – a *modus vivendi* of sorts – he wrote that the US and its allies should embark on a geopolitical and military grand strategy to contain Soviet expansive tendencies. In his testimony before the US Congress in 1947, Kennan stated that the US should "support free peoples who are resisting attempted subjugation … by outside forces".[2]

In April 1950, the United States' National Security Council Report, NSC-68, articulated Kennan's vision. The report argued "that the best course of action was to respond in kind [confronting the hostile design of the Soviets] with a massive build-up of the US military and its weaponry".[3] NSC-68 outlined several courses of action:

Including a return to isolationism; war; continued diplomatic efforts to negotiate with the Soviets; or 'the rapid building up of the political, economic, and military strength of the free world'. This last approach would allow the United States to attain sufficient strength to deter Soviet aggression. In the event that an armed conflict with the Communist bloc did arise, the United States could then successfully defend its territory and overseas interests.[4]

When the United States decided to build up its political, economic and military strength to counter Soviet expansionism, the US Navy developed "a maritime strategy to support Joint Staff [The Joint Chiefs of Staff] planning for a confrontation with the Soviet Union".[5] It was a blue water strategy that would contribute to the overall containment strategy by conducting offensive operations with aircraft carriers capable of launching aircraft that could carry nuclear bombs to strike the Soviet homeland.

During the first two decades of the Cold War, US Navy and Royal Navy CVBGs could freely operate in the Norwegian Sea, the Mediterranean and/or the North Pacific without too much concern that Soviet air and or naval assets would track them. However, that began to change when first, the Soviet Union developed its own nuclear weapons capability, and with that capability, Soviet strategy saw that the next war would not be a conventional one. It would quickly escalate to the use of nuclear weapons, to include the use of nuclear weapons at sea.[6]

Second, to counter US and British CVBGs, the Soviet Navy, under the leadership of Admiral Sergei Gorshkov, adopted an asymmetrical approach, "what the Soviets described as a scientific-technical 'revolution' in military affairs".[7] Captain First Rank V. Anufriyev of the Soviet Navy described the approach in a classified article that appeared in a USSR Ministry of Defence publication in 1962 and was translated in a former Top Secret Central Intelligence Agency (CIA) memorandum disseminated in 1977:[8]

Project 613 (Whiskey-class) patrol submarine. (NARA)

Project 644 (Whiskey twin-cylinder) SSG. (US DoD Image Database)

As a consequence of the high mobility of the carrier strike large units, the concealment of their actions, and their deeply echeloned defense, the organization of combat against them at sea is a very complex and difficult matter that obviously will require a considerable effort of the forces not only from the navy but also from the other branches of our Armed Forces.[9]

This revolution kept one part of Stalin's plan for a large conventional Soviet Navy; it continued building submarines: "The medium-range Whiskey (Project 613)-class diesel boats – incorporating features of the German Type XXI U-boat … were mass-produced … and when the last unit was completed in 1957 a total of 236 had been built."[10]

An earlier classified CIA Intelligence Memorandum disseminated in 1971 had come to the same conclusion:

The Soviets view the submarine as their primary naval weapon system. The Soviet navy now has some 335 submarines, the largest submarine fleet in the world. About 55 of them have a strategic strike mission. The remainder – some 280 attack submarines – is the principal force for strategic defense against Polaris ballistic missile submarines, for countering aircraft carriers, and for interdicting sea lines of communication. The attack submarine force is also an important contributor to ocean surveillance.[11]

Several of the Whiskey-class submarines were retrofitted with surface-to-surface (SS) anti-ship cruise missiles; the P-5 *Pyatyorka* (the NATO-designated SS-N-3 Shaddock) anti-ship cruise missile was fitted onto this submarine.[12]

The Soviet Navy modified several of its destroyers and small fast attack craft to be fitted onboard with the Soviet Army's SS missile the P-1 *Strelka*, which was designated by NATO as the SS-N-1 Scrubber. The Soviet Navy quickly replaced the Scrubber with the first mass-produced anti-ship cruise missile, the P-15 *Termit*, designated by NATO as the SS-N-2 Styx. This missile was also installed onboard Soviet Navy destroyers and small fast attack craft.[13]

In addition to arming destroyers and submarines with anti-ship cruise missiles, the Soviets developed and operationalised air-to-surface missiles (ASMs). They were fitted on the Soviets' first jet-powered heavy bomber, the Tupolev Tu-16 – NATO-designated Badger – with the first, the Raduga KS-1 *Komet*, designated by NATO as the AS-1 Kennel (ASM).[14]

However, as Captain Anufriyev wrote, this revolutionary combined arms concept required:

> constant surveillance of the strike carriers and their support forces even in peacetime. This will enable us to determine at any given moment, even if only approximately, the area in which they are located and the probable nature of their activity. With this information we can then deduce correctly whether they are preparing for a surprise attack and within what time frame and from which areas this attack should be expected.[15]

To provide a reliable, operational indications and warning (I&W) and a tactical tracking and targeting capability of US and British carrier strike groups, the Soviets established a two-step intelligence collection process. At the operational level, the first step was to surveil US naval bases and associated infrastructure to determine whether carrier strike groups and supporting forces were preparing to depart, and the second was to deploy a tactical at-sea tracking and targeting capability.

Anufriyev's article also identified the following operational I&W indicators of US Navy intentions:

- planned or unplanned exercises of large strike units in US coastal waters;
- a considerable increase in the combat training of all operational formations;
- the rapid and concealed movement of diverse types of large units out to sea;
- the mobilisation of a considerable number of ships from the merchant fleet;
- strengthening of security at naval bases, individual ports, and the most important naval depots, with the partial evacuation of the families of servicemen and civil personnel;
- the reduction or complete cancellation of leave for the personnel of operational large units;
- a sharp increase in air defence forces and means;
- preparation and transfer of shore staff personnel of the fleet to sheltered command posts;
- the preparation and putting into service of a large number of combat ships and naval aircraft from the reserve.[16]

Several sources were available to the Soviets to provide them with operational I&W regarding US Navy intentions at US naval bases and operations in US coastal waters. One source was categorised as open source intelligence. Through newspapers, radio and television, it was possible to put together indications of ship movements. Another source of intelligence was the Soviet Union's signals intelligence (SIGINT) collection station located on Cuba. Additionally, the Soviets deployed spy ships along the US east and west coasts; ships that could give operational warning regarding US Navy ship movements. Finally, the Soviets could obtain information on US Navy ship movements from agents and intelligence officers assigned to Soviet embassies and consulates.

Space was another source of gathering intelligence on US and NATO navies: "Since the early 1960s, space systems have become an integral part of Soviet military capabilities, providing intelligence collection, command and control, targeting of strategic and conventional weapons, navigation, and warning of an Inter-Continental Ballistic Missile launch."[17]

During the 1960s and through the mid-1970s, the Soviet Union's space-based intelligence collection systems such as photoreconnaissance satellite systems became available to Soviet naval intelligence. These early satellites averaged about two weeks in orbit.[18] They were film-based imagers that brought photographic film back to earth to be processed and analysed. These satellites could photograph US and NATO naval bases and obtain indications of force composition and at-sea readiness. However, the time delay between the first film exposed over the intended target and the last film being exposed would be more than a week. Adding the time for de-orbiting, recovering the negatives to be processed and then analysis of the film, the value to Soviet awareness of US/NATO naval intentions could support only strategic/operational intelligence-level awareness.[19]

Additionally, the Soviets developed orbiting rudimentary electronic ocean reconnaissance satellites (EORSATS) that could detect electronic transmissions. EORSATS collected electronic transmissions emitted from aircraft and ship radars, while radar ocean reconnaissance satellites (RORSATS) obtained radar images of ships. Radar image resolution was sufficient to detect and classify the ship as a small or large target (i.e., determining whether the target imaged was large enough to be an aircraft carrier). This combined capability could give the Soviets operational and quasi-tactical warning.[20]

At the tactical level, a reconnaissance variant of the large four-engine, turboprop-powered strategic bomber, the Tupolev-designed and NATO-designated Tu-95 Bear bomber, provided the Soviet Navy with the capability to track and target US carrier strike groups. The Tu-142 Bear F became the primary maritime reconnaissance aircraft.[21] As the Soviets developed longer-range anti-ship cruise missiles, such as the SS-N-3 Shaddock, the Bear F provided targeting (geo-positioning coordinates) information for over-the-horizon attacks. Additionally, specially built reconnaissance and surveillance ships complemented aerial reconnaissance/surveillance platforms.

The Soviet merchant marine and fishing fleets provided another source of both operational and tactical intelligence to the Soviet Navy. By the 1970s, the Soviet Union had built a large merchant navy that had its ships sailing in all the world's oceans: "In the twenty-eight years between 1946 and 1975 … the Soviet Union raised its place on the list from twenty-third to sixth largest merchant marine."[22] In addition to providing needed income as well as leveraging political influence to third world countries, "all Soviet flag ships [any and all] had the requirement to immediately report the sighting of any non-Soviet naval vessels".[23] Furthermore, "This created a global mobile monitoring capability and, compilation of such reporting over time provided a pretty good ocean surveillance capability."[24]

However, Captain Anufriyev wrote: "Therefore, to spot it [a carrier strike group] may require many days of uninterrupted scanning of a broad expanse of ocean. Not a single country, not even the strongest militarily, now has nor will it likely have in the future a sufficient amount of the force and means necessary to this kind of scanning."[25]

Nevertheless, Anufriyev failed to mention, most likely for security reasons, that Soviet space-based collection systems had the potential for shortening I&W time. Admiral Gorshkov summarised the Soviet Navy's 'revolutionary' concept: "The course taken required the construction of an ocean-going fleet, capable of carrying out offensive strategic missions. Submarines and shore-based naval aircraft, equipped with nuclear weapons [missiles or torpedoes], have a leading place in the program. Thus, there began a new stage in the development of the fleet and of its naval science."[26]

At the beginning of the Cold War, and even through the subsequent 30 years of the struggle, the US and NATO navies interpreted the Soviet Navy's revolutionary concept to mean that in wartime, Soviet submarines would interdict not only carrier and amphibious task groups, but the critical trans-Atlantic sea lines of communication (SLOC). With that perception, the US Navy and NATO navies embarked on the development of a robust ASW capability designed to conduct operations against the huge numbers of Soviet submarines that could be deployed to interdict the SLOCs.

However, this understanding was a misperception on the part of the US and NATO. Commander Robert Herrick, USN Ret, understood this, as he explained in his seminal work published in 1968, *Soviet Naval Strategy: Fifty Years of Theory and Practice*:

Regardless of this infrequently mentioned Soviet appreciation of the fact that their largely submarine navy is primarily a weapon of the strategic defense [ballistic missile submarines are part of an offensive strategy], Western writers have repeatedly portrayed the Soviet Navy as an offensive, high seas fleet designed to contest for command of the seas. It appears particularly difficult for United States and British naval officers and writers, steeped as they are in the Mahanian tradition of naval operations by high seas fleets, to appreciate the position of a weaker naval power and think realistically about the problems involved in developing and implementing a strategically defensive strategy.[27]

The B-36 Peacemaker. (US Air Force photo 040210-F-9999G-002)

USS *Forrestal*, CV-59. This photo was given to the author by the CORTRON 8 commander, Commander Virgil Snyder, USN. (Official USN photograph #709323)

As a defensive strategy, the Soviets did not intend to interdict transiting carrier strike groups, but to attack them when they came within the Soviet defence zones. These zones comprised the Norwegian Sea, the North and Baltic seas; the Sea of Japan and North Pacific and the Mediterranean Sea. In the Mediterranean, the zone was the inland sea's eastern basin, between the island of Crete and the shores of the Levant (Turkey, Syria, Israel and Egypt).

The Barbel-class submarine, the USS *Blueback*, SS-581. (NHHC 78763)

Gearing-class destroyer USS *Fiske* DD-842, with Second World War configuration and FRAM conversion. (NHHC 102953 and NHHC 102964)

TTPs, such as nuclear-powered submarines, guided missiles and the Soviet revolution in military affairs, mentioned previously, promised to alter the next war at sea in favour of the submarine.

The third battle did not start off as the US Navy and Royal Navy had expected. The immediate post-Second World War years of the late 1940s witnessed both navies suffering massive reductions in the number of operational ships, submarines and aircraft. They also faced competition for resources from their respective air forces.

For the US Navy, the competition resulted in a fight to determine which services would hold the monopoly on strategic nuclear weapons. The US Navy witnessed the cancellation of a new class of super aircraft carriers, beginning with the USS *United States*, due, in part, to the decision by the newly created Department of Defense (DoD) to rely on the US Air Force Strategic Air Command's long-range bombers to deliver nuclear bombs.

However, in the early 1950s, the US Navy began building the first super carriers with the introduction of the USS *Forrestal*, CV-59. Additionally, several of the US Navy's Second World War-designed Essex-class aircraft carriers and all three of the Midway-class carriers were modernised to operate long-range, jet-powered strike aircraft capable of delivering nuclear bombs.[30]

Also, the US and the British,

As Norman Polmar and Edward Whitman wrote: "Ironically, for some 35 years of the Cold War the US and other NATO Navies were preparing, training, and exercising to fight a Third Battle of the Atlantic. It was, however, a battle that was neither planned nor prepared for by the Soviet leadership."[28] Owen Cote has added: "The US Navy's global Cold War ASW effort therefore constituted the third great battle for control of the seas against the submarine, albeit one that remained a peacetime effort."[29]

The first two great battles for the Atlantic were against Germany's U-boats during the Great War of 1914–18 and the Second World War of 1939–45. The Allies' innovative technologies, tactics and procedures (TTPs) overcame the U-boat challenge. However, the new

with their NATO partners such as Canada and the Netherlands, began to invest in ASW technology. The US and British navies initiated major submarine and destroyer/frigate-building modification programmes, which emphasised improved active and passive sonar systems and ASW weapons possessing increased ranges. Both navies also recognised that they needed faster submarines and ASW ships to fight the anticipated Third Battle of the Atlantic. They recognised that as a platform, the submarine might prove to be best for detecting, tracking and sinking other submarines. Both navies began a two-track programme for ASW submarines. The first took the US Navy's newest Second World War-designed fleet submarines and converted them under the Greater Underwater Propulsive Power (GUPPY)

USS *Kearsarge*, CVS-33, with S-2 Tracker ASW aircraft and SH-3 Sea King ASW helicopters. (NHHC KN-13416)

programme.[31] The GUPPY conversions streamlined the hull and sail/fin to improve speed. They were also equipped with snorkels and increased battery storage capacity. The British converted their latest Second World War Amphibian-class (or A-class) submarines in the same manner.

The second track that both navies took was to design purpose-built anti-submarine submarines, or SSKs. The Royal Navy built the Porpoise-class and Oberon-class submarines. The US Navy built three SSKs based on the latest Second World War-designed hulls and GUPPY streamlining conversions. They possessed a huge bow dome that housed a passive sonar array. Additionally, the US Navy produced three advanced-hull submarines of the Barbel class.

The S-2 Tracker was the first purpose-built ASW aircraft for the US Navy. (US Navy photograph by PHC Mahlon K. Miller, USN)

Based on the prototype submarine, the USS *Albacore* AGS-569, the Barbels had a teardrop-shaped hull. This hull form would become the standard hull shape for succeeding generations of nuclear-powered submarines. With the introduction of nuclear-powered attack submarines (SSNs), the US Navy dropped the SSK concept in favour of the SSN for hunting and killing submarines.

Both navies also embarked on improving their respective surface ASW capabilities by modernising their Second World War destroyer and escort destroyer (frigate) classes, as well as building modern versions of the classes with improved sonars and weapons. What the GUPPY programme was to submarines, the US Navy's Fleet Rehabilitation and Modernization (FRAM) programme was for its Second World War destroyers. The Royal Navy also had its version of FRAM for its destroyers and frigates.

Both navies merged several technologies into both the FRAM conversions and the new classes of destroyers and escort destroyers/frigates – high-performance sonars (active and passive), lightweight ASW torpedoes, ASW rockets, helicopters and airborne drones.

Besides ASW helicopters and drones, fixed-wing aircraft and large helicopters formed a key element for the US and British ASW

The USN version of the B-24, the PB4Y. (NHHC 80-G-44506)

Lockheed P-2V Neptune. (NHHC NH 92979)

High-Frequency Direction Finding (HF/DF, or 'Huff Duff') to detect U-boat radio transmissions. Both systems could obtain a line of bearing on the U-boat, which they could then attack by aircraft firing machine guns and/or rockets, following up with aircraft dropping depth charges or the newly developed torpedo that homed in on the submarine's engine noises. The escorting destroyers would manoeuvre to the last known position to ensure the kill.

The US Navy reintroduced the HUK concept in the 1950s, modifying nine of its Second World War Essex-class aircraft carriers into ASW carriers (CVSs). The British did not convert carriers for that single purpose. Each one of the Essex CVSs operated purpose-built aircraft and helicopters from their large flight decks. These aircraft combined search capabilities – radar, sonobuoys and Magnetic Anomaly Detection (MAD) systems – with attack capability (torpedoes, nuclear depth bombs, air-to-surface rockets).

Another innovation from the war was the fielding of land-based, long-range maritime patrol aircraft (MPA), flying specifically as aircraft that would detect, track and attack submarines. Using existing airframes, the US Army Air Corps, US Navy, Royal Navy's Fleet Air Arm and Royal Air Force Coastal Command formed ASW squadrons that carried air-to-surface radar, high-powered searchlights, HF/DF, MAD sensors, sonobuoys, depth charges and homing torpedoes.[32]

force structure. Both navies brought dedicated shipborne ASW aircraft and large helicopters to sea.

During the war, both navies had built and sent to sea small aircraft carriers as convoy escorts with aircraft to battle the U-boat menace. Then, as more of these 'Jeep' carriers became available, they formed the centrepiece of dedicated hunter-killer (or HUK) groups, comprising a single carrier with as many as six escorting destroyers and/or DEs. The escort carrier group was not tied to a specific convoy. Instead, they operated in areas where submarines were known to be congregating.

The aircraft that operated from these escort 'Jeep' carriers were not purpose-built to conduct ASW. However, they were modified to carry air-to-surface radar to detect surfaced submarines and

The 1950s saw the US Navy and NATO air forces design purpose-built, land-based MPAs with the sole mission to serve as ASW platforms. The US Navy introduced the P-2 Neptune, which was followed by the P-3 Orion, while the RAF had the Avro Shackleton, followed by the Nimrod MPA. The Canadians introduced their own design, the Canadair Argus, and later their version of the P-3 Orion, the Aurora MPA. Other naval powers, such as France and Japan, developed their own MPAs.

Both land-based and ship-board aircraft, as well as surface ships and submarines, carried improved sensors and weapons that were developed during the war. The US Navy and its NATO allies, in their

Soviet Zulu-class submarine overflown by a P-3 Orion MPA. (NHHC K-71395)

Cold War at Sea effort, made a huge investment in ASW-oriented intelligence collection, platforms, operations, tactics, technology and training during the first 30 years of the period. One such

massive investment was in what became several underwater sound surveillance systems, such as ITASS and follow-on passive towed array sonars.

2
THE UNSEEN STRUGGLE TAKES A TURN

As the US Navy and its NATO allies confronted the massive number of submarines entering the Soviet Navy's order of battle (OOB), the US Navy countered the threat with a technological trump card that became a game changer for ASW. The technology it brought forward to counter a potential Third Battle of the Atlantic found its roots in the First Battle of the Atlantic, the Great War of 1914–18.

The Royal Navy and the French Navy first applied two rudimentary submarine detection technologies during the Great War's Battle of the Atlantic. The first was a prototype active sonar system that sent high frequency (HF) sound waves through the water. These sound waves reflected back to the receiver when bouncing off an underwater object – a submarine. The British continued developing active sonar after the war. By the middle of the 1920s, the Royal Navy had deployed on several of its destroyers the first generation of active sonar, euphemistically called ASDIC (Anti-Submarine Detection Investigation Committee).

The second was technology to detect underwater sounds generated by a submarine. A submerged submarine's ability to operate undetected by listening devices (hydrophones) is directly

related to the acoustic signature it generates in the water. Its acoustic signature is a composite of sounds it makes whilst operating its machinery; machine vibrations go through the submarine's hull and into the water, radiating three-dimensionally in all directions. A submarine's turning propeller(s) is another source of sounds. As it turns, a propeller generates bubbles which then collapse (cavitation), creating a shock-wave sound. The faster a propeller turns, the louder the sound it creates. The design of the propeller, including the number of blades and the shape of each blade, are additional factors that will create cavitation unique to the propeller. Another source of sound comes from the submerged submarine's hull itself as it moves through the water, creating turbulence. Taken as a whole, a submarine's noise is a unique signature which will vary with the submerged vessel's depth, speed and the water conditions through which it is moving.

Water conditions can also create an ambient noise level surrounding the submarine, and this will affect its acoustic signature. Wave action on the ocean's surface is a major contributor to the natural water conditions that create sound. There is a direct

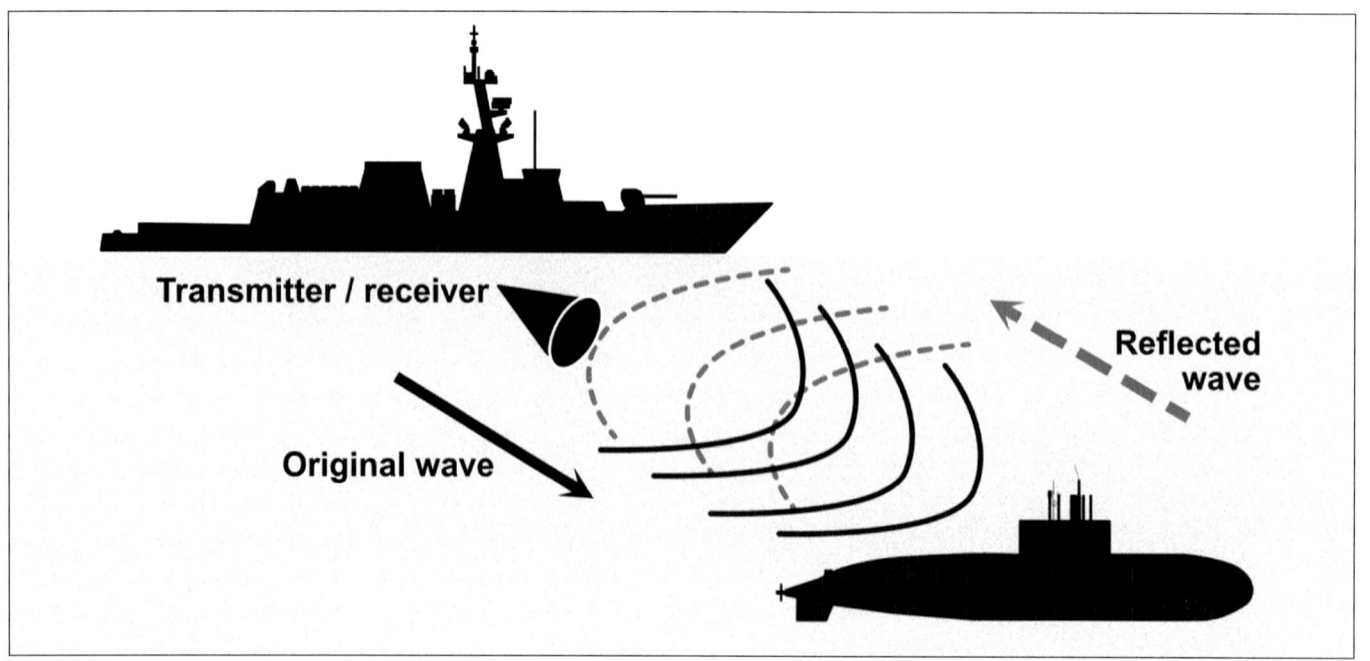

Active Sonar. (Mark Thompson)

correlation between wind speed and sea state. Obviously, the higher the wind speeds, the greater the wave action, and thus the higher the ambient noise level. Another source contributing to the ambient noise levels of the ocean is biological – sea life. Sounds generated from the creatures of the deep are thoroughly unpredictable. A third source is man-made; the sounds generated by vessels moving through the water, as well as those originating from ashore such as power plants and manufacturing sites, can add to the ambient noise of any given body of ocean and sea. However, unlike the unpredictability of sounds emanating from the natural world, man-made sounds can be tonally consistent and catalogued as belonging to a specific hull type.

In 1917, at the US Navy's Experimental Station New London in Connecticut, Dr Harvey C. Hayes constructed a hull-mounted and a towed array passive sonar system that successfully detected a submerged US Navy submarine 2,000 yards away in Long Island Sound. The system was placed aboard the Pauling-class destroyer USS *Jouett*, DD-41. On the destroyer's hull, situated on its port and starboard side forward near the bow and below the waterline, was an array of 12 hydrophones. They were set 1ft apart and encased in rubber. The length of the hull-mounted arrays was 40ft. In addition to the two hull-mounted arrays, two towed arrays, each with another set of 12 hydrophones, were set 1ft apart and encased in a neutrally buoyant gum rubber hose. Both 40ft arrays were set at 100ft below the surface and extended 300–500ft behind the *Jouett*. Hayes gave few details of his array construction or self-noise, but his system configuration was farsighted, since he removed left/right ambiguity and attempted passive ranging using the hull/towed-array baseline.[1]

With the end of the Great War, the US Navy discontinued research and development work on passive sonar, especially towed-array passive sonar. Some interest in passive sonar detection was revived towards the end of the Second World War, when merchant ships acquired a towed passive system to detect incoming torpedoes. But during the 1950s, the Office of Naval Research (ONR) in Washington, DC brought Harvey Hayes' work back to life. Under the ONR's direction, the Chesapeake Instrument Corporation constructed and tested several towed arrays.[2]

But, the development of passive towed-array sonar was part of a much larger developmental effort by the US Navy in passive underwater detection of submarines – a super-secret, seabed-deployed, passive surveillance system that became known as SOSUS. Edward Whitman has written: "Born … of early Cold War strategic necessity … the Navy's pioneering SOSUS became a key, long-range early warning asset for protecting the United States … providing

USS *Jouett*, DD-41. (NHHC 111-SC-7062)

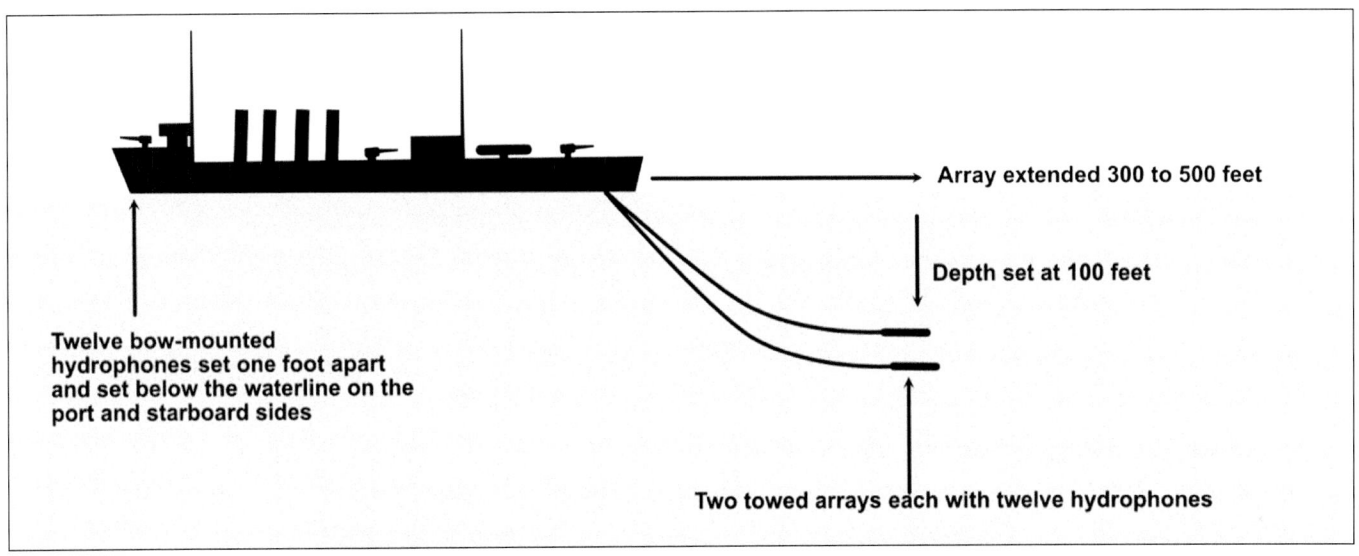

Array extended 300 to 500 feet

Depth set at 100 feet

Twelve bow-mounted hydrophones set one foot apart and set below the waterline on the port and starboard sides

Two towed arrays each with twelve hydrophones

The Hayes passive towed array. (Mark Thompson)

vital cueing information for tactical, deep-ocean, anti-submarine warfare."[3]

Beginning with SOSUS, ITASS and follow-on passive towed arrays had their genesis in the development of oceanographic and engineering inventions that emerged between the two world wars. One invention of the early 1920s was the Sonic Depth Finder (SDF): "Not only did the

A bathythermograph as carried by a US Navy destroyer or destroyer escort in the 1960s. (Tin Can Sailors)

SDF advance the state-of-the-art in acoustic technology, but it also facilitated detailed depth and ocean-bottom surveys with a speed and accuracy never before available using lead-line techniques."[4] Later, in 1937, scientist Maurice Ewing of Lehigh University made a groundbreaking discovery "while doing seismic refraction experiments in three-mile-deep water in the North Atlantic". Setting off underwater explosions as his sound source, Ewing recognised a series of pulsing echoes from the explosions that were caused by the sound reflecting between the ocean floor and the sea surface. He discovered the 'deep sound channel'; sound could travel through this channel hundreds, if not thousands of miles from its source and could be detected by strategically placed hydrophones.

As Dr Whitman wrote in his paper for *Undersea Warfare Magazine*: "Almost simultaneously, another crucial element appeared with the invention and refinement of the Bathythermograph by scientists at the Massachusetts Institute of Technology (MIT) and the Woods Hole Oceanographic Institution."[5] This device could continuously measure and correlate ocean temperature to depth. This, in turn, made it possible to determine "how underwater sound speed varied with distance below the surface – the *sound velocity profile* (SVP)". The bathythermograph supported Ewing's findings that a transmission path (sound channel axis) existed that trapped sound, depending on water temperature and pressure that increases with depth, and carried it in sound waves with minimum signal loss.

Ewing continued experimentation during the war years. One result was the development of "an air-sea rescue system known as SOFAR – for Sound Fixing and Ranging".[6] The system required downed pilots to drop small explosive charges into the deep sound channel, where the sound of the explosions would travel for thousands of miles to

variously placed seabed-mounted hydrophones along the east coast of the US and Canada. These hydrophones would triangulate the sound and determine the general location of the downed pilots. The war ended before anyone thought to use the SOFAR channel for submarine detection.

However, with the start of the Cold War and the associated threat that the growing number of Soviet Navy submarines posed to the Western allies, the US Navy looked to academia for ASW technological solutions. In 1946, the Navy, through the advisory committee that it established during the war, the Committee on Undersea Warfare, sought suggestions as to how it should develop a capability to counter the Soviet submarine threat.[7]

The result of the US Navy's request was the creation of Project HARTWELL:

Project HARTWELL was initiated by the Navy as a short-term intensive assault on the technical barriers that now limit the effectiveness of anti-submarine and anti-marine warfare. The group's function was to explore the potentialities inherent in old and new methods: suggest future long-range programs, and formulate recommendations that could be used by the Navy to guide research and development.[8]

This MIT-sponsored effort gathered top scientists and naval officers to determine what technologies could be applied to detect, classify and identify submerged submarines. The committee recognised Ewing's SOFAR findings and associated technology as holding tremendous potential to passively detect submerged submarines at long ranges.

Project HARTWELL's report recognised Ewing's findings:

One of the most promising developments in underwater listening appears to be the use of audio frequencies below 500 cycles. At these frequencies, sounds apparently penetrate the shallow thermal layers and propagate to great distances in the deep sound channel. This frequency range is particularly important for submarine detection, because there is evidence that there are strong peaks in machinery noise both from Diesels and battery-operated submarines at these frequencies even when propeller cavitation is absent. The low frequencies are also known to have a very low attenuation.[9]

The report went further in its recommendations by stating the need for continued research,

to determine the limits of integration time that can be employed to advantage with signals of various lengths … it is essential to know more about the propagation of low-frequency sounds … Experimentation should be carried out with ships, submarines, buoys, helicopters, remote-controlled vessels, and shore stations to determine the optimal organization of search sonars … Further experimentation should determine the best way of integrating search sonar into overall weapon systems.[10]

The proposals led the ONR later in 1950 to award a contract to American Telephone and Telegraph (AT&T) to develop a seabed-placed surveillance system based on long-range sound propagation.[11] Coinciding with constructing the surveillance system, AT&T adapted its sound spectrograph, which was invented to analyse "speech sounds into a similar device called LOFAR – for Low Frequency Analysis and Recording – designed to analyze low-frequency underwater signals in near-real time".[12] This machine, using an electrostatic stylus that blackened 'special' paper, swept across the paper, recording waterborne noise including discrete frequencies, 'tonals', correlated with distinct submarine signatures. The overall effort by AT&T and its partners in academia and industry was highly classified. The US Navy named the project JEZEBEL.[13]

Project JEZEBEL, together with partner research organisations known under the codename Project MICHAEL, allowed researchers to obtain a greater understanding on how sound propagates through the water. Their findings were amalgamated to form the design and deployment of a full-size seabed array of hydrophones designated Project CAESAR; the first SOSUS.

The Navy installed the first SOSUS array off Eleuthera Island in the Bahamas early in 1952. After a series of successful detections against US Navy diesel submarines, it decided to build and install identical arrays along the entire east coast. The hydrophone detections were transmitted via cables to the newly built SOSUS processing facilities identified as Naval Facilities, or NAVFACs. By 1957, Project CAESAR's SOSUS arrays and attendant NAVFACs "had been established at Bermuda, Shelburne (Nova Scotia), Nantucket, Cape May, Cape Hatteras, Antigua, Eleuthera, and Barbados".[14] By the time the three Dealey-class DEs were fitted with their ITASS arrays and processing vans in 1970, "there were 24 NAVFACs and similar installations on the coasts of Britain and Norway".[15]

As mentioned previously, the ONR had directed Chesapeake Instrument Corporation to construct and test several towed arrays. The requirement for a 'towed' version of SOSUS was twofold. First, from a political standpoint, SOSUS could not cover large expanses of the world's oceans and seas; some countries bordering these bodies

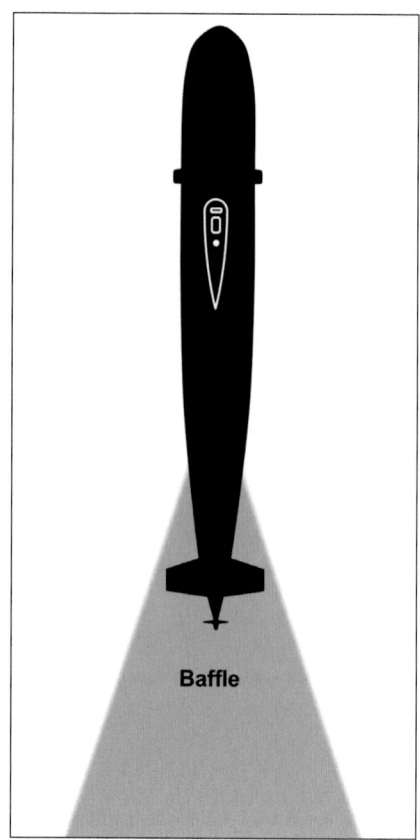

Aft acoustic blindness due to hull baffling for both submarines and surface ships. (Mark Thompson)

of water were not allied to the United States or they were neutrals. Second, the US Navy's submarine community was "confronting the problem of aft acoustic blindness due to hull baffling".[16] At the time, a submarine's active and passive sonar array was located on its bow. The array was placed there in order to reduce the noise generated by the submarine itself; its machinery noise and that caused by the submarine travelling through the water. The forward placement made the sonar more effective, but it created a blind spot. This was caused by the submarine itself blocking the sonar's ability to detect underwater contacts directly aft of its course, as well as by the sound generated by its own propeller(s) cavitation and the overall wake produced by the submarine as it travelled through the water. The higher the speed of the submarine, the more pronounced its wake and its blind spot – its baffles. The same can be said for ships.

To counter the potential threat of being 'tailed' by an enemy submarine, a submarine captain would 'clear his baffles' by executing a 180-degree port or starboard turn to bring the submarine's forward sonar to search the aft sector. This tactical manoeuvre was certainly a necessary one, but it was potentially a dangerous one as well. If the submarine was being followed, the risk of collision was very real.

During the late 1950s, the Chesapeake Instrument Corporation built and tested a series of passive towed-array sonars. Small-diameter, cable-like tossed arrays were built, as well as 3-inch diameter arrays with hydrophones in flexible rubber tubes. One array was towed from the sail of the USS *Albacore*, and the Chesapeake Instrument Corporation conducted a sea trial of large-diameter arrays in the Bahamas in the summer of 1961.[17]

In 1964, the former US Navy coastal minesweeper USS *Redpoll*, then the Oceanographic Research Vessel (ORV) *Sir Horace Lamb* belonging to Columbia University and stationed at the university's Field Station at St David's, Bermuda, was selected to take onboard a Chesapeake Instrument Corporation-designed towed array.[18]

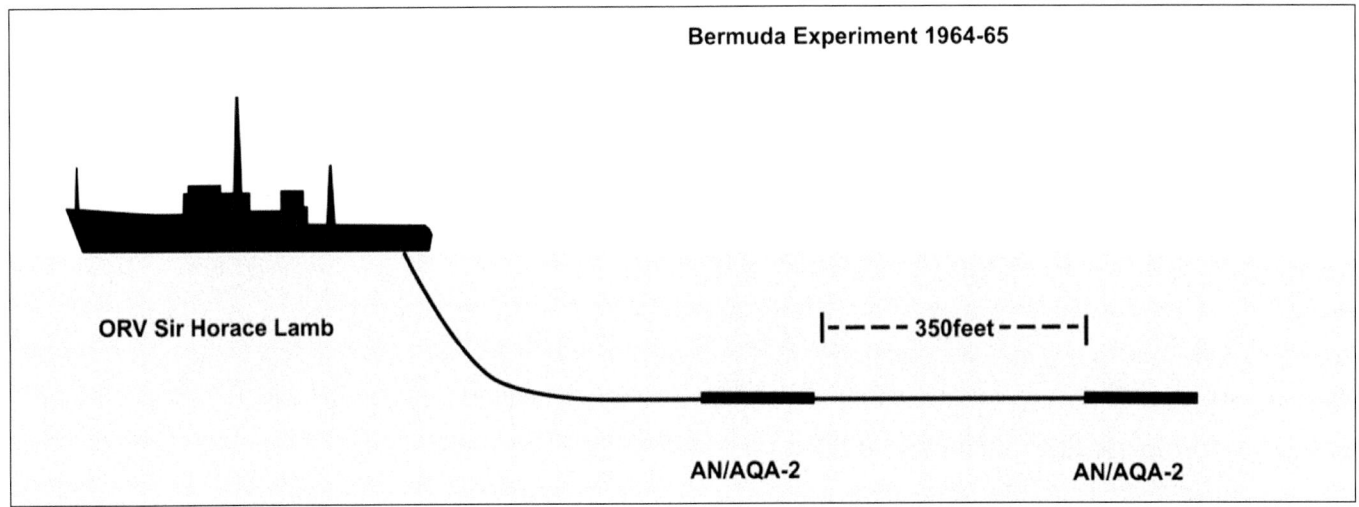

The ORV *Sir Horace Lamb* passive sonar towed array. (Mark Thompson)

Chesapeake Instrument Corporation engineers designed a horizontal array with two AN/AQA-2 'JEZEBEL' Airborne LOFAR sonobuoys and fixed them 350ft apart.[19] They borrowed the two JEZEBELs from the US Naval Air Station Bermuda's ASW squadron that was based on the island at the time.

Beginning in 1964 and concluding in 1965, the *Sir Horace Lamb*, with the Chesapeake Instrument Corporation's long baseline towed array, conducted a series of tests off Bermuda and the Bahamas against US Navy diesel submarines. With the array sending acoustic data to the ship's Correlation Detection Gear (known by its acronym CODAR), the sensor successfully detected US Navy snorkelling submarines.

The tests probably had the submarines diving and surfacing, as well as operating at various speeds on the surface and submerged. More importantly, the tests had these diesel submarines operating submerged using their snorkels. It appears that the tests' greatest success occurred toward the end of the trials; in May 1965, the array detected one snorkelling submarine at a range of 67 miles.

But as Dr W. Carey said when he and his team briefed the Chief of Naval Operations' (CNO) staff in the Pentagon later in 1965 on the results of the test, "Even if we know there's a submarine seventy miles away, what can I do about it?" The US Navy did not have an integrated system (platform/sensor/weaponry) with the capability to destroy a submarine at such distances. Carey added: "It would be several years before a total system concept would evolve for the use of towed arrays on surface ships."[20] The next step, the development of passive towed arrays, would come in a relative short time.

During the next 12 months, the 'what next' seemed to languish. But in 1967, the DoD Deputy Director of Research, Development and Engineering commissioned Bell Technical Laboratories (BTL) to study whether the hydrodynamics of the Mediterranean Sea would serve as a medium for passive towed array sonar to detect submerged submarines. BTL conducted tests in the Mediterranean for several months in 1967, and the study "resulted in a recommendation that towed arrays be deployed in the Mediterranean for submarine surveillance".[21]

Just before Christmas 1967, DoD Deputy Director Dr G. Sabastien brought together manufacturers of towed arrays at a meeting in the Pentagon. He presented a one-hour briefing on the problem of detecting submarines in the Mediterranean. Besides BTL, each manufacturer – Hughes Aircraft Company, Litton and Chesapeake Instrument Corporation – gave a one-hour presentation. Sabastien sent the presentations to the US Naval Underwater Sound Laboratory (USNUSL) at New London, Connecticut. The USNUSL

VADM Charles Martell, USN, Director of ASW Programs (OP-95), CNO. (NHHC Series USN1063812)

wrote specifications for a Mediterranean Surveillance System. The specifications were given to Naval Sea Systems Command (NAVSEA), and then released to the manufacturers, who attended the meeting in December for bids. The request for proposals required the manufacturers to present their bids in just 28 days. On 29 May, the USNUSL received the bids and recommended to NAVSEA that the Chesapeake Instrument Corporation be awarded the contract to produce three towed array systems. Chesapeake Instrument Corporation was the lowest bidder.[22]

However, NAVSEA considered that the programme required a large company, such as Hughes Aircraft, to carry out the contract. NAVSEA saw that only a large company could perform what was considered a difficult task to develop and build such a system. However, Vice Admiral (VADM) Charles Martell, USN, had a different opinion. Martell was the CNO's Executive Director of ASW Programs (OP-95), and he disagreed with NAVSEA's recommendation to give the contract to Hughes.[23] He had reviewed the results of the hydrodynamic testing to determine the level of ambient noise in the Ionian Sea. The scientists reported that the Ionian had extremely high and low ambient frequency noise levels, which were caused by marine life and ship traffic. He calculated that such an intense level of ambient noise would allow a passive towed array to detect a submerged submarine only inside a range of 3,000 yards.[24] This was not acceptable, as Soviet submarine torpedoes and missiles had a range in excess of 3,000 yards.

Martell did not reject going ahead with producing a passive towed array system, but he considered Hughes' bid to build three systems at $12 million too expensive. He instead gave the contract to the Chesapeake Instrument Corporation as they had placed their bid at $4 million: "Give it to them. It's not going to work anyway."[25] The Chesapeake Instrument Corporation thus won the contract to build ITASS.

Chesapeake Instrument Corporation built three systems that the US Navy designated as the AN/SQR-14 ITASS. The towed array consisted of 16 electronic modules and four vibration isolation and stability modules. The entire array was about 600ft long and had a 40ft nylon drogue line to prevent the end modules from fishtailing. All the modules were filled with oil under pressure and were electrically and mechanically connected to each other.

3
OUT OF NEWPORT

The Mediterranean and Naples await

Thursday, 1 January, New Year's Day 1970, found the USS *Hammerberg*, *Courtney* and *Lester* pier side with their sister ships USS *John Willis* (DE-1027), *Van Voorhis* (DE-1028) and *Hartley* (DE-1029) at the US Naval Station (NAVSTA), Newport, Rhode Island. All six ships were 'cold iron'; that is, all six were receiving steam and electricity from the shore, and not producing power from their own boilers. All six were in reserve 'cadre status'. Each ship had a commanding officer, but not the full complement of officers and ratings.

However, 1970 would witness major changes to the operational status of four of the DEs. All would trade their 'cadre status' to return to operational status with the Atlantic Fleet. However, their role as DEs, possessing a robust ASW armoury, would be altered. They would be stripped of most of their weaponry and converted to operating a new design of passive towed array sonar – ITASS. They would become tailships.

At the time, the DEs of Escort Squadrons (CORTRONs) 8, 10 and 14 were stationed at Newport, Rhode Island. Newport was the homeport for the Commander of Cruiser-Destroyer Force Atlantic and several destroyer and DE squadrons. It was also the home of several subordinate commands within the greater Newport naval base. Besides the Naval War College, the tenant commands included the Naval Academy Prep School and the US Navy's Officer Candidate School (OCS).

During the late 1960s, when the sailors of the ships of CORTRON 8 were stationed at Newport, the town adjacent to the naval base was a typical US Navy town. Dr William Dudley, former director of the US Naval Historical Center (now the Naval History and Heritage Command, NHHC) remembers when he was a cadet at the Navy's OCS and a junior officer aboard the USS *Cromwell*, DE-1014. In his correspondence to the author, he wrote:

> The Newport that I knew in the 1960s was a sailors' town, at least along the water front. Driving along Thames Street, we had our

From left to right: USS *Dealey*, DE-1006, USS *Hammerberg*, DE-1015, USS *Courtney*, DE-1021, USS *John Willis*, DE-1027 and USS *Cromwell*, DE-1014. (Tom Sobeck, USS *Hartley*, DE-1029)

choice of bars, pawn shops, dance studios, and small restaurants, strip joints and probably a few brothels. One notable strip joint was the Blue Moon where the strippers would flaunt their wares. As OCs [Officer Candidates] we were told to stay away from that place. The main place we gathered as junior officers was at The Moorings where the Fall River girls congregated on weekends. This was all a far cry from the fru-fru hair salons, boutiques, upscale restaurants, and nautical clothing stores of the post-Vietnam era. To go to nicer places we would start at the Viking Hotel, on Bellevue, and later we gathered at The Pub for a more collegiate crowd (girls from Salve Regina and Wheaton College) where we drank beer while listening to the Kingston Trio, Joan Baez, and Peter Seeger on the juke box. For a good steak dinner we went to Angelo's. For a really special date we'd go have a meal at the scenic Castle Hill Inn Restaurant on Ocean Drive along the approach to Narragansett Bay. For those who had to stay close to Piers 1 & 2, there was the Datum – not much of a place, but the nearest one for a drink, or the Naval War College's Officers' Club. For a nice day-sail on a weekend you could rent a knockabout sloop from the naval base marina and head out to the Bay. This was at the time when the Newport Folk Music Concerts were popular. Also, the America's Cup races had been revived and we sometime caught a glimpse of them, heading out to Block Island Sound. Those were fun times.[1]

From a junior enlisted sailor's experience of being homeported in Newport, Electricians Mate Seaman Joseph Szep, USNR, remembers Thames Street in downtown Newport and its attractions very well:

I began to fraternize with others [the local girls] at the local bars with my buddies while we did our "bar-storming" up and down Thames Street all the way down to Narragansett Avenue … I recall that on Thames Street were Frankie's Cafe, Night Owl Bar & Pub, Bird in Hand, Clancy's Bar & Grill, and the Narragansett Bar & Grill … as for sleaze joints there was the Blue Moon.[2]

For Szep and the other bachelor sailors on the DEs, there were more things to do in Newport than going to the bars:

During the late spring and into the late fall, my shipmates and I would head up to Boston to see many a baseball game [Boston Red Sox] at Fenway Park … I also drove my Navy buddies to the Aquidneck Lanes to go bowling. After that we would head back to the Newport YMCA to watch TV and discuss amongst ourselves what our next move would be during the evening coming up.[3]

Newport was certainly more than just a Navy town. Besides being the home of several US naval installations, Rhode Island was known as 'America's First Vacationland'. Those of "the wealthier and 'more exclusive classes' were attracted to shoreline destinations along lower Narragansett Bay" and Newport.[4] During the late nineteenth century, "moneyed industrialists from New York and farther south hired architects to create summer 'cottages'"[5] — opulent structures reflecting the owners' wealth and status.

By the 1930s, Newport had become the epicentre of America's yachting world. In addition to their summer cottages, "the Vanderbilts, the Astors, the Manvilles, JP Morgan and many more all brought their luxurious sailing yachts to Newport … For over fifty years of the twentieth century, the most coveted sailing race in the world was held in Newport – the America's Cup."[6] The staff of COMCORTRON 8 (Commander, Escort Squadron 8), together with

the crews of the *Courtney, Hammerberg, Lester,* and *Van Voorhis,* were present during the preparations for the 1970 America's Cup race that was held at Newport in September. However, they departed Newport prior to the commencement of the race. But even with all hands busy preparing for the Atlantic crossing and homeporting in Naples, Italy, they would have seen the magnificent 12-metre-class sailing yachts preparing for the race.

The officers and men of CORTRON 8 ships would have rubbed elbows with the entire spectrum of American society during the fading days of the 1970 summer tourist season. "With the end of the war, … more and more Americans … began to take vacations, as vacations with pay had been extended to the majority of US industrial workers by the end of the decade."[7] However, there was a lingering cloud over the town, as well as for most of the Americans – The Vietnam War. During the Vietnam War, an increasing number of Americans opposed the US involvement. By 1970, only a third of the population believed that the US had not made a mistake by sending their armed forces to fight in Vietnam. Szep recalled:

Being onboard the *Courtney,* the mood was somewhat mixed about our commitment in Vietnam. As to what the crew thought was about 50% against the war, and 50% for the war. Some guys were 'Gung-Ho', being very eager to get into action for 'God and Country'. The others were those who … blamed the entire war on our politicians. We kept our thoughts to ourselves. But, we were grateful for being in the Navy and not being drafted to become 'cannon fodder'.[8]

New Year's Day 1970 found the future tailships in various states of modification that would reconfigure them to be tailships. The reconfiguration began with *Hammerberg*. After experiencing significant engineering problems earlier in 1968 and a three-month Atlantic/Mediterranean deployment later in the year,[9] *Hammerberg* was towed to Boston on 3 April 1969. Under the command of Lieutenant Commander (LCDR) J.E. Tedder, USN, major work was accomplished, including the expansion of *Hammerberg's* "communications spaces and the addition of much new equipment, to include the installation of a new gun mount, and the removal of the Weapon Alfa … The overhaul was completed on 2 October; about one month later due primarily to difficulties with the engineering plant."[10]

In January, *Van Voorhis,* under the command of LCDR William W. Pippenger, USN, had its DASH (Drone Anti-Submarine Helicopter) equipment removed to make way for ITASS, and on 8 February, it was towed out of Newport for the Bethlehem Steel Shipyards in East Boston to begin its actual conversion. During the rest of February, its ITASS equipment was installed. Its DASH hangar was reconfigured to berthing for the additional crew, who would be assigned to operate ITASS. *Van Voorhis* completed the transition, and for the next four months it would conduct refresher training (REFTRA) out of the US Naval Station, Guantanamo Bay (GITMO), and then be the lead tailship to test ITASS off Eleuthera in the Bahamas. The ship would then return to Newport to prepare for deployment with its sister tailships to the Mediterranean.[11]

The *Courtney,* under the command of LCDR Richard T. Reimann, USN, continued moored alongside at NAVSTA Newport until Sunday, 11 January 1970. On Monday morning, 12 January, it was taken under tow to be moved to the Boston Naval Shipyard via the Cape Cod Canal, arriving at the Boston Navy Yard that night.

Courtney remained in dry dock through most of February. During the two months that followed, its aft twin 3-inch gun was

Three of the DEs under tow at Naval Station Newport. (NARA)

removed and the ITASS van, with its large cable reel and service tray, was installed. On Wednesday, 25 February, *Courtney* left dry dock and moored alongside at Pier Number 4. While it was alongside, modifications continued through all of March. Midway through April, *Courtney* got underway to conduct sea trials on Thursday, 16 April.

LCDR Reimann put his tailship through its paces. *Courtney* successfully tested its engines and conducted man-overboard and general quarters drills. It returned to the Boston Navy Yard that evening. One week later, on Thursday, 23 April, Reimann took *Courtney* back to sea again. This time it conducted an extensive engineering test, working up to a full power run. With its speed increasing, the tailship conducted numerous course changes. It took *Courtney* 15 minutes to go from 15 knots to 23 knots. Securing from the full power run, the ship began testing its steering gear with its twin rudders. Coming to a full stop, Reimann ordered all back full. It continued going full astern for 13 minutes.

Later, *Courtney* conducted sonar noise levels with its AN/SQS-4 sonar at various speeds, ranging between four and 22 knots. Coming to a complete stop, it had a sonobuoy deployed in the water. At various course changes and different speeds, *Courtney* conducted echo ranging with its AN/SQS-4 sonar by sending transmissions and having them bounce back off the sonobuoy, returning to the sonar.

That night, *Courtney* continued steering at various courses and speeds while conducting radar radiation patterns with its AN/SPS-5D surface search radar against a buoy. The tailship continued operating through the early morning hours on Thursday the 24th, returning alongside Pier Number 4 at Boston Naval Shipyard at 0930 hours.

Courtney remained pier side through the rest of April until Wednesday, 13 May, when it was towed from the Boston Navy Yard to a civilian yard across the harbour, the Bromfield Shipyard of East Boston, for additional work that would prepare it for the upcoming three-year Mediterranean deployment. On Thursday, 4 June, it departed Boston for the last time and headed south at 20 knots to the northern entrance of the Cape Cod Canal and back to its homeport at NAVSTA Newport, arriving just before sunset.

With Reimann in command, *Courtney* departed Newport on 16 June for her REFTRA at GITMO. However, *Courtney* took a circuitous course toward Cuba. During the pre-dawn hours of Thursday, 18 June, *Courtney*'s log recorded that the ship "started streaming research gear at 0637".[12] It continued to stream the array off the Virginia Capes training area through the entire morning and afternoon hours.

After breakfast, Reimann sent the crew to general quarters (GQ), and a series of drills began. Reimann was preparing the crew for the rigour they could expect to receive at the hands of the GITMO REFTRA staff. This included live firing exercises with its sole twin 3-inch/50-calibre gun. With securing from GQ, the ship held steering casualty drills, culminating just before the ship's bosun piped the midday meal. In the afternoon, the ship resumed drills to include small-arms practice, in which the ship's company had an opportunity to fire the antiquated weapons from their small-arms armoury – the M1 Garand rifle, Browning automatic rifle, Browning machine gun and the iconic Colt 45 pistol. During his time as the *Courtney*'s CO, Reimann was known to toss a live grenade off the ship's bridge wing.

Courtney arrived at GITMO during the morning of 21 June. On Sunday, 22 June, Commander Fleet Training Group Guantanamo (COMFLETRAGRU GITMO) arrived with his staff to conduct a GITMO arrival inspection critique and brief officers on the unique features of GITMO Bay.

For the next week, the ship and its crew were put through a series of exhausting drills and exercises. All of these activities were conducted under the watchful eyes of the training group staff. *Courtney* passed its hell week and was certified as combat ready, returning to Newport in time for the Fourth of July holiday. The vessel would remain in Newport, except for day cruises to exercise the ship, until it departed for Naples during the last week in August.

On Wednesday morning, 26 August, *Courtney* departed Newport Naval Base for the last time and headed out to sea for its new homeport, Naples. It departed with other units of Task Group 80.2 (TG 80.2). As Officer in Tactical Command (OTC) of TG 80.2 COMCORTRON 8, Commander D.E. Crawley, USN, also had under his command USS *Hammerberg*, DE-1015, LCDR L.G. Anderson, USN, commanding, and USS *Van Voorhis*, DE-1028, commanded by LCDR W.E. Pippinger, USN. The *Van Voorhis* deployed because the USS *Lester*, DE-1022, was still fitting out in preparation for its three-year deployment to the Mediterranean.[13]

Later that afternoon, whilst on a course of 166 degrees, speed five knots, *Courtney* commenced streaming its tail. Reimann had his tailship turn to starboard no less than 10 degrees an average of every five minutes. The number of changes in course and the shortness of time between course changes did not seem to be related to the ship's ITASS purpose to detect and obtain a bearing on a submerged submarine's acoustic transmissions. It seems as though Reimann was gauging how far his ship could alter course and not endanger the towed array.

On Saturday, 29 August, all three ships practiced deploying and retrieving their tails, approximately 380 nautical miles (nm) northeast of Bermuda. Later that day, all three tailships came alongside the Sacramento-class fast combat store ship, the USS *Seattle* AOE-3, to refuel (UNREP – underway replenishment).[14] Once the UNREP concluded, the three diminutive tailships formed up on the *Seattle* and continued their trans-Atlantic cruise.

On Sunday, 30 August, the four ships joined the ships commanded by COMCRUDESGRU 8 (Commander Cruiser-Destroyer Group 8) for the cruise to Naples. The flagship was the former Second World War heavy cruiser of the Baltimore-class, the USS *Columbus* CG 12. It had been reconfigured as an Anti-Air Warfare cruiser to become one of the three Albany-class missile cruisers. Accompanying the *Columbus* was the recently reclassified guided missile destroyer, the USS *Mitscher* DDG (Destroyer Guided Missile) 35, and another guided missile destroyer of the Coontz-class, USS *Dahlgren* DDG 12. The remaining destroyers were Second World War destroyers of the Sumner and Gearing-classes that had been modernised under the FRAM II programme. These were the Gearing-class destroyers USS *Meredith* DD 840, USS *Perry* DD 844, USS *Charles R. Ware* DD 865 and USS *Stribling* DD 867. The Sumner-class destroyer USS *Sumner* DD 692 was also included.

The FRAM programme involved upgrading these Second World War destroyers into ASW specialists. Each FRAM destroyer received a new ASW suite, to include the new Anti-Submarine Rocket (ASROC), carrying a single ASW torpedo/missile, which was installed in a 'pepper box' launcher amidships. Each FRAM destroyer was rebuilt to house a helicopter hangar and flight deck for the DASH and each FRAM ship's machinery was thoroughly overhauled. Additionally, new electronics were installed (radar and electronic countermeasures equipment) and an active variable depth sonar array system was installed on the stern.

On Tuesday, 1 September, Commander Crawley, COMCORTRON 8, transferred to the cruiser to meet with the COMCRUDESGRU FLOT 2 Commander and his staff. Crawley briefed them on ITASS.

With Crawley aboard the cruiser, a slight embarrassment occurred on that afternoon watch when *Courtney* attempted to exercise its 3-inch/50-cal guns. It commenced firing at a target

sled, but after a few rounds were fired, the left bore became fouled (jammed). *Courtney* tried firing again in an attempt to clear the bore, but the attempt was unsuccessful. 'Cease fire' was ordered again. Reimann ordered a 30-minute waiting period in accordance with hang fire-misfire procedures. After 30 minutes, the leading gunner's mate removed the round from the breech.[15] With the end of the 'firepower display', Crawley returned to the *Courtney* via high-line transfer.

On Saturday, 5 September, *Courtney*, *Hammerberg* and *Van Voorhis* detached from the main group, and on the following day the tailships of CORTRON 8 came under the command of Commander Sixth Fleet, specifically under the Commander of ASW Sixth Fleet, Task Force 67 (TF67). With that they became designated as Task Group 67.3.

On Wednesday, 9 September, CORTRON 8 ships arrived at Naples and moored along the sea wall together, with *Hammerberg* alongside *Courtney*'s port side and *Van Voorhis* on the port side of *Hammerberg*. They were now at their new home.

As for *Lester*, LCDR S.H. Edwards took his ship from Newport to the Boston Navy Yard, arriving on 25 February. During the next four months, it was docked and reconfigured similarly to its two sisters. "During her overhaul, her major systems were overhauled, two new communications spaces with a more complex and sophisticated radio system were added, and all auxiliary equipment for Weapon Alfa, just prior to overhaul, were offloaded." On 18 June, *Lester* left the yard, returning to Newport.[16]

On 3 August, Edwards returned his ship to Boston. This time it was taken in hand by "Boston's General Shipyard for the installation of ITASS foundations and associated cabling".[17] The reason the entire system was not fitted when it was in Boston was, as mentioned previously, that only three systems were manufactured by the Chesapeake Instrument Corporation. *Van Voorhis* would transfer its tail to *Lester* once it arrived in Naples.

After successfully completing a four-week GITMO REFTRA and Operational Readiness Inspection (similar to *Courtney*'s and *Lester*'s experience), Edwards returned his DE to cooler climes in Newport on 26 September. Upon its arrival, he began preparations for shifting *Lester* to a new homeport in Naples, remaining in Newport until late October. It entered Sixth Fleet's operational area on 7 November, arriving in Naples on the 9th.[18] The tailships were now back together in their new home.

4

THE BEAR AND THE EAGLE: A MEDITERRANEAN CONFRONTATION

The Soviet naval activity in the Mediterranean remained at a high level … Indications are that the Soviet Mediterranean Fleet will maintain approximately 45–50 units in Mediterranean waters.[1]

The tailships and their men would be operating in the Mediterranean for the next three years in one of the world's most intensive maritime and naval environments. For the US Navy's Sixth Fleet, its operations above, below and on the Mediterranean Sea were in many ways as extensive as those of the Seventh Fleet, operating off the waters of Vietnam. However, each day, the Sixth Fleet's aircraft,

ships and submarines, and their crews, found themselves sharing a great inland sea – unique in its physiography, hydrologic features and climate – with thousands of commercial vessels and the aircraft, ships and submarines of the Soviet Navy's Fifth *Eskadra*.

The Physiographic and Hydrologic Characteristics of the Mediterranean Sea

The setting for the almost daily interaction, and at times confrontation, between US/NATO and Soviet naval and air forces was within a largely enclosed, intercontinental sea that stretches west to east from the Atlantic to Turkey, a distance of approximately 2,500 miles. Its north–south extent from Croatia to Libya is approximately 500 miles.[2] Using Sicily as a geographic centre, and dividing the Mediterranean in two, the westward half from the Straits of Gibraltar to Sicily is subdivided into three primary basins – east of Gibraltar lies the Alboran Basin, eastward of that is the Balearic Basin, with the Tyrrhenian Basin between Corsica/Sardinia and Italy/Sicily.

To the east of Sicily are two major subdivisions. The Ionian Basin has Italy, Sicily, Albania and Greece bordering it to the north, whilst Libya is its southern border. It is in the Ionian Sea that the deepest sounding in the Mediterranean has been recorded – 16,000ft. As with the sea floor between Sicily and North Africa, there is a submarine ridge between Crete and Libya. This upwelling divides the Ionian from the next subdivision, the Levantine Basin, with the Aegean Sea containing numerous islands; Turkey, Syria and Israel form its northern and eastern borders, while Egypt forms most of its southern border. Finally, between Italy and Albania lie the Straits of Taranto and to the north of these is the Adriatic Sea. The Adriatic separates Italy from the Balkan countries, which was Yugoslavia during the time the tailships operated in the Mediterranean.[3]

The physiography of the western division is dominated by the Straits of Gibraltar in the west and the Strait of Sicily in the east, whilst the Strait of Messina separates Sicily from Italy. The western division has prominent continental shelves created by the effluents from the Ebro River of Spain. The shelf extends eastward, underpinning the Balearic Islands of Menorca, Majorca and Ibiza. To the north, along the French southern coast, the effluents from the Rhone River have formed another extensive continental shelf. But as one moves eastward of Marseilles and through the Italian Riviera, the shelf narrows somewhat all the way down Italy's west coast, extending only west and southward, underpinning Corsica and Sardinia. The sea floor beyond these continental shelves is cut by numerous canyons and troughs.

An important off-shore physiographic feature, that transiting Soviet submarines would take advantage of when travelling submerged east–west, is the very narrow continental shelf, ranging from the Straits of Gibraltar all the way toward the western entrance of the Strait of Sicily. Off the coasts of Morocco, Algeria and Tunisia, this continental shelf's gradient plunges sharply, providing a terrain backdrop to help conceal the presence of a submarine.

Entering the Strait of Sicily, a transiting submerged submarine can travel over an extensive shelf that has depths rarely exceeding 1,500ft from the surface. This prominent underwater feature widens eastward and south off the entire east coast of Tunisia to western Libya, despite some distinctive troughs and valleys leading eastward into the Ionian Sea.[4] Along the Libyan coast, the shelf begins to narrow considerably towards Benghazi, rounding eastward toward Derna in Libya. The rest of the Ionian and Levantine Basins possess considerable depths, averaging over 6,000ft.

Superimposing hydrologic data over all these features, one can begin to see a complicated underwater picture. As with all bodies of water, the Mediterranean hydrodynamics have three layers of water density or mass. These layers constitute an important factor for submarines operating in the Mediterranean, as well as those ASW forces attempting to detect and track them.

The surface layer depth varies from 250–1,000ft, the intermediate layer depth ranges between 1,000ft and 2,000ft, whilst the deep layer, "containing the great bulk of Mediterranean water – occupies the remaining zone … In general, the water of this layer is homogeneous."[5]

The Mediterranean's salinity and temperature are two additional factors to consider for submarines and ASW forces alike. For the surface layer, as a consequence of evaporation occurring throughout the Mediterranean, "there is a continuous inflow of surface water from the Atlantic Ocean".[6] The flow continues eastward from Gibraltar, paralleling the North African coast, and is the most consistent feature of the Mediterranean's current circulation. This surface water flows mostly anti-clockwise throughout the Mediterranean's two primary divisions, and it is at its most robust during the summer, when evaporation is at its zenith. Therefore, in the summer months, the surface layer's salinity, temperature and density increase considerably. The highest temperatures in the Mediterranean during the summer months are off the Libyan coast – the Gulf of Sidra – with a mean of 88°F/31°C, and the waters between Cyprus, Turkey and northern Syria, at 86°F/30°C. Of course, water temperatures at the surface drop during the autumn and winter months.

The physiographic and hydrographic features described above were major factors for consideration when the tailships deployed their passive sonar arrays. Much success or failure of ITASS operations rested on taking these features into consideration.

Maritime and Naval Considerations

From a maritime perspective, the Mediterranean witnessed on a daily basis approximately 2,000 ships and craft underway within its great expanse. At this time in its history, the Mediterranean was a major commercial SLOC between the western Eurasia landmass and the western hemisphere. This was despite having the Suez Canal closed to seaborne traffic since the June 1967 Arab-Israeli War. With the thousands of merchant ships and fishing craft of all sizes and descriptions on the Mediterranean, the tailships faced a constant challenge of avoiding collision, especially the threat of an errant merchant or fishing vessel cutting the cable, with attached sensors being towed astern. For the Oceanographic System Technicians (OTs) operating ITASS, the Mediterranean would prove a noisy sea and a challenge to detecting, classifying and identifying submerged Soviet submarines.

From a naval perspective, the Mediterranean was the fulcrum of the Cold War at Sea. Each day, when the tailships found themselves operating as individual units or as tactical pairs, they shared the Mediterranean with more than 40 surface ships and submarines belonging to the Soviet Navy's Fifth *Eskadra*.

Since the 1967 Arab-Israeli War, the operational scope and sheer number of aircraft, ships and submarines assigned to the Fifth *Eskadra* had expanded dramatically.[7] The war had shown that the Soviets were handicapped in their ability to shape its course, because they did not possess an effective counter-weight to the Sixth Fleet and its NATO partners. By the time the three tailships entered the Mediterranean in October 1970, the Fifth *Eskadra* was operating the largest number of 'Out-of-Area' submarines in the vast Soviet submarine force.[8]

As the Sixth Fleet Command History for 1971 noted in its Anti-Submarine Warfare section:

The Soviet submarine level continues to average slightly over eleven deployed units while Sixth Fleet ASW assists have remained steady. Although some qualitative improvements have been made, the Soviets have also improved and the number one threat to the Mediterranean is the Soviet submarine force. Effective 26 November, 1971, ASW in the Mediterranean was given first priority. Dedicated to the task were 13 P-3 aircraft, 3

ITASS destroyer escorts, 15 destroyers, a squadron of ASW helos [helicopters], a cruiser, 3 submarines and 2 patrol boats. Coordinating the effort is Rear Admiral W.F. Clifford, Jr., Deputy for ASW, Sixth Fleet."[9]

A Foxtrot SS anchored at the Gulf of Hammamet Soviet fair weather anchorage in the summer of 1972. Note the Soviet sailors in swimsuits. The Fifth *Eskadra* flagship, a Don-class auxiliary submarine depot or tender ship (AS). (Author's photograph)

The backbone of the Soviet submarine force in the Mediterranean belonged to the large class (62 Soviet units built) of diesel-electric powered, long-range attack submarines (SSs), known by the Soviet Navy as the Project 641 *Podvodnaya Lodka* (*PL*) submarines;[10] NATO designated them as Foxtrot-class submarines.

The design was an evolutionary one that found its origins in the Second World War German Type XXI diesel-electric submarines. The first units became operational with the Soviet Navy beginning in 1958, with the last unit completed in 1973; by that year, the class was considered obsolete.

The number of Foxtrots operating against the Sixth Fleet and NATO in the Mediterranean ranged from

This photograph amply illustrates the observation upon the design of the Juliett-class that "The submarine's configuration is not optimized for either surface or submerged speed." (Norman Polmar, *Guide to the Soviet Navy*, used with permission)

six to eight submarines on any given day. All of these submarines came from the Soviet Northern Fleet based above the Arctic Circle at submarine bases located on the Kola Peninsula. US Naval Intelligence understood that, once in the Mediterranean, the newly arrived Foxtrots would transit toward and then position themselves in the major choke points found within the region. Because of its battery capacity, a Foxtrot could lie in wait to ambush US/NATO ships as they transited through the narrow confines of a choke point such as the Strait of Messina.

It was estimated that, depending on the number of Foxtrots available, one could operate in the westernmost choke point of the Mediterranean, the Alboran Sea. Positioned as such, a Foxtrot had the ability to sortie through the Straits of Gibraltar into the Atlantic to intercept US/NATO ships as they approached the Mediterranean.

A second submarine was understood to operate between Sardinia and Tunisia. A third would find the Tyrrhenian Sea advantageous, so that it could monitor Sixth Fleet activities at Naples, Gaeta and Maddalena.[11] A fourth Foxtrot was estimated to operate in the Strait of Sicily, with a fifth one off the east coast of Sicily, monitoring the Strait of Messina, as well as the comings and goings of Sixth Fleet and NATO ships in Augusta Bay. Along Augusta Bay's shoreline is a huge petroleum refinery complex, where US and NATO tankers would go to take on fuel, lubricants and water.

Further to the east, a sixth Foxtrot was believed to be operating in the waters between Crete and the Libyan coast, with a seventh east of Crete and west of Cyprus and an eighth off the Levant – the

Israeli, Lebanese and Syrian coasts. The major support base for the Fifth *Eskadra* was located in the Syrian port of Latakia, where the occasional Foxtrot would come alongside a Soviet Navy auxiliary repair ship that was based there. Periodically, a Foxtrot would appear at Split, a major port in the former Yugoslavia, for maintenance.

In addition to the Foxtrots, the Soviets would periodically deploy another diesel-electric powered submarine; the Soviet Project 651 cruise missile submarine, *Podvodnaya Lodka Raketnaya Krylataya* (*PLRK*), designated by NATO as the Juliett-class cruise missile submarine (SSG).[12] Sixteen units of the class were built, with the first one entering the Soviet Navy's OOB in 1961.[13] The final unit was commissioned in 1969. As with the Foxtrots, the last Juliett was considered obsolete when it was commissioned. However, several of them remained in service through the 1980s.

The Juliett's design was based upon its primary weapon system, the P-5 *Pyatyorka* missile, the NATO-designated SS-N-3 Shaddock anti-ship cruise missile. As with other Soviet/Russian submarines, the Juliett was doubled-hulled. The outer hull was built above the pressure hull; one pair of cruise missiles was positioned forward of the sail, while the second pair was aft of the sail. With the Juliett riding on the surface, each pair would raise its two missiles together into the missiles' firing position.

Several salient recognition features of the class directly related to the fitting of its cruise missiles. The first was the large sail, which was centrally positioned on the hull. The size of the sail was attributed to the mounting of a large radar antenna housed in the forward

The Front Door tracking and mid-course guidance radar for the SS-N-3 Shaddock. (www.hazegrey.org)

Project 671 *Podvodnaya Lodka Atomnaya* Victor I SSN. (Open source)

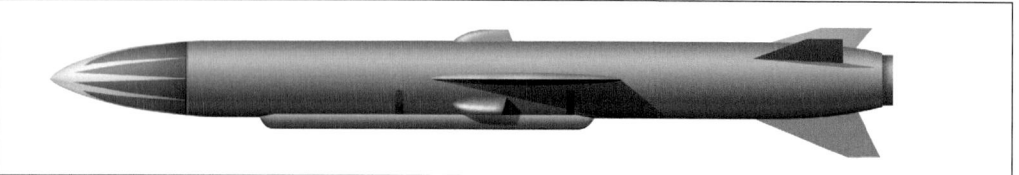

The P-70 Amethyst, known by NATO as the SS-N-7 Starbright Anti-Ship Cruise Missile. (Open source)

section of the sail. Designated by NATO as the Front Door radar, its role was to track and provide mid-course guidance for the Shaddock missile. To activate the radar, the forward part of the sail would swing open, something akin to the opening of a clam shell.[14] Another feature associated with the Shaddock missile was the two large openings positioned on either side of the outer hull behind each cruise missile launch tube. The openings were designed as blast deflectors that would take the exhaust blast from the missile up and outboard from the submarine.[15]

Two state-of-the-art, second-generation nuclear-powered submarines rounded out the Fifth *Eskadra*'s submarine OOB when the tailships began operations. The first was the Project 671 *Yorsh Podvodnaya Lodka Atomnaya* (*PLA*), or in NATO parlance, Victor I SSN. The second was the Project 670 *Podvodnaya Lodka Atomnaya Raketnaya Krylataya* (*PLARK*, cruise missile nuclear submarine), or as designated by NATO, the Charlie I SSGN.

The Victor I was armed with a combination of Type 53 torpedoes or the *RPK-2 Vyuga* (Blizzard), designated by NATO as the SS-N-15 Starfish anti-submarine missile. It could carry a conventional or nuclear depth charge.[16] The *Vyuga* was

Port side view of a Charlie I-class SSGN. (Author's collection)

A Kresta I *BRK/RKR* missile cruiser. (NHHC 1143720)

comparable to the US Navy's RUR-5 ASROC. Both weapons would be fired from six bow-mounted torpedo tubes. US Naval Intelligence considered the Victor I as a submarine that was developed to specifically counter the US Navy's nuclear attack submarines. But with a Victor I in the Mediterranean, Naval Intelligence believed the submarine's primary mission to be that of a carrier killer.

A Kynda-class *BRK/RKR* missile cruiser. (NHHC 1172678)

The second type of Soviet nuclear submarine that was operating in the Mediterranean when the tailships conducted operations was the Charlie I SSGN. This SSGN originally carried eight *P-70 Ametist* (Amethyst) missiles, the NATO-designated SS-N-7 Starbright solid fuel cruise missiles. This missile was replaced by the *P-120 Malakhite*, the NATO-designated SS-N-9 Siren. These missiles were arranged in two parallel rows inside the outer hull and forward of the sail. They could travel just below Mach 1 and could strike a

Kresta II-class *BPK* large anti-submarine ship. (Open source)

surface target with either a conventional warhead or a nuclear weapon. The Starbright's range was 35nm, while the Siren could hit a target out to 65nm. Unlike the Juliett, the Charlie I could fire its missiles while submerged at periscope depth (PD). Additionally, unlike the Juliett's SS-N3s, the Starbright did not need mid-course guidance radar on the Charlie I. Once a targeting solution was obtained, the missiles were fired.

The ability to fire its sea-skimming cruise missiles underwater made the Charlie I less vulnerable to ASW countermeasures. Unlike a traditional torpedo-equipped submarine (nuclear or conventionally powered), the Charlie I could attack from all azimuths and at ranges beyond those of escorting destroyers using active sonars. To defend

itself, a CVBG needed to detect and prosecute submarines such as the Charlie I at greater ranges and at a full 360 degrees from the centre of the battle group. This was the rationale for introducing passive towed array sonar.

To add to the complexity of countering such a submarine, the Charlie I could carry twelve Type 53 torpedoes or twelve SS-N-15 Starfish from six torpedo tubes located on its bow.

As a rule, the Soviets would try to have one SSN/SSGN deployed to the Mediterranean for every US Navy aircraft carrier operating there. The role of these submarines was to sink US Navy aircraft carriers when the 'bubble went up'.

The surface force of the Fifth *Eskadra* consisted mostly of auxiliary-type ships. Of the 40-plus ships, just over a dozen were combatants; the rest were intelligence, repair and replenishment ships. The combatant's role would depend on the individual ship's function. The chart at the end of this chapter shows the Fifth *Eskadra*'s 1972 OOB of submarines, warships and intelligence collection ships as taken from the author's notes.[17]

Combatants that would be assigned to strike US and NATO warships were surface-to-surface equipped missile ships. During the period the tailships were operating in the Mediterranean, it was not unusual to have one Soviet Navy *Bol'shoy Raketnyy Korabl* (*BRK*, large missile cruiser) in the Mediterranean from three different classes;[18] the NATO-designated Kresta I, the Kynda-class guided missile cruisers (CG) or the Kresta II-class CG.

The first two classes of missile cruisers were equipped with SS-N-3b Shaddock surface-to-surface missiles (SSMs). The Kresta I carried just four Shaddocks, whilst the Kynda carried eight with another eight reloads. The Kresta I cruisers would sail from the North Fleet base of Severomorsk in the Kola Peninsula to deploy for approximately six months in the Mediterranean. The Kynda cruisers came out of the Soviet Black Sea Fleet at Sevastopol to sail into the Mediterranean via the Dardanelles – the Turkish straits.

The third cruiser class to make an appearance was identified by NATO as the Kresta II guided missile cruiser. One can see this class was basically an improved Kresta I CG, but it possessed larger missile capacity, with varied electronics and radars. One major identification feature was the huge "long-range, three-dimensional air-search and early warning radar, sitting atop

Kashin-class DDG (*BPK* large anti-submarine ship). (US Department of Defense)

Primorye-class AGI. (NARA)

IL-38 May MPA/ASW. (Author's collection)

Table 1: Soviet Fifth Eskadra Order of Battle 1971 (derived from author's notes)

Class	Russian designation/terminology	English translation	NATO designation terminology	Number of Units
Submarines				
Project 641	*Podvodnaya Lodka/PL*	Submarine	FOXTROT SS	6
Project 651	*Podvodnaya Lodka Raketnaya Krylataya/PLRK*	Cruise Missile Submarine	JULIETT SSG	1
Project 679 Yorsh	*Podvodnaya Lodka Atomnaya/PLA*	Submarine (nuclear)	VICTOR I SSN	1
Project 670 Skat	*Podvodnaya Lodka Atomnaya Raketnaya Krylataya/PLA*	Cruise Missile Submarine (nuclear)	CHARLIE 1 SSGN	1
Surface Warships				
Project 1123 Kondor	*Protivolodochnyy Kreyser/PKR*	Anti-Submarine Cruiser	MOSKVA CHG	1
Project 70E	*Kreyser/KR*	Cruiser	Sverdlov CLG	1
Project 1134A Berkut A	*Bol'shoy Protivolodochnyy Korabol/BPK*	Large Anti-Submarine Ship	KRESTA II CG	1
Project 61	*Bol'shoy Protivolodochnyy Korabol/BPK*	Large Anti-Submarine Ship	KASIN DDG	5
Project 56A Spokoinyy	*Eskadrennyy Mononosets/EM*	Destroyer	KOTLIN SAM DDG	1
Project 56 PLO	*Eskadrennyy Mononosets/EM*	Destroyer	KOTLIN MOD DD	1
Project 30bis	*Eskadrennyy Mononosets/EM*	Destroyer	SKORYY DD	1
Project 35-M	*Storozhevoy Korabl/SKR*	Patrol Ship	MIRKA II FF	2
Project 35	*Storozhevoy Korabl/SKR*	Patrol Ship	MIRKA I FF	1
Project 770	*Srednyy Desantnyy Korabl/SDK*	Medium Landing Ship	Polnocny LSM	2
Intelligence				
Project 393A	*Gidrograficheskoye Sudno/GS*	Hydrographic Vessel	Mirnyy AGS/AGI	1
Project 394B	*Gidrograficheskoye Sudno/GS*	Hydrographic Vessel	Primor'ye AGS/AGI	1
Project 539 W	*Sudno Svyazy/SSV*	Communications Vessel	Okean AGI	1
Project 860	*Gidrograficheskoye Sudno/GS*	Hydrographic Vessel	Samara AGS/AGI	2
Project 861M	*Sudno Svyazy/SSV*	Communications Vessel	Moma AGI	3
Project 310 Batur	*Plavuchaya Baza/PB*	Floating Base	Don AS	1
Project 1886 Batur	*Plavuchaya Baza/PB*	Floating Base	Ugra AS	1

of the cruiser's large pyramid-shaped mast".[19] Its primary weapon system was the NATO-designated SS-N-14 Silex rocket-propelled anti-submarine weapon carrying a homing torpedo. It was also estimated that the Silex was a capable weapon against surface ships.[20]

These missile cruisers would be supported by up to five multi-purpose Project 61 large anti-submarine ships (BPK), the NATO-designated Kashin-class DDGs. Besides having a robust armament

of two twin-76mm dual-purpose guns, a quintuple mount of 21-inch torpedoes and a battery of Gatling guns, the Kashins carried a considerable arsenal of surface-to-air missiles (SAMs), the SA-N-1B Goa.[21]

Besides their own active and passive sensors, the major submarine and surface combatants summarised above also relied on off-board cueing for detecting, identifying and tracking USN/NATO

Tu-16 Badger bomber. (Author's collection)

combatants from several sources – dedicated tactical intelligence ships and reconnaissance aircraft.

For the former, the Fifth *Eskadra* had at its disposal about a dozen intelligence ships that could be found throughout the Mediterranean. It was not uncommon for a tailship to sight several different classes of Soviet intelligence collection ships. One of the more capable platforms was the Project 394B *Gidrograficheskoye Sudno/Korabl' Razvedyatel'nyy* hydrographic/intelligence ship, the NATO-designated Primorye-class auxiliary intelligence collection ship Auxiliary General Intelligence (AGI). This class carried numerous electronic intercept antennas, together with a robust onboard SIGINT (communication and electronic) receiving, processing and dissemination capability.[22]

Another reconnaissance, surveillance and strike asset for the Fifth *Eskadra* was embodied in two types of land-based aircraft. Prior to being pulled out of Egypt in 1972, the Soviets had based at an Egyptian Air Force base near Cairo two aircraft squadrons; one was the IL-38 May maritime patrol (MPA)/ASW aircraft and the other the medium bomber/reconnaissance aircraft, the Tu-16 Badger.

These submarines, operating with the Fifth *Eskadra*'s surface units, would manoeuvre against the carrier battle groups so as to win 'The Battle of the First Salvo'.[23]

5
ARRIVAL: SORTING THINGS OUT

Bella Napoli!

After an uneventful transit, the tailships arrived in Naples on Wednesday, 9 September. All three ships were directed to moor along the *Molo San Vincenzo*, a mole that formed a large breakwater protecting Naples' inner harbour. Each ship had to moor Mediterranean-style, or with a method euphemistically called Med-mooring.[1]

Med-mooring, the most common way vessels of all sizes moored harbour-side in the Mediterranean, required each ship to reverse in perpendicular to the *molo*. As each tailship slowly moved into position, it dropped its anchors; letting them pay out a short distance before sending out stern lines to awaiting longshoremen on the mole. This required a deft level of ship handling by each captain.

LCDR Reimann backed *Courtney* in first. LCDR Anderson followed, backing *Hammerberg* in and mooring on *Courtney*'s port side. It was then LCDR Pippinger's turn: he backed *Van Voorhis*, mooring on the port side of *Hammerberg*. Fenders were deployed and lines were passed between each ship, and a brow (walkway) was deployed between each ship. But the ships were moored too far away for a brow to be set to the mole.

This method of mooring would become routine for the tailships. Med-mooring restricted access to the ships. To go ashore, the ships' companies would have to use their own ships' boats, or use one of the 50ft utility boats from the destroyer tender, the USS *Cascade*, AD-16. Like the tailships, *Cascade* was also Med-moored in the harbour. Neapolitan water taxis could come alongside to pick up or drop off the crew from Fleet Landing situated on Naples' International Pier. Small boats operated by local watermen would also pick up garbage from the ships. Heavily chlorinated fresh water from Naples' water system was available from a water line that ran down the *molo*.

Although direct access to the *molo* was inconvenient, it did have its upside, preventing many of the enterprising Neapolitans from obtaining easy access to the ships in an attempt to sell their wares. Lack of direct access to the shore would come in handy the following year, when terrorists began to target US facilities and personnel across Europe. However, lack of direct access to the shore did pose significant challenges, as *Lester*'s former supply officer, Jack Flanagan, wrote about the comings and goings of CORTRON 8 sailors between ship and shore:

All three tailships are Med-moored. The Molo San Vincenzo is on the left. (SF2 David Truby, USN)[2]

A typical Neapolitan taxi captain and his boat would take US sailors to shore. (Author's collection)

USS *Courtney*, DE-1021, entering Naples harbour. (CDR Mark D. Tabing, USN Ret)

Lester was pier side … in Naples only twice during my time aboard. The first instance was in March of 1972 when I reported on board. The second was in September of 1973 as the ship prepared to head back to the states to be decommissioned.

In all other instances … we had to use navy small craft (e.g., 50 foot utility boats, LCMs [Landing Craft Mechanized], officers' boats, captain's gig, etc.) to get from the Fleet Landing out to the ship or vice versa. This was no small thing for a number of reasons:

Boats ran on a set schedule, meaning if you'd just missed a boat you'd have to wait 30 or 60 minutes for the next scheduled run. Waiting around for a boat was a huge time waster. Additionally if you lived ashore just barely missing a run from Fleet Landing could prevent your getting back aboard in time for morning quarters.

Occasionally a scheduled boat simply wouldn't make a run due to mechanical or crew difficulties … or … for extreme weather conditions … There could be more passengers waiting than the boat's capacity. Some boats were particularly unsuited for the task [such as the *Cascade*'s LCMs] … or so-called 'Mike'

Fleet Landing on the Molo Angioino, Naples. (Jerry Montgomery, USS *Lester*)

USS *Cascade*, AD-16, and *Denebola*, AF-56, with the tailships, 13 March 1971. (NHHC K—88830)

boats which are designed to drive up to and lower their bow ramp on to a beach. These were often used as work boats to haul cargo and vehicles around the port of Naples. When used to haul passengers they offered large capacity. The downside was a rough ride, passengers' clothes/uniforms were often stained/ripped, the lack of seating and/or grab rails made it difficult for dozens of standing passengers in the well deck of the boat to travel safely in rough weather. Often the boats were not covered so there was no shelter in case of rain. Embarking/disembarking alongside the *Cascade/Lester* could be sporty depending upon sea conditions.[3]

US Navy Support of the Ships Homeported in Naples

By the time the tailships and their sailors arrived to set up housekeeping, a very large contingent of US and NATO commands and facilities were already operating in Naples: "There are five major military activities operating in Naples – Headquarters of Allied Forces Southern Europe (NATO) [AFSOUTH]; Commander Fleet Air Mediterranean [COMFAIRMED]; US Naval Support Activity [NSA NAPLES]; Naval Air Facility; and Naval Communications Station [NAVCOMSTA NAPLES]."[4]

Maintenance and material support to the tailships were very different from the support to other units that were forwardly deployed to such ports as Yokosuka in Japan or Rota in Spain. Naples lacked the US Navy infrastructure that Yokosuka and Rota provided, such as utilities (electrical and steam power), cranes, dry docks, fuel oil bunkering, maintenance and repair shops.[5] A major challenge for the tailship crews was that they lacked the onboard equipment and personnel expertise to perform any but the most rudimentary maintenance and repairs.[6]

However, they were not completely without logistics support. For many years, the Sixth Fleet had homeported a destroyer tender, such as the USS *Cascade*, AD-16. *Cascade* possessed heavy repair machinery, a forge to cast metal fittings, advanced electronics repair and carpentry shops. Just as important, *Cascade*'s ship's company had experienced senior enlisted sailors to man those shops.

As with other destroyer tenders, *Cascade* provided 'hotel services', such as steam, electricity and fresh water to those ships requiring such services. This allowed the tailships to go 'cold iron' when they required extensive maintenance and/or repair of their engineering systems. Going alongside and shutting down the power plants allowed the ships' engineers 'snipes' to take a break from the constant need to be on duty every third day when in port; sometimes the 'snipes' were placed on port and starboard watches (12 hours on, 12 hours off). Unfortunately, despite *Cascade*'s best efforts to keep the tailships operational, the wear and tear to these vessels became all too obvious by 1973. What did not help the situation was that the tailships had to compete with the entire Sixth Fleet for *Cascade*'s maintenance support; Sixth Fleet always had priority. Overall, as Jack Flanagan related, "it's not the same as having regular access to shoreside maintenance and repair facilities".[7]

Flanagan's observations about the lack of maintenance support to the tailships was officially stated in Sixth Fleet's Command History for 1971:

The lack of dedicated shore based support for the small ships now homeported in Naples makes their maintenance difficult and frustrating.[8] Pier facilities with hotel services are not available. Cold iron services provided by the CASCADE are adequate but since this is the only tender available in Sixth Fleet, her services must be provided first to ships in Tender Availability and are not always available for the small boys. CASCADE also has some problems in maintaining her engineering plant, since she cannot adequately isolate parts of her plant for maintenances while maintaining her engineering load. Twice during the period of this report prudent engineering required that a destroyer provide cold iron services to the tender. Dedicated pier space with adequate fresh water, steam, and 50 cycle power is a vital need for ships which must maintain themselves on a long term vice deployed basis.[9]

Support to the Ships' Companies in Naples

There was a US Navy shore support facility in Naples. It was centred at the Naval Support Activity (NSA) Naples located in the Agnano area of the city, roughly six miles away, or 20–45 minutes through traffic-clogged roads by car from Fleet Landing. Travel by bus would take much longer.[10]

Originally, NSA Naples was established in the early 1950s to support US Navy personnel assigned to the NATO base of AFSOUTH. Over time, the facility expanded with other commands to include the tailships' reporting command, Commander Task Force 67 (CTF 67), as well as Commander, Anti-Submarine Warfare, Sixth Fleet (COMASWSIXTHFLT) and Commander Fleet Air Mediterranean (COMFAIRMED).

NSA's primary support to the men of CORTRON 8 and their dependents was a commissary, Navy Exchange, Housing Assistance Office, a DoD-operated school for kindergarten-age children through to 12th-grade high school students, naval hospital, movie theatre and large recreation area located within an extinct volcano that was named Carney Park.[11] Tailship crews and dependents took advantage of these facilities as best they could. There was no outreach specifically directed at homeported ships.[12]

Modern Naples: What Awaited the Americans – *Bella Napoli*

The following is from the US Navy's monthly magazine describing what awaited a sailor homeported in Naples: "Celebrated the world over for its beauty, Naples lies along the semicircle formed by the enchanting Bay of Naples, over which rises the cone of Mount Vesuvius. It is the commercial, cultural and artistic center of southern Italy and one of the important ports on the Mediterranean."[13]

But the beauty of the city, the energy of its people and the wealth of Naples as the capital of an independent kingdom – the Kingdom of the Two Sicilies – had changed markedly when the sailors and their families arrived in 1970. During the nineteenth century, Naples lost its primacy in Italy and was relegated to the periphery of European affairs. The completion of Italian unification in 1861, in particular, had a devastating effect on the city and surrounding province of Campania, which were then subjected to "a series of fiscal and tariff measures that precipitated a spiralling economic decline".[14]

Mussolini's neglect of the city's needs, coupled with the destruction of the city by Allied bombing and Nazi sabotage, left Naples at its historical low point. The celebrated Australian war correspondent and historian Alan Moorehead wrote after the Allies arrived in Naples in October 1943: "For anyone who loved Italy it was a bitter experience to come to Naples. The traditional talents of the people, their charm and generosity, seemed for a time to have vanished in the savage and abject struggle for existence." However, during the three decades that followed the war, Naples had made a recovery of sorts; one that was very much a partial exercise. What faced the tailship sailors of CORTRON 8 and those with families was a city and immediate countryside that had "experienced a long, slow, and decidedly uneven economic recovery" from the Second World War.[15]

What the Americans saw before them was a city that:

… seemed to be locked in a never-ending downward spiral. Noise, water and air pollution reached dangerous levels [on some days it was nearly impossible to see Mount Vesuvius for the air pollution]; schools deteriorated; garbage went uncollected; and hospitals, sewers and museums lapsed into various states of disrepair. Year after year, the city remained at-or-near the top of Italian municipalities in a number of negative categories: it had the highest level of infant mortality; the greatest level of infectious disease; the most substandard housing; and even the greatest number of rats. A cholera outbreak in 1973 was followed by a major earthquake in 1980. Tourists fled, industries languished, and crime soared.[16]

The tailship sailors who were married and brought their families to Naples had their own experiences; some were similar, whilst others were unique from both a positive and negative perspective.

Unlike other US Navy facilities, Naples had no on-base housing. It was Navy policy to have Americans assimilate as much as possible with Neapolitans and within Naples and its surroundings. Those wishing to have a place ashore for themselves and their families had to find somewhere to rent through the Navy's Housing Assistance Office at Naval Support Activity (NSA) Naples. Through the assistance office, each sailor negotiated the lease with the landlord, then he would be subject to the vagaries of the individual landlord for the life of the lease. However, working with the Italian landlords was generally a good experience, as for the most part they enjoyed the Americans for their regular monthly rents.[17]

For those single sailors who could rent an apartment or a villa, life ashore in Naples, between periods at sea, was a singular experience. A *Courtney* sailor's experience was typical:

A lot of us shipmates lived in Licola. We would regularly visit any of 6–8 different apartments of friends. I don't remember knowing anyone from other ships. *Courtney* boys stuck together.[18] … Life in Licola was very sweet. We were all very close. Some guys had girlfriends and there were always women around … I did date one Italian girl, but that was very rare amongst my friends.

We spent a lot of time on the beach which was right across [from] or right behind our apartments. My favorite day was to go to a local market and get some Provolone cheese, Prosciutto ham, and some wonderful homemade rolls and lie on the beach with friends.

The other thing we had in common was music. Music was always playing. We all bought the newest records and played them loudly. Truthfully, most of the Licola guys were the drug users from the ship.[19]

Radioman Third Class Richard Eriksson had been serving in Naples prior to joining the *Van Voorhis* at Newport in 1970 before the ship went to Boston to be fitted with its ITASS gear. During the ship's refit in Boston, he married his fiancée. Shortly after *Van Voorhis* arrived in Naples, Eriksson had made his way to the NSA housing office and obtained a rental:

I had liberty and found an apartment to rent just outside of the Naval Communications Center [co-located with NSA Naples]. I went downtown to the telephone center in Naples and called my wife, telling her to sell our 1964 Dodge and use the money to buy an airplane ticket to Naples. We lived there from 1970 to 1972 and our daughter was born at the Naval Hospital up on the hill.[20]

Another radioman, Steve Magistro, was a single sailor and *Courtney* was his home during his entire time in the Mediterranean:

I lived aboard ship and obviously didn't have to deal with living arrangements. I did make many trips to NSA with RMC Jack Simpson in his 1969 Ford Torino to eat lobster tail after returning from a cruise. I also frequented my two favorite bars, the El Morocco and the San Francisco. Other than that, it was life aboard the *Courtney*.[21]

Another *Courtney* sailor, Oceanographic System Technician (OT) Second Class Steve Kendall, had a comparable experience:

I lived on the *Courtney* even though others lived ashore. I was single and it was convenient to live on the ship for I didn't have to worry about missing the liberty boat in the morning thus missing quarters, I could get to my bunk in minutes instead of driving to outlying areas where most [of] the guys lived either with their families or splitting rent with a buddy. I could avoid the liberty boat rush and go ashore on liberty at my leisure, and there were always plenty of crew mates that would be available to 'Steam' with. I spent time at Capodichino waiting for the ship with one of the cooks so the chow wasn't too bad. It is always good to make friends with a cook. The food was at least as good as what I could cook for myself and there were plenty of restaurants on the beach to fill in the gaps.

The down side was you were regularly tapped for some duty section help/drill or leaned on by those sad-eyed married guys to stand their duty for them. We liked their wives so we would sometimes cave in.

The *Courtney* was my home throughout my tour including the time the ship was in dry dock, except for the occasional invites to spend the night with friends who lived ashore. Living onboard during the time in dry dock, one realized how dependent a ship is on the water it sails in. It got extremely hot in the berthing compartments and sleeping took place on deck and/or in the air conditioned van.

During the dry dock period, food was served on the *Hammerberg* who was tied up nearby, or you could buy it from a nearby small Italian restaurant. *Courtney*'s bottom was scraped and inspected and when we were refloated it was a sigh of relief, for sleeping conditions improved immensely.[22]

These experiences varied, depending on whether the sailor or officer was accompanied by his family. One immediate difference was that senior enlisted and officers had a navy person (sponsor) who lived in Naples and was familiar with the ins and outs of Neapolitan life, and they were a big help getting the sailor and his dependents settled in at their new home. Lieutenant Jack Flanagan aboard *Lester* recalled that his sponsor "had made arrangements for Carol [Jack's wife] to stay at the Pensione Monte Spina, not too far from both NSA and the NATO Base (AFSOUTH) in Bagnoli". Shortly after his wife's arrival, the young navy couple moved into the fifth floor at 157B Via Manzoni in a multi-storey apartment complex in Naples' Posillipo area.

Flanagan continued:

The building was clean and well-maintained … very spacious … all the floors except for the kitchen and bathroom had a greenish gold onyx tiles. Large windows opened up on two sides of the (corner) living room and the outboard sides of the dining room and two bedrooms. Outside of the windows were rollup persianes (i.e. shutters that could be lowered to ward off the midday heat) … There was only one other American family in the building when we moved in.[23]

Lieutenant Steven Edwards was aboard *Lester*. He had left his wife and his two boys in Newport when he took his tailship to Naples. As with many married men with a family, Edwards' family joined him in Naples. Unfortunately, what occurred for so many of the families when they stepped off the airplane at Naples airport was that their sailor was at sea. However, as an officer or a senior enlisted man, Edwards had a sponsor in Naples who met the families when they arrived and coordinated the travel, arrival, housing, etc., with them. Edwards recounted:

I don't recall any details except that it was nearly flawless. We of course were at sea. But all my wife can recall is she and the boys, and our dog left Newport and arrived at the American Hotel without a bump. The car also arrived on schedule. I wish I knew who was in charge cuz it was a logistical miracle. Airline tickets, busses, transfers, drive from Rome to Naples, hotel rooms etc., all without any confusing problems for the families.[24]

Claire Kelso was the wife of a *Courtney* sailor. Her husband did not have a sponsor, as he was a junior petty officer and a navy reservist on two years of active duty. Luckily, he was able to arrange to have someone meet Claire and their baby daughter at the airport. She recalled:

I remember arriving at the airport in Italy in June of 1971 with one-year-old baby Erin in my arms and expecting to be met by my husband, John. However, the USS *Courtney* had been deployed and I was met by Bob Shipman, who I learned was our next-door neighbor at the apartment John had rented for our little family. Bob had a photo of Erin and me and introduced himself, explaining that the *Courtney* had a schedule change and that John had asked him to meet Erin and me at the airport and get us settled into our apartment. I was naturally disappointed, since John had been in Italy for some time before our arrival, but I had to make the best of it. Then in the middle of the night, I heard someone coming through the front door, and it was John. Due to mechanical problems, the *Courtney* had returned to Naples earlier than planned. So, our little family was together again![25]

Ensign Jim Haddock, who was prior enlisted, remembered the junior sailors who served with him aboard *Lester* and what conditions they faced while homeported in Naples:

As for the junior enlisted sailors, they were, overall, good young men who put up with some miserable living and working conditions. A majority were there as an alternative to the draft and Vietnam. They worked hard when properly led, but their daily lives were constrained with poor living conditions aboard ship and limited opportunities for recreation in Naples, and a few of them acted out. A very few were married and lived ashore, but they struggled to make ends meet on an E-3 or E-4 salary."[26]

Haddock continued about life for his enlisted sailors:

The single sailors did not have much to look forward to being in Naples. Near the port, there was a very spartan USO and the Seaman's Club which was used mostly by merchant sailors. There were some service clubs at the AFSOUTH base and at the Naval Support Activity, but they were quite far away from the port. Transportation [local buses] in the evening was a problem, and the shipboard sailors (except the CPOs [Chief Petty Officers]) did not patronise them. There was an active bar scene in downtown Naples near the port. A few became steady customers, and two or three got into trouble with the shore patrol or the Italian police every once in a while – most often, drunk and disorderly, but, also, selling sea-store cigarettes, urinating on street corner shrines, etc. Once in a while, a romance ashore would bloom, usually ending in a broken heart. I do remember one GM3 [Gunners Mate Third Class] who married an Italian girl he met in port. I ran into them at the Navy Exchange in Norfolk [Virginia] five or six years later. They were still madly in love, but I don't think either of them had learned much of the other's language yet. Most of the junior, single sailors made a home on the ship and waited for it to be over.[27]

Oceanographic Systems Technician Third Class (OT3) Jim Whyte arrived aboard *Lester* in March 1973. By that time, the ships of the squadron had been homeported in Naples for two-and-a-half years. Many of his fellow OTs had already established apartments ashore. Whyte was able to buddy up with his fellow OTs:

For a part of the time I lived in Licola Lido. During the summer months, especially August when the entire country of Italy is on vacation, the traffic would rival, or even surpass, the worst of the Jersey Shore traffic. I was very fortunate in that the second apartment I lived in, and shared with two other sailors, was literally right on the beach. Our back door opened onto the sand. Lots of parties, and most of the time locals mingled with sailors.[28]

Whyte continued by recounting how some Neapolitan food dishes had a certain way of catching up on Americans:

Something I found difficult to relate was the Italian taste in certain street food. One time a few of us went to this amusement park in Naples and outside the entrance someone was selling chunks of various animal viscera. Another were [sic] the vendors of mussels, sold with a whole lemon. One of our division members must have had some bad mussels over the holidays because on our next cruise he turned very yellow. He had contracted hepatitis and was evacuated from the ship, and the rest of us had to get gamma globulin shots. He later returned, good as new.[29]

During the summer of 1973, Naples also experienced an outbreak of cholera. This was nothing new for the city, as it had experienced similar outbreaks through the course of its 2,000-plus year history. Historically, city officials were constantly watching for outbreaks of disease, especially in the overcrowded slums of the city. The first few cases were initially identified in April:

Officials suspected that the source of the cholera was raw mussels from the Bay of Naples, so the government banned their sale, and stepped up inspections of restaurant kitchens. The streets were sprayed with a bleach solution, and the city suddenly became very clean. The government even began to plan a system to collect and treat its sewage instead of dumping it into the bay, as had been done for more than 2,000 years.[30]

Peter McCammon, the former commanding officer of the tender USS *Graham County*, recounted that Neapolitans considered lemon juice would disinfect their food. Lemons thus became extremely scarce during the summer. But when the government lifted the ban on mussels from markets and restaurants, the displays of mussels were surrounded by lemons.[31]

The Lancet medicinal science magazine reported:

From August to October 1973, a cholera El Tor outbreak, with 127 laboratory-confirmed cases, occurred in Naples, and its surroundings. There were 12 deaths. The route by which the infection was introduced has not yet been tracked down but it seems likely that it reached Naples via infected mussels imported from Tunisia or via healthy or infected carriers who arrived in Naples by air or sea from an endemic area. The dissemination should be attributed to mussels' eating habits. The infected were mainly adults and old people with no statistical difference between sexes.[32]

Not one American sailor or their dependents contracted cholera, as all were inoculated against the disease before they left the US for Naples.

However, some negative experiences came from unexpected quarters. For one, Steve Edwards of the *Lester* remembers what his wife experienced as a 'destroyer wife', and it was not from a Neapolitan: 'After a wives affair hosted by COMFAIRMED ladies association and including the newly arrived "destroyer wives", one wife of a fairly senior staff officer commented to my wife, "frankly we wished you destroyer people had never arrived" … NICE!'[33]

As with life in general, it is what one makes of any situation. For the wives of the sailors, Claire Kelso's experience living in Naples was pretty typical:

I met several other women whose husbands were stationed on ships that were part of the Sixth Fleet in Naples. We formed some strong bonds and supported one another through the ups and downs of Navy family life … When the ships were deployed, the wives and children got together to cook, enjoy meals, play cards, watch each other's children when needed, to laugh and sometimes to cry. We had some great times at the beautiful swimming pool at Allied Forces South in Naples. We also made a few memorable trips to 'Shoe Alley' where we purchased beautiful Italian-made shoes, sandals, and handbags that were slightly less than perfect at cut rate prices. When it was time for the ships to return to port, we changed gears, cleaned house, and prepared for our husbands to return. We loved our 'girl time' and we loved our 'couples time'.[34]

Professionally, tailship sailors improvised as required to keep their ships operational under conditions that were something less than what they would have expected if homeported in CONUS (Continental United States). For many of them and their families, living in Naples and Italy was pretty much a rude awaking. Some adapted and enjoyed their time in Naples and Italy writ large. Some were able to take leave and travel throughout Italy and parts of Europe as well. As a sailor's wife, Claire Kelso's experience was typical:

Since we were living on enlisted pay, our budget didn't allow for much travel. John's parents came to visit from the States in the summer of 1972, and together we traveled to England to visit John's extended family there. Later that year, Erin and I flew to Barcelona with a few other 'Courtney wives' to meet the ship and spend some family time on the beautiful Barcelona beaches. I still remember the fabulous food and the Sangria!

Others did not enjoy their time in Naples and could not wait to get back to CONUS. But for the most part, the experience of tailship sailors and their families living in Naples was typical, as Claire Kelso wrote:

Our return to the States in 1973 was bittersweet. I had missed my family back home and couldn't wait to see them again, but

I would miss my Navy family and the experiences I had in Italy. Thankfully, we kept in touch with three of the families with whom we bonded in Naples, and our friendships continued after we all returned home to the States.[35]

6
OPERATIONAL PLANNING CONSIDERATIONS

The United States Sixth Fleet in the Mediterranean is faced with a Soviet naval challenge more than 25 times greater than five years ago.[1]

Developing an operational plan requires the commander to know two interdependent factors. The first is the intelligence situation pertaining to OOB, capability and intention of the enemy; the second is the geographical space the enemy occupies.

Intelligence Situation

The following summary from the official Sixth Fleet Command History for 1970 indicates the level of Soviet naval activity and OOB confronting the Sixth Fleet and NATO in 1970, serving as a backdrop to tailship operations:

Information available concerning the status of potential hostile forces ranged from satisfactory to marginal. Intelligence for support of nuclear and conventional war operations was satisfactory for the European Soviet Bloc regions. The intelligence support for the same operations in possible threat countries of the eastern and southern Mediterranean littoral improved significantly.[2]

Sixth Fleet's intelligence report further added that Soviet Mediterranean naval activity remained at a "high level", with a 20 percent increase in the number of unit operating days for the calendar year compared to 1969.[3] Sixth Fleet intelligence indicated that the number of operational units (surface combatants, submarines and auxiliaries) would be maintained at 45–50 units during the winter months.[4]

Furthermore, Sixth Fleet intelligence emphasised that Fifth *Eskadra*-assigned survey ships (AGSs) were conducting a high degree of hydro-acoustic operations during the period. Sixth Fleet was especially concerned that these single and multi-ship survey operations were concentrated at key Mediterranean choke points – "Hurd Bank, southern approaches to the Strait of Messina, southwest Adriatic, Aegean, Straits of Gibraltar and eastern coast of Sardinia".[5] Ironically, these operations appeared to mirror US Navy hydro-acoustic operations prior to the tailships entering the Mediterranean.

With regard to the Soviet air threat posed to the Sixth Fleet and NATO:

Additional capabilities which included: extensive use of naval air reconnaissance and surveillance aircraft in Egypt consisting of 6–11 TU-16 BADGER and 4 BE-12 MAIL aircraft all with Egyptian markings. In addition the Soviets deployed AN-12s and IL-18 (ASW) aircraft to the UAR [United Arab Republics] … Some of the AN-12s probably SIGINT configured. The helicopter carrier MOSKVA deployed to the Med twice and the LENINGRAD made her maiden Mediterranean deployment during March 1970.[6]

Of importance to the tailships, Sixth Fleet intelligence saw that a

subtle shift took place in Soviet SSM deployments. Prior to 1970 the force level usually included 2–3 SSM surface ships and one submarine … this has shifted to one surface SSM platform and two (sometimes three) SSM submarines … The new CHARLIE class SSGN initiated regular Mediterranean patrols in 1970.[7]

This shift took place in recognition of the vulnerability of their surface SSM 'shooters' (SSM-equipped ships) to Sixth Fleet 'tattletale' tactics that would have a Sixth Fleet destroyer follow the Soviet, and if it appeared ready to fire off its missiles, the US destroyer would open fire first.

Russian sources stated that Charlie I-class SSGNs were introduced into the Mediterranean in 1970 as part of the Soviet Navy's global *OKEAN* (Ocean) exercise. Two of the SSGNs operated in the Mediterranean during the first months of 1970. Submarine K-25 completed its Mediterranean deployment on 9 April, whilst K-143 did so on 30 April. The Charlies' departure left a significant gap in the number of Soviet nuclear submarines operating in the Mediterranean through the summer. Only as a response to the Jordanian Crisis did three Victor I SSNs enter the Med. K-53 arrived in November, departing from the western Mediterranean on 23 December, whilst K-147 and K-323 arrived in December, leaving on 24 February 1971. The submarine SSM gap was partially filled when the Juliett K-67 entered the Mediterranean in September for a four-month deployment.[8]

Of course, the ever-present Foxtrot-class submarine was another factor in tailship operational planning. As mentioned previously, Foxtrots were deployed in the many Mediterranean choke points. However, by the time the tailships began operations, several Foxtrots were also operating in the Mediterranean's eastern basin, in response to Sixth Fleet carrier and amphibious operations (Operation DEEP EXPRESS) in the same region during the Jordanian Crisis. Of the nine Foxtrots in the Mediterranean in October, four were operating in the eastern basin, with Foxtrots B-2 and B-4 actively conducting reconnaissance against DEEP EXPRESS.[9]

Another aspect of Sixth Fleet's intelligence assessment, one that was pertinent to the tailships, was the fleet's need for additional forces and authorised operating hours, capable of constant surveillance and intelligence collection against the increased numbers of Soviet Mediterranean naval forces.[10]

The overall assessment of Soviet Fifth *Eskadra* capabilities and intent highlighted above would be factored in any given Sixth Fleet operational plan and associated tactical deployment (to include tailship deployment). The intelligence assessment hinged on the latest intelligence collection and analysis by the US Navy's Ocean Surveillance Information System (OSIS). OSIS was developed as the

A typical Classic Bullseye AN/FRD-10 HF/DF circular antenna array. (Library of Congress HABS HI-522-B-1)

result of "a staff study approved by the Director of Naval Intelligence in 1964 [that] endorsed the development of a comprehensive information processing system for ocean surveillance information".[11] Commander of the Sixth Fleet, Vice Admiral David Richardson, supported the system's creation because of the need for a dedicated Mediterranean surveillance capability in response to increased Soviet activity.[12] By 1970, "OSIS emerged … as the highest expression of the Navy's OPINTEL [operational intelligence] art".[13] By the time the tailships entered the Mediterranean, OSIS had evolved into an all-source intelligence collection, analytical and dissemination system providing the most complete information on Soviet naval operating forces.

OSIS consisted of a global network of SOSUS facilities, HF/DF stations (called Classic Bullseye[14]), signals and communication intelligence (SIGINT/COMINT) collection systems and imagery reconnaissance satellites (IMINT).[15] Additionally, US and NATO ships and aircraft provided sighting reports, including photography and motion picture footage of Soviet ships and submarines. These reports were incorporated in the latest intelligence provided to the planners.

The heart of the system was the Fleet Ocean Surveillance Information Center (FOSIC), co-located at the headquarters of the US Navy's Office of Naval Intelligence (ONI), Suitland, Maryland. It supported the three FOSICs and the two Fleet Ocean Surveillance Information Facilities (FOSIFs). For CTF 67 and CORTRON 8 staff, the FOSIF located at Naval Station Rota, Spain (NAVSTA Rota), provided the OPINTEL on Soviet aircraft, surface and subsurface units in the Mediterranean.

Established in 1970, FOSIF Rota "began as a specialist OPINTEL cell supporting Sixth Fleet operations".[16] The FOSIF "focused upon systematized collection, processing and dissemination with an eye to I&W intelligence; exploitation of Soviet command, control, and communications (C3) activity; more efficient surveillance".[17] Each morning, at 0500 hours Greenwich Mean Time, the FOSIF would disseminate, at the SECRET NOFORN level, a message that would provide the best available position reports on Soviet aircraft, surface and subsurface units in the Mediterranean, as well as declarations of Soviet Black Sea Fleet warships and naval auxiliaries scheduled to transit through the Bosphorus Strait, as stipulated by the Montreux Convention. This report would also inform Sixth Fleet of Soviet naval units transiting to the Mediterranean from North Fleet and Baltic Fleet bases.

The 'Sixth Fleet 1970 Command History' was succinct regarding the intelligence value that FOSIF provided to Sixth Fleet units: "FOSIF has been of immense value in providing the most accurate intelligence and estimates rapidly to all levels of command. In the future FOSIF will expand its operations to cover larger aspects of the SOVMED [Soviet Mediterranean] problem."[18]

Climatic Considerations

The Mediterranean climate is characterised by dry summers and mild, wet winters. The main cause of the Mediterranean's dry summer is the subtropical ridge extending northwards during the summer from Africa and migrating south during the winter months due to increasing north–south temperature differences.[19] Seasonal changes in the Mediterranean can bring dramatic and hazardous weather conditions; March/April and October/November can have severe storms and high seas, which affected ITASS operations.

Mediterranean Hydrodynamics

Admiral Isaac C. Kidd, USN, the Sixth Fleet commander, fully appreciated the unique hydrodynamics of the Mediterranean. His assessment is worth noting in full:

The Mediterranean is probably the worst body of water on the face of the earth in which to find a submarine, bar none. The hot winds off the desert for instance rapidly evaporate the surface water. The residual salt sinks. It causes a great turbulence, and variations in salinity. This in turn affects the paths of sound waves as they travel, just like a light going through a prism as it hits these walls of different chemical density. They bend. The fish down here, the marine life, are very chatty creatures. They just jabber away all the time and create a very high ambient noise level … The bottom of the Mediterranean Sea is configured like the interlocking rings of the Ballentine's beer ad, where each of those rings is like the lip of a cup. The cup is deep in the center; so you have these cups close to each other and as you move from bowl to bowl, things in the bowl make noise. The noise tends to reverberate back and forth between the sides. The chemical composition of the water in these bowls varies, depending on where they are in relation to the prevailing winds. The density contributes to the noise. Consequently, all of these factors outlined greatly affect the ability of antisubmarine ships to find submarines.[20]

Mediterranean hydrodynamics consist of three layers of water mass: a surface layer with depths from the surface ranging between 250–1,000ft; the intermediate layer ranges between 1,000ft and 2,000ft; whilst the deep layer that sinks to the bottom ranges from 2,000ft to well over 5,000ft. A separate bottom layer is missing. Each layer exhibits differences in density, salinity and temperature, and these variances are directly related to the depths of the subdivisions (the seas) of the Mediterranean. They greatly influence how effectively submarine hunters can operate a passive sonar system such as ITASS.[21]

The rivers that flow into the Mediterranean replace about one-third of the water lost through evaporation. Because evaporation is so great, especially during the summer months, colder surface waters from the Atlantic continuously flow through the Straits of Gibraltar. Most of this surface water flows eastward along Africa's north coast – coincidentally, the route Soviet submarines took as they transited in or out of the Mediterranean. As it moves eastward, this flow diminishes, but it is still detectable through the Sicilian Strait and all the way to the Levant. Correspondingly, only a small amount of water enters the Mediterranean from the Black Sea through the Bosphorus.[22]

Salinity also varies throughout the Mediterranean's surface layer, although that layer is uniformly salty. As evaporation, salinity, density and temperature increase, the surface layer sinks. It pushes the bottom water layers westward through the Straits of Gibraltar, increasing the inflowing water from the Atlantic. The Mediterranean is like a breathing organism, inhaling surface water and exhaling deep water.[23]

The Mediterranean's surface water layer circulates anti-clockwise in each of the two major basins. However, if one divides the inland sea in half west to east, the northern half consists of numerous islands that create many smaller eddies and localised currents. This only adds complexity to the overall circulation pattern of the Mediterranean. Additionally:

> Sound propagation characteristics in the major Mediterranean basins … were well known from the surface to 100 feet below the primary layer, but was limited for the Med's deep sound channel, where a relatively long wave length, low frequency, passive towed array is designed to operate. The high ambient noise in the Med, a result of fairly shallow depths and a high concentration of surface traffic, was another element.[24]

Tides are not a major consideration throughout the Mediterranean. There is little difference between high and low tides.

Water temperature was another factor in determining how to deploy the ITASS array. During the summer months, water temperatures of 80°F (26.6°C) were common. The mean temperature for the Mediterranean's eastern basin in August is approximately 88°F (31°C). The waters in the Gulf of Sirte, off the coast of Libya, as well those in Turkey's Gulf of Iskenderun, routinely register such temperatures.[25]

Water temperature was also a factor for Soviet submarines. Conditions for Soviet submariners in the Mediterranean during the summer months were comparable to those of Soviet Foxtrot-class submarines operating in Cuban waters during the Cuban Missile Crisis of 1962:

> The diesel Foxtrots proved unsuitable for the operation. The boats, especially in that climate, were hot; temperatures inside reached 50°C (122°F), forcing the crew to cool off by sitting neck deep in water. The boats lacked cooling systems for their batteries, which greatly complicated recharging. The Foxtrots furthermore had to surface often to receive instructions from Moscow and recharge batteries.[26]

With intelligence and weather/hydrodynamic data, the planners determined tailship operating areas and individual tracks that they would follow. However, once at sea, it was not unusual for any one of the tailship commanders to disregard the plan and plot their own tracks.

ITASS Operational Planning Process

The CTF 67 and CORTRON 8 staffs planned upcoming tailship operations from the top floor of the six-storey NSA Naples administration building, located within the greater NSA compound. The compound was situated in the town of Agnano, a suburb west of Naples proper in the shadow of the active volcano, Solfatara. When the wind was just right, the smell of sulphur filled the air.

The top floor housed the executive offices of Rear Admiral Pierre Charbonnet, USN, Commander Task Force 67 (CTF 67) ASW Force Sixth Fleet (COMASWFORSIXTHFLT), and Rear Admiral William Clifford, USN, the Deputy Commander, who was also the officer in charge of the Operations Center for the command. The Operations Center was manned 24/7, and behind the vaulted door, both staffs worked out tailship operational plans and tactical deployments. This process was an iterative one, and for the CORTRON 8 Commander and his staff, a frustrating experience.

CTF 67 planners would review the intelligence reports and develop a SECRET level operational order to be disseminated to CORTRON 8 and the individual tailship(s). CTF 67's operations staff would decide on the general location for the ship tracks, such as the eastern Ionian Sea.

The CORTRON 8 staff was often frustrated that the CTF 67 staff responsible for laying down the tracks did not understand the intricacies of ITASS or the capabilities of the ageing ships and hull-mounted radars and sonars. They did not plot tracks on actual Mediterranean nautical charts. Instead, they drew tracks on blank plotting charts, writing latitude and longitude markings in longhand along the margins. When CORTRON 8 staff plotted the coordinates on actual Mediterranean charts, they found that the tracks were often placed over water too shallow for a tailship to effectively deploy its towed array, or were inside of territorial waters. This was obviously not acceptable, because countries on the North African coast were not friendly toward US Navy operations; Libya especially. US Rules of Engagement stipulated that air and surface units must operate 30 miles beyond any given coastline.[27]

Additionally, the distance between successive tracks (more than one track would be part of the overall operation) as laid down by CTF 67 staff officers was so great that it required a tailship to exceed its maximum speed of 27 knots (not one of the three DEs could reach, nor sustain, 27 knots). It was not uncommon that an operation required a 30-knot speed overall to travel to the next ITASS track start point. COMCORTRON 8 and his staff would address these problems, many times "on the fly, doing the best they could with the orders they were given".[28] It was only later in the squadron's Mediterranean deployment that COMCORTRON 8 staff went to CTF 67 Operations Center prior to an ITASS "operation to review and re-plot the tracks – injecting tactical reality".[29]

Also, a typical plan did not address the potential benefit of advance coordination with the deployed P-3 Orion ASW squadrons operating over the Mediterranean; two squadrons deployed to the Mediterranean on a six-month rotation, with one squadron flying out of NAVSTA Rota, Spain, whilst the other flew out of NAVSTA Sigonella, Sicily.

The Rota-based squadron flew missions over the western Mediterranean and the Atlantic side of the Straits of Gibraltar.[30] The Sigonella-based squadron conducted missions over the Strait of Sicily, the Ionian Sea and south to the Gulf of Sirte, then east toward the Levant.[31] In addition to operating out of Sigonella, squadron aircraft often flew to NAVSTA Soudha Bay on the Greek Island of Crete, from which to stage search operations over the Mediterranean's eastern basin.

Rota-based squadron aircraft flew well away from the Algerian coastline, while P-3 missions out of Sigonella kept well away from the Libyan and Egyptian coastlines. It was often serendipity when a P-3, flying over a tailship's operational area, was able to fly against a tailship submarine contact. However, if an aircraft was not available, a tailship that was 'hot' with a submarine contact could request an aircraft from CTF 67, which usually had an aircraft on ready alert status. Only through COMCORTRON 8's initiative was coordination improved between the ships of the squadron and the P-3 squadron aircraft.[32]

With the latest intelligence, operation planners also reviewed weather information. The Fleet Weather Center, Rota Spain, provided the planners with the latest weather predictions and ocean water conditions. The effects of weather and hydrodynamic conditions on tailship operational planning and tactical deployment can be understood at two interrelated levels – seasonal variations and weather and hydrodynamic predictions within a given season.

Support to Sixth Fleet Units

CTF 67 plans for tailship operations did not involve tailships providing direct tactical ASW support to Six Fleet units, especially CVBGs. The reason was because carriers received direct tactical ASW support from their own air wing, as well as from their escorting destroyers and land-based aircraft, and US Navy nuclear-powered attack submarines.

US Navy SSNs operated in the Mediterranean, and they were available to provide tactical ASW. Although they were not integrated into the CVBG OOB (this would come later, when at least two SSNs were officially integrated into a CVBG OOB), it was taken for granted that a US Navy SSN would operate, either directly against a Soviet SSN/SSGN by tracking the submarine's movement, or it would go ahead of the CVBG's position of intended movement and/or the CVBG's selected operations area, and 'sanitise' it to make sure Soviet submarines were not in the area.

Also, when available to the Sixth Fleet, an entirely dedicated ASW task group would augment the tactical support to Sixth Fleet CVBGs. The task group would consist of an Essex-class CVS operating

ASW aircraft and helicopters, such as the twin-engine S-2 Tracker and SH-3 Sea King respectively.

However, when the tailships began operating in the Mediterranean, the dedicated ASW carrier task groups were being phased out because they were considered too expensive. They were being replaced by reconfigured carrier air wings. These multi-

The USS *Sunfish*, SSN-649. (NH 1139759)

USS *Wasp*, CVS-18, with S-2 Trackers and SH-3 Sea Kings. (NHHC 97510)

The Light Airborne Multi-Purpose System (LAMPS) SH-2 Seasprite helicopter. (U.S. Defense Imagery: DN-SC-87-08838)

helicopters, such as the Kaman Aircraft Corporation SH-2 Seasprite. OTSC Chief Ralph Rooney related that, "we [*Courtney*] ran tests with LAMPS equipped ships. It was fun, but other than some closely controlled tests, ineffective."[33]

Additionally, the long-range, four-engine, land-based P-3 Orion fixed-wing ASW aircraft and SSNs would provide direct tactical support to the CVBGs. The Essex-class CVS USS *Wasp*, CVS-18, was one of the last ASW carriers to operate with the Sixth Fleet when tailships were present. During the first two months of 1971, the *Wasp* and its escorts operated with the Sixth Fleet and participated in ASW operations against Fifth *Eskadra* submarines.[34]

CORTRON 8 and CTF 67 staffs considered most, if not all, of the above factors in planning tailship operations.

purpose air wings were equipped with fighter, attack, electronic warfare, refuelling and airborne early warning aircraft, and ASW

7
SPECIAL HYDROGRAPHIC OPERATIONS: OCTOBER–DECEMBER 1970

It did not take long for the tailships to begin operations under the guise of 'special hydrographic operations'. After three weeks in Naples, during which the ships and squadron staff sorted things out, all three tailships prepared to depart on Wednesday, 30 September for their first dedicated ITASS operations. Reimann's *Courtney* and Anderson's *Hammerberg* would head out to commence ITASS calibration tests in the Tyrrhenian Sea using the Second World War veteran and GUPPY-converted submarine, USS *Threadfin*, SS-410, as a cooperative target.[1] Vollmer would take *Van Voorhis* to the Ionian Sea for its first ITASS operation using another Second World War-era GUPPY-converted submarine, USS *Clamagore*, SS-343, as a target.[2]

Courtney and *Hammerberg* departed Naples on 30 September, and during the early hours of 1 October began streaming their ITASS arrays in the Tyrrhenian Sea. At 0800 hours, CDR C.C. King took *Threadfin* from Naples to begin operating with the two tailships. At 1500 hours, King ordered his boat to submerge. Once underwater, *Threadfin* "commenced steering various courses at various speeds and depths",[3] these manoeuvres providing an opportunity for the tailships to obtain solid acoustics on *Threadfin*.

During the next 72-hour period, both ships made frequent course and speed changes (speeds alternating between five and 12 knots).[4] This continued until the late evening of 4 October, when Reimann ordered *Courtney*'s array to be retrieved. Then he headed his ship back to Naples, arriving on 5 October.

Hammerberg and *Threadfin* continued operating together, "conducting oceanographic equipment evaluation" until late on Wednesday, 7 October, when Anderson ordered the array to be retrieved and King headed his submarine for Naples. Arriving off Naples harbour on 8 October, *Threadfin* conducted a small boat transfer of personnel to be put ashore (one can assume these individuals were part of the exercise). With the transfer completed, King took his submarine back out to sea and headed for Malaga, Spain.[5]

Just after midnight on 8 October, *Hammerberg* rendezvoused with the USNS *S. P. Lee*, T-AGS-31, to conduct additional tests of the tailship's oceanographic equipment with the oceanographic research ship, which had been in "the Mediterranean and operated out of Naples conducting environmental acoustics tests for the 6th Fleet".[6] The operation continued through the morning, after which *Hammerberg* retrieved its array and Anderson headed his tailship towards Naples, arriving on 9 October.

Whilst *Courtney* and *Hammerberg* were busy calibrating their ITASS gear with *Threadfin*, Vollmer took *Van Voorhis* down the west coast of Italy and passed through the narrow northern neck of the Strait of Messina and into the Ionian Sea for his tailship's first ITASS operation.

Steaming through the Strait of Messina in total darkness was always an exciting time for the men of the squadron, and this was no exception for those aboard *Van Voorhis*. All personnel on

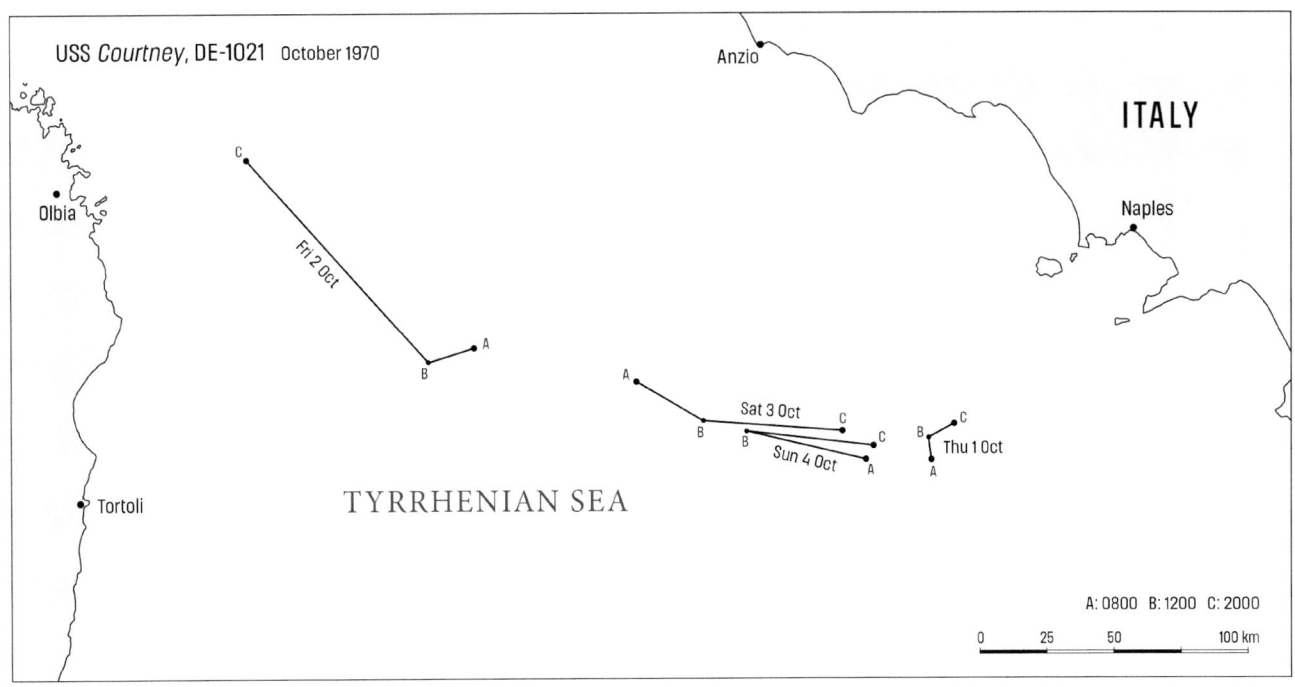

Courtney with *Hammerberg* conducting ITASS calibration tests using Threadfin as a cooperative target during October 1970. (Map by Paul Hewitt based on *Courtney* October 1970 Deck Log Book)

USNS *S.P. Lee*, T-AGS 31. (NHHC NH85028)

the bridge, in the Combat Information Center (CIC) and below in the engine room were on high alert as the tailship approached the narrow northern opening of the strait. One could feel the heightened awareness of all on the bridge when Vollmer took over the manoeuvring of the ship from the officer of the deck (OOD). The junior OOD, together with the ship's lookouts, strained their eyes for surface contacts, while the OOD along with the radarmen in the CIC monitored the radar displays to determine the closest point of approach (CPA) to the numerous ferries and commercial vessels darting back and forth between Sicily and the Italian mainland. This imposing challenge, however, was nothing compared to the task of avoiding the countless little wooden fishing boats that appeared visually or on the radar screen at the very last minute.[7] It was not unusual for the CIC watch team to go through the phonetic alphabet labelling system on surface contacts three times before passing through the first 20 miles of the strait, which added considerable stress to the ship's radarmen responsible for determining the CPA

range and time for each contact. Once clear of the strait, Vollmer secured the special sea and anchor detail. With that, the stress level on the bridge and in the CIC fell precipitously.[8]

Heading south from the strait, *Van Voorhis* steamed to Augusta Bay, Sicily, before beginning its special hydrographic operation. Shortly after anchoring on the morning of Friday, 1 October, the ship prepared for a routine change of command ceremony. During the midday watch, LCDR Vollmer was relieved of command by LCDR A.M. Hunt, USN. After the change of command, *Van Voorhis* remained at anchor through the night and weighed anchor with its new captain on the following day.[9]

Van Voorhis began its first special hydrographic operation by streaming its array later on Saturday, 3 October. The tailship steamed south until reaching a point approximately 35 miles east by north-east of Malta, astride the major east–west Mediterranean shipping lanes that night. Retrieving the array prior to midnight, the tailship headed due east, paralleling 36 degrees north latitude, and during the following day the vessel deployed its array.[10]

Hunt had *Van Voorhis* stream its array back and forth on an east–west course paralleling 36 degrees north for the next five days. Hunt broke off the operation on Friday, 9 October, and headed his tailship back to Augusta Bay to refuel. After having refuelled and watered, the tailship returned to its operating area, reaching it early on Saturday morning.[11]

USS *Andrew Jackson*, SSBN-619. (NHHC 1081069)

USS *Clamagore*, SS-343. (Open source)

anchoring just before midnight on the 12th.[14]

This was an unusual encounter. First, nuclear deterrent patrol areas were, and are to this very day, highly classified.[15] However, it was known through open sources that SSBNs had been operating in the Mediterranean since 1963. As reported in the *Washington Post*, President Kennedy had announced in a news conference during the last week in January 1963, "that Polaris missiles would go into the Mediterranean to supplant the Italian and Turkish bases".[16] This reporting was further amplified in an *Army Times* article published on 23 February:

The dismantling of our fixed-site intermediate range ballistic missiles (IRBMs) now located in Turkey and Italy is a belated recognition of the fact that weapons which can almost surely be knocked out by a surprise attack are not very effective deterrents against such an attack … The IRBMs are to be replaced by three US fleet ballistic missile submarines armed with Polaris missiles, which will be assigned to duty in Mediterranean waters under the operational command of the US Sixth Fleet.[17]

As a result of the Cuban Missile Crisis, President Kennedy agreed to withdraw the missiles if Premier Khrushchev would withdraw his missiles from Cuba.[18]

Van Voorhis continued its special operation until midday on Monday, 12 October, when Hunt received a message to head south with all possible speed and rendezvous with the Lafayette-class nuclear-powered ballistic missile submarine USS *Andrew Jackson*, SSBN-619, under the command of CDR L.G. Valade, USN.[12] Retrieving the array, Hunt steered to meet with the 'boomer boat'. Arriving two hours later at the rendezvous, *Van Voorhis* took up position 1,000 yards off the surfaced *Andrew Jackson*'s port quarter and stopped engines.[13] The tailship sent its motor whaleboat over to the submarine.

Van Voorhis remained dead in the water (DIW) for several minutes before slowly moving ahead at three knots. The motor whaleboat took onboard a single passenger from *Andrew Jackson*. At 1457 hours, with the ship's boat retrieved, and *Andrew Jackson* returning to the depths of the Ionian Sea, Hunt increased speed to 15 knots and headed his ship back northward toward Augusta Bay. Averaging 21 knots, Hunt brought his tailship into Augusta Bay,

Van Voorhis' log mentions the submarine only by name and does not indicate the reason for the rendezvous. One can only speculate that the reason for the rendezvous was to transfer one of the submarine's crew for a medical emergency. It could explain the tailship's destination; the US Navy had a fully staffed medical facility at NAS Sigonella, not far from Augusta Bay. *Van Voorhis* stayed anchored at Augusta Bay through Tuesday afternoon, when it weighed anchor and headed back out to resume its special operation, streaming its array nine hours later.

That *Andrew Jackson* had surfaced to rendezvous with *Van Voorhis* within the major east–west Mediterranean shipping lane was certainly an unusual event. With *Van Voorhis* operating its passive sonar to the north of not only the east–west shipping lane, but where the SSBN was operating, one wonders if *Van Voorhis* was tasked to determine whether its ITASS could differentiate the boomer's

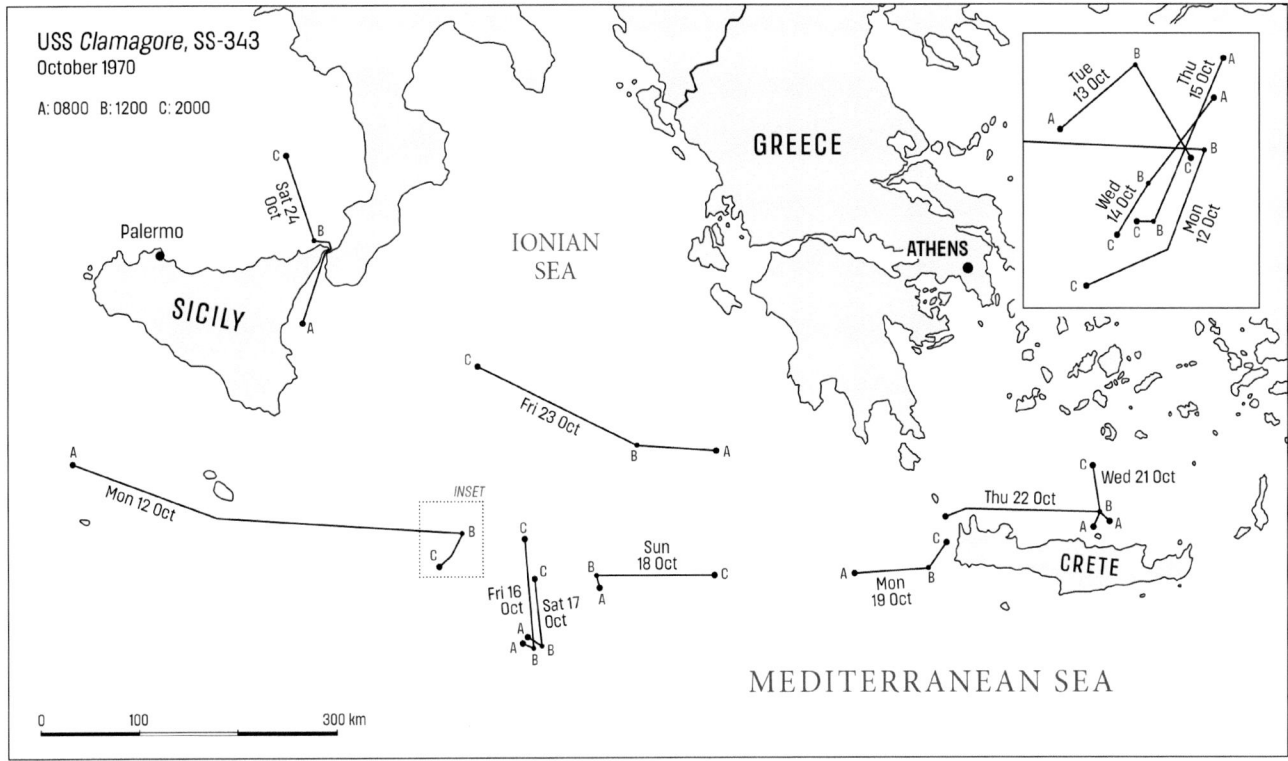

The track shows *Clamagore*'s ITASS patrol, while operating with *Van Voorhis* in October 1970. The rectangle represents a notional ITASS detection 30nm north and south of the DE's east–west track. (Map by Paul Hewitt based on *Clamagore* October 1970 Deck Log Book)

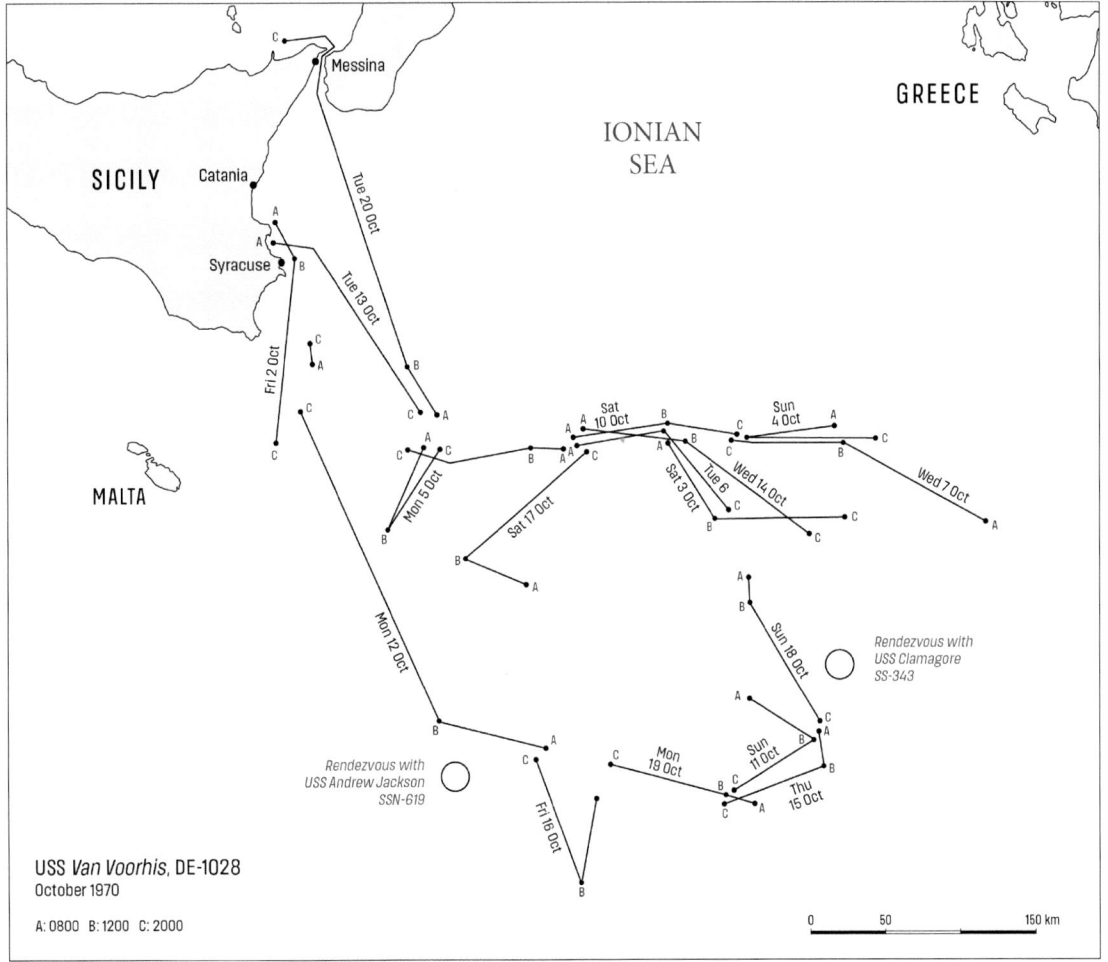

Van Voorhis' tracks (13–17 October) and (18–20 October) showing the rendezvous with *Clamagore* and *Andrew Jackson*. (Map by Paul Hewitt based on *Van Voorhis* October 1970 Deck Log Book)

acoustics from those of the numerous surface ships; a logical area for an SSBN to hide. A few days later, another rendezvous occurred.

Operating in the same area of the Ionian Sea was the diesel-powered submarine USS *Clamagore*, SS-343, under the command of CDR W.G. Mine, USN. This submarine had entered the Med on 1 September.[19] Missions for it and sister submarine USS *Cutlass*, SS-478, appeared to be twofold: 1) to counter the Soviet Fifth *Eskadra* units; and 2) to serve as opposition forces during Sixth Fleet and NATO exercises. They would also be available to the tailships to test their ITASS.

While on the second leg of the tailship's special operation, Hunt received a message to rendezvous with *Clamagore*. On 18 October, Hunt steered his tailship toward the submarine's port quarter and closed to 600 yards from the submarine. According to the ship's log, *Van Voorhis* completed a small boat transfer; LCDR J.R. Combemale, USN, arrived onboard.[20]

This transfer did not appear to be one of a medical or emergency leave need, because with the conclusion of the transfer, Hunt took *Van Voorhis* back on its track and deployed the array, continuing the rest of its special operation until Tuesday, 20 October. *Van Voorhis* returned to Naples the following morning.

The rendezvous with *Andrew Jackson* and *Clamagore* point toward the reason for *Van Voorhis*' 'oceanographic test'; to determine how well the ITASS could detect, classify and track the acoustic signatures of a US Navy SSBN and an SS.

Two days after *Van Voorhis*' return to Naples, Reimann took *Courtney* back out to sea, heading for the eastern Mediterranean. On Saturday morning, while Reimann was taking *Courtney* across the Ionian Sea toward its operating area, two Egyptian-based Soviet Tu-16 Badger aircraft overflew the tailship. It is debatable whether this was an incidental contact by the Soviets, as *Courtney* and its sister ships routinely operated their AN/SPS-5 surface search radar. As mentioned previously, this radar was a unique electronic emitter that identified to the Soviets that one or more of the tailships were at sea. Using their HF/DF capability, it would be easy for the Badgers to obtain a line of bearing on *Courtney*'s radar and vector toward the emission.[21] After the overflight, the Badgers headed out to continue their reconnaissance mission.

On Sunday, 25 October, *Courtney* arrived at the position to deploy its tail. It was approximately 45nm south-west of the island of Liviko Pelagos, which lies due south of Crete, where the tailship commenced its operation.

For the next five days, *Courtney* conducted ITASS operations within a geographic box, euphemistically called the Levantine Basin Patrol area, which was centred halfway between Crete to the north and Libya to the south, and coincidentally in the same general area in which *Van Voorhis* and *Clamagore* operated the previous week. Within the box, *Courtney* streamed its array on a series of parallel tracks running north-west to south-east.[22]

During this phase of the deployment, Reimann was well aware of the need to ensure the security of the 'special' system aboard. He conducted several general quarters drills as well as exercising the ship's repel borders team. When called away from their duty stations, the team, numbering 30 men, deployed tactically throughout the ship. With the team in position on the main deck and upper decks, the ship's 3-inch gun was fired using fragmentation rounds. The team would then open fire with 45-cal pistols, M-1 Garand rifles, Browning automatic rifles and 30-cal machine guns toward the splashes created by the exploding 3-inch rounds.

While *Courtney* was operating its tail, Task Group 60.1, the USS *John F. Kennedy*, CVA-67 (Carrier Fixed Wing) battle group, was approximately 270nm to the east of *Courtney*'s operating area. Operating south-west of Cyprus within a geographically defined box called 'Bravo Station', the *Kennedy* Task Group (TG) was conducting East Mediterranean Guard operations:[23]

Political and military unrest [the Jordanian Crisis] and tensions continued throughout the Eastern and Southern Mediterranean, requiring the Sixth Fleet to remain alert to respond to possible contingency operation requirements. Units of the Sixth Fleet responded and were prepared for possible contingency operations in the Middle East between 9 September and 31 October … At least one carrier task group is nominally positioned east of Malta.[24]

The *Kennedy* TG continued operating on Bravo Station until the early evening of 30 October, when the carrier and its escorts broke their modified location (MODLOC) and began their westward transit to Naples.[25]

A Near Disaster

On Friday, 30 October, and prior to the *Kennedy* TG departing their station, Reimann ordered the tail to be retrieved. *Courtney* headed northward to pass around the eastern tip of Crete, and then steam west toward Soudha Bay to refuel. This transit should have been routine; but then the unexpected occurred.

Just after midnight on 31 October, as *Courtney* was rounding the north-east tip of Crete off Cape Sidero, the tailship "lost fires in 1A Boiler due to loss of suction from fuel oil service tank".[26] With Reimann and his navigator on the bridge, *Courtney* was now DIW. Unable to light the emergency diesel generator, *Courtney* was completely without electrical power. This meant the navigator and those in the CIC could not use the surface search radar to accurately determine their position in relation to the shore, nor could the ship's radio alert Sixth Fleet as to the situation. Shortly, the navigator obtained visual bearings from Cape Sidero lighthouse and the island of Paximadha. With these visual sightings, he informed Reimann that *Courtney* was now drifting south toward the rocks.

Without delay, Reimann called away the special sea and anchor detail and ordered one of the ship's anchors to be dropped. He realised his ship was still in deep water, but he hoped, if *Courtney*'s power could not be restored, that the anchor would catch on the bottom before his ship grounded on the rocks.

While the deck personnel were busy with the ship's anchor and the operations department personnel were determining the ship's position, the engineering department personnel stood up a bucket brigade to transfer fuel oil from the forward fuel tank to the after tank to restore suction to the boilers. But without electricity to operate the ship's force draft blowers, there would not be enough forced air to light the boilers. Reimann ordered all ship doors and hatches to be opened to provide enough of a draft of air down into the ship's hull to fire the boilers. At 0138 hours, enough oil had been transferred to the aft tank to enable suction to the 1A boiler. *Courtney*'s log states that at 0140 hours, power was restored, and by 0154 hours the tailship was proceeding toward Soudha Bay. Prior to midday, *Courtney* secured alongside the refuelling pier at Soudha Bay.[27]

While *Courtney* remained moored in Soudha Bay to affect repairs and provide the ship's company with a run ashore, Hunt took *Van Voorhis* back to sea on 1 November to conduct special operations in the same area south-east of Crete in which *Courtney* was intended to operate. They were to operate their tails as a tactical pair, and were to use *Clamagore* as a target.

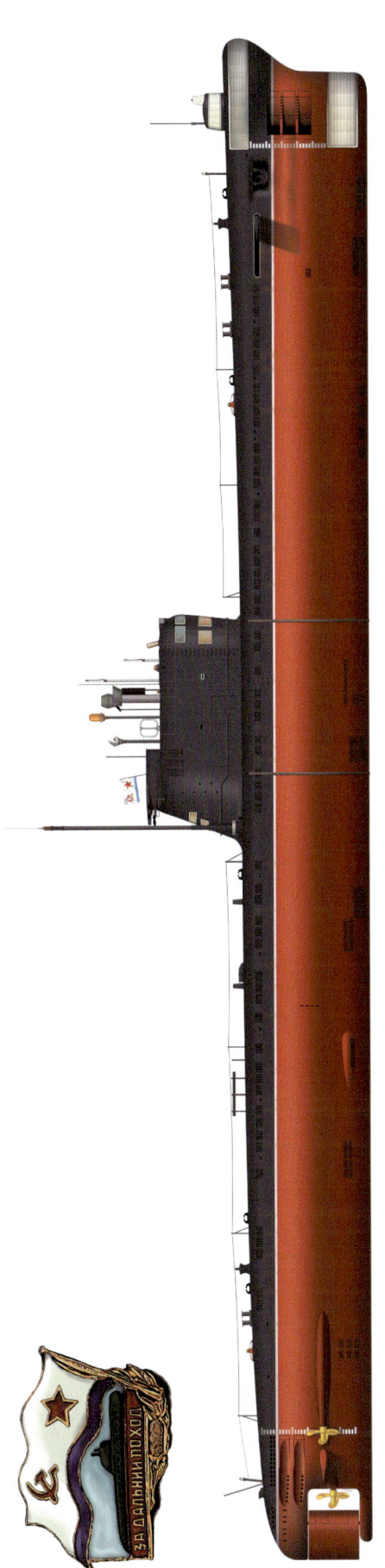

The Foxtrot-class was the NATO reporting name for the Soviet Project 641 class of diesel-electric patrol submarine. A total of 58 were built, of which six to eight Foxtrots operated in the Mediterranean at any given time between 1970–1973. US/NATO intelligence estimated this class operated in the many choke points found in the Mediterranean. The Foxtrot's performance and armament were comparable to those of most other non-teardrop hull designs built for other navies. However, when not on battery power, its three propellers made it noisier than most Western designed subs. (Artwork by Anderson Subtil)

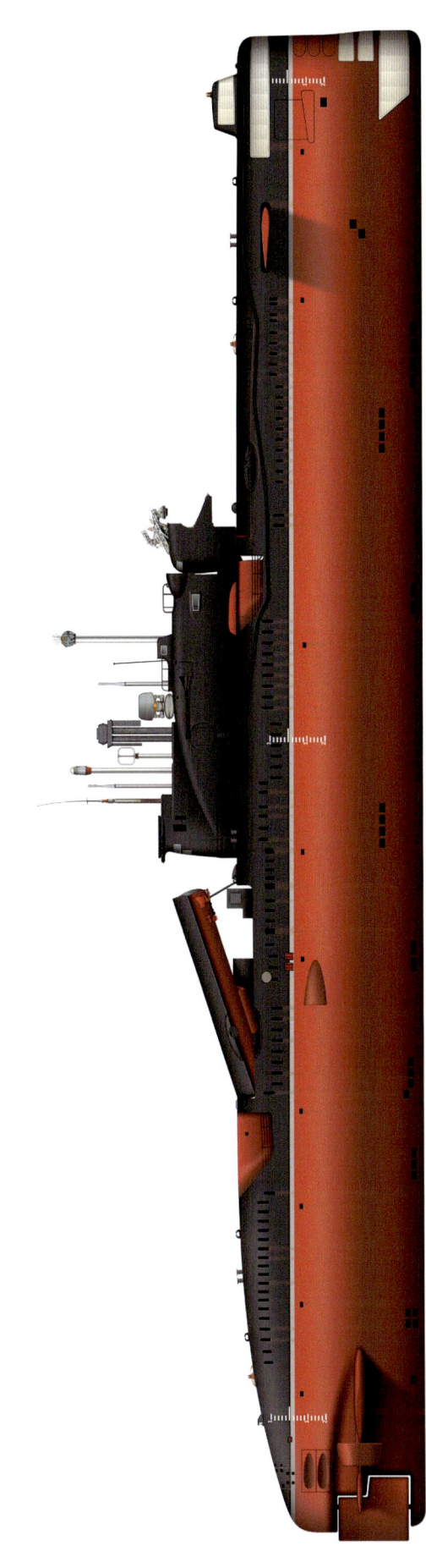

The Juliett-class was the NATO reporting name for the Soviet Project 651, a diesel-electric submarine armed with four SS-N-3a (Shaddock) cruise missiles. Launching the missiles required the submarine to surface. A total of 16 units were built. From October 1971 through March 1972, four of the class operated in the Mediterranean. (Artwork by Anderson Subtil)

The Victor I-class was the NATO reporting name for the Soviet Project 671 nuclear-powered attack submarine (SSN). A total of 16 were built. They were the first teardrop hull-shaped submarines designed to conduct ASW operations. However, only seven Victor Is were in commission at the time the Tailships began their Mediterranean operations. That may explain why only three of the class deployed (sporadically) to the Mediterranean between 1971–72. But, by 1973, there were 11 in commission and this allowed the Soviets to keep at least one Victor I constantly deployed in the Mediterranean. With the Yom Kippur War, the Soviets deployed three of the class into the Mediterranean to counter the presence of three US Navy carrier battlegroups. (Artwork by Anderson Subtil)

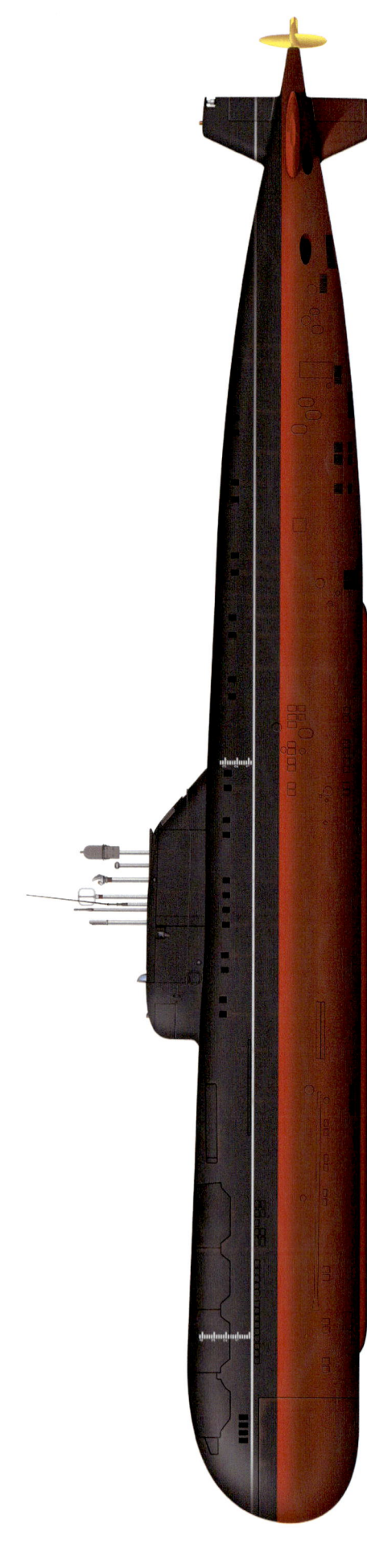

The Charlie I-class was the NATO reporting name for the Soviet Project 670 nuclear-powered cruise missile submarine (SSGN). A total of 11 units were built. They were the first class of Soviet submarines that could launch their eight SS-N-7s (NATO designated Starbright) anti-ship cruise missiles (ASM) while submerged. Between 1970 and 1973, four of the class deployed to the Mediterranean. In 1972, each of the three Charlie Is deployed in the Mediterranean for a 90-day period. (Artwork by Anderson Subtil)

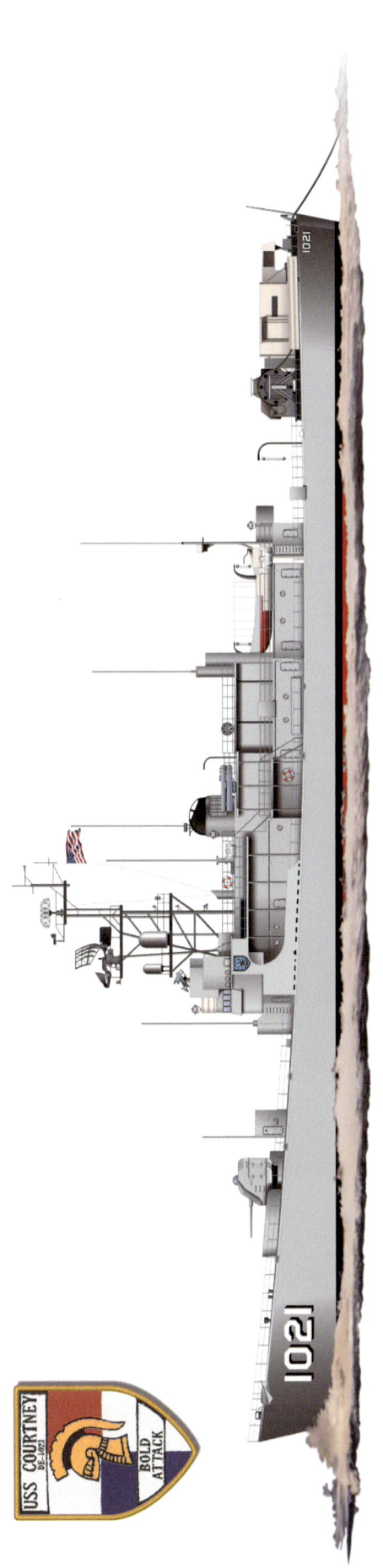

The USS *Courtney* was the only member of the Dealey/Courtney-class that was not modified to accommodate the DASH helicopter system. Instead, *Courtney* was reconfigured as a squadron flagship with command and staff cabins built aft of her funnel and above the main deck. (Artwork by Anderson Subtil)

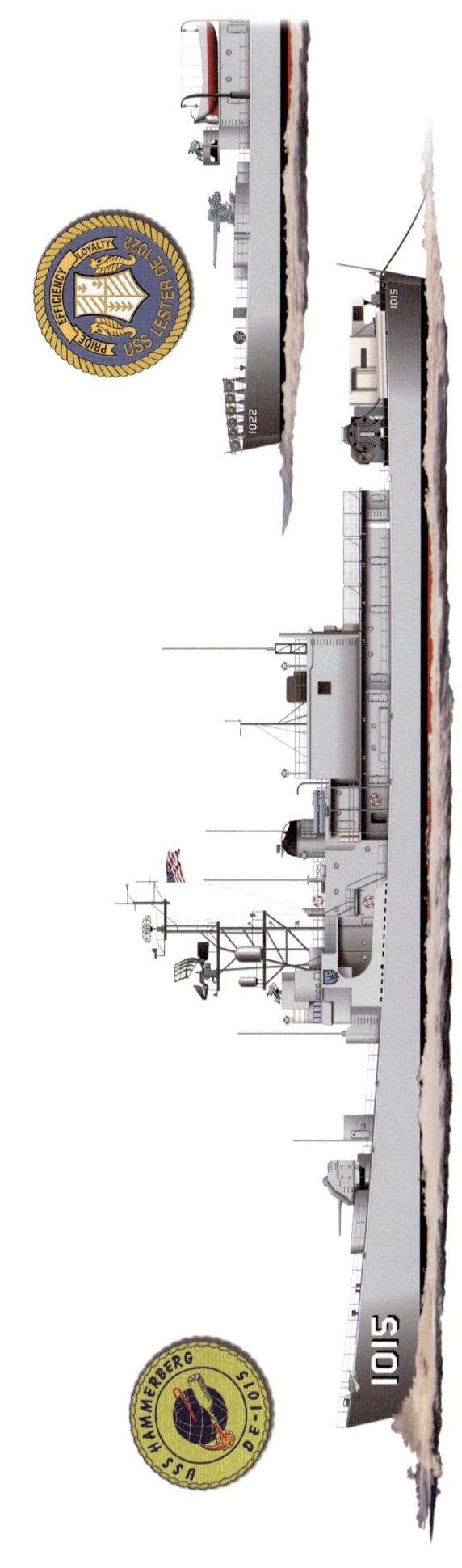

The aft ends of the *Hammerberg* and *Lester* were reconfigured from the original Dealey/Courtney-class configuration (upper right) with a hangar and flight deck to accommodate the DASH helicopter system. With their deployment to the Mediterranean, DASH was removed and the hangar converted to crew quarters and extra storage space. (Artwork by Anderson Subtil)

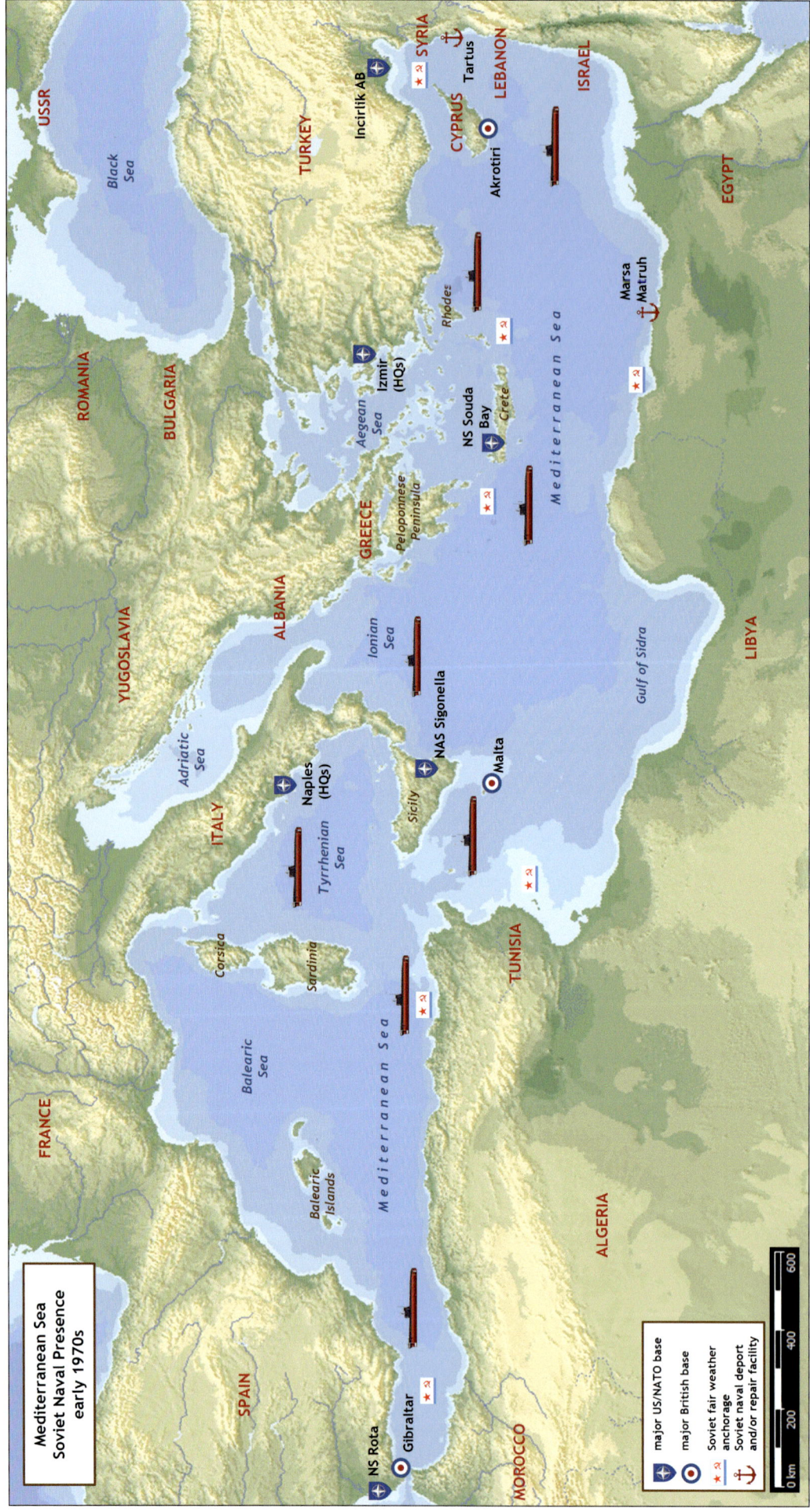

In addition the major bases and fair weather anchorages throughout the Mediterranean in the early 1970s, the above map shows the chokepoints typically patrolled by Soviet submarines during this era. (Map by Tom Cooper)

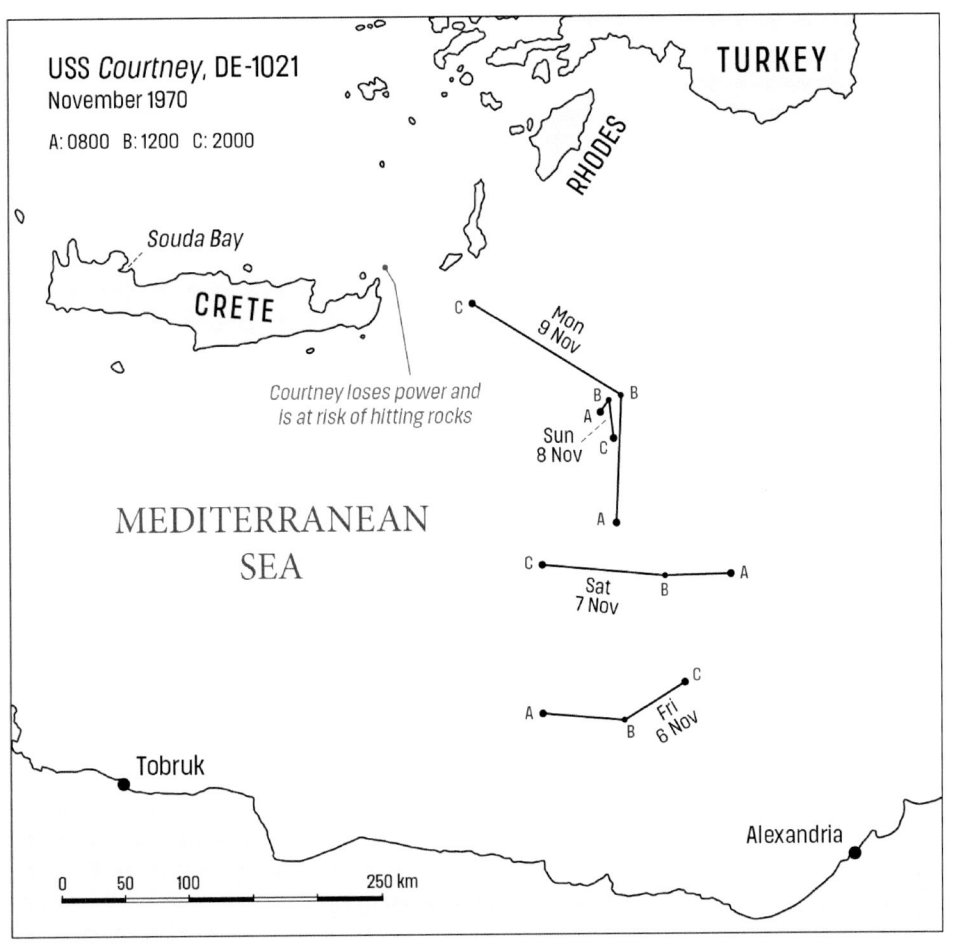

Courtney's tracks against *Clamagore*, 6–9 November. (Map by Paul Hewitt based on *Courtney*, *Van Voorhis* and *Clamagore* November 1970 Deck Log Books)

On 3 November, *Van Voorhis* rendezvoused with *Clamagore* 120nm west of Elafonissi, Crete, and began its special operations against the submarine. The operation continued throughout the next day. It was during these first hours that the submerged *Clamagore* commenced snorkelling. Through the rest of 4 November, *Clamagore* repeatedly surfaced on snorkel, submerged, commenced snorkelling and increased speed to ensure its propellors would cavitate.[28]

Clamagore generated enough noise to give *Van Voorhis* plenty of acoustic data with which to obtain and maintain a track on the submarine. This was despite the fact that both were operating in a heavily trafficked part of the Mediterranean, including an acoustically noisy group of US warships operating within the same area. *Van Voorhis* and *Clamagore* continued travelling east by south-east for the next 24 hours. *Clamagore* continued snorkelling, surfacing then diving, changing speeds and running its diesel engines, either

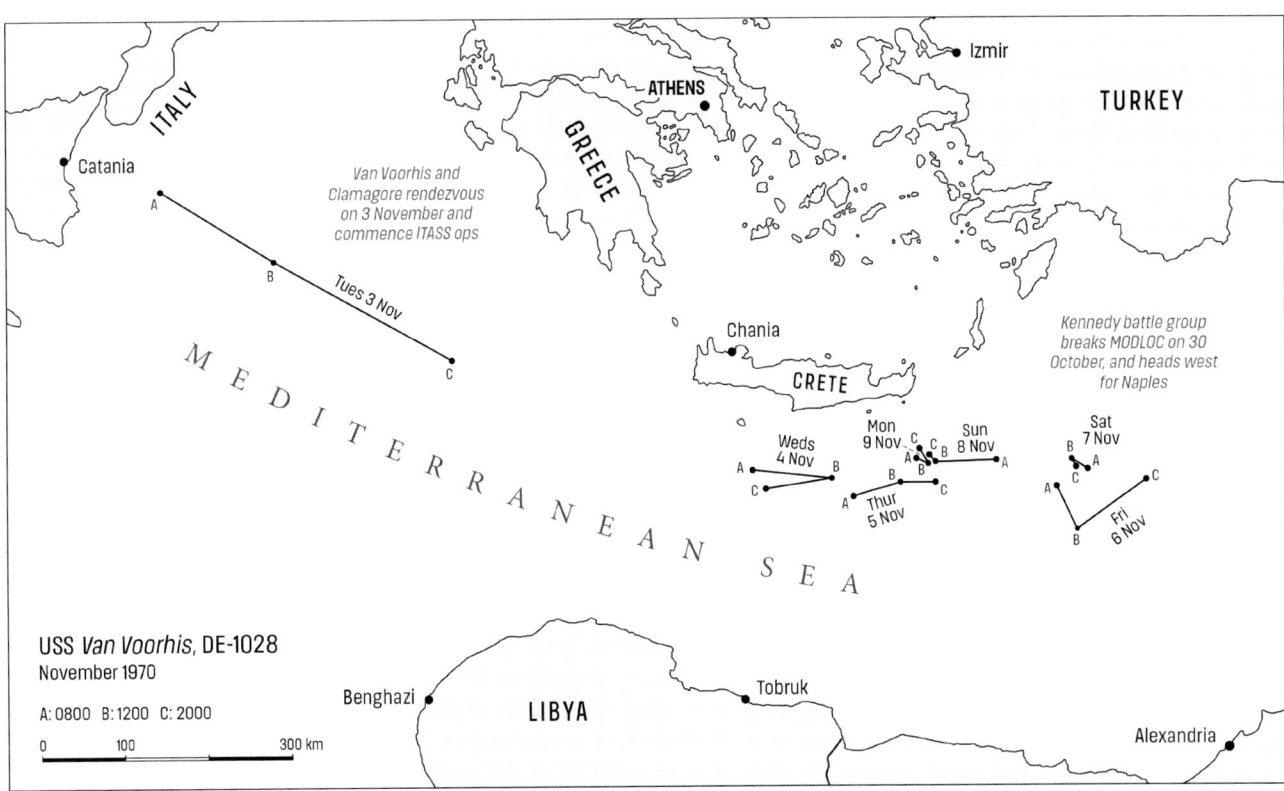

Van Voorhis's tracks against *Clamagore*, 3–9 November 1970. (Map by Paul Hewitt based on *Van Voorhis* and *Clamagore* November 1970 Deck Log Books)

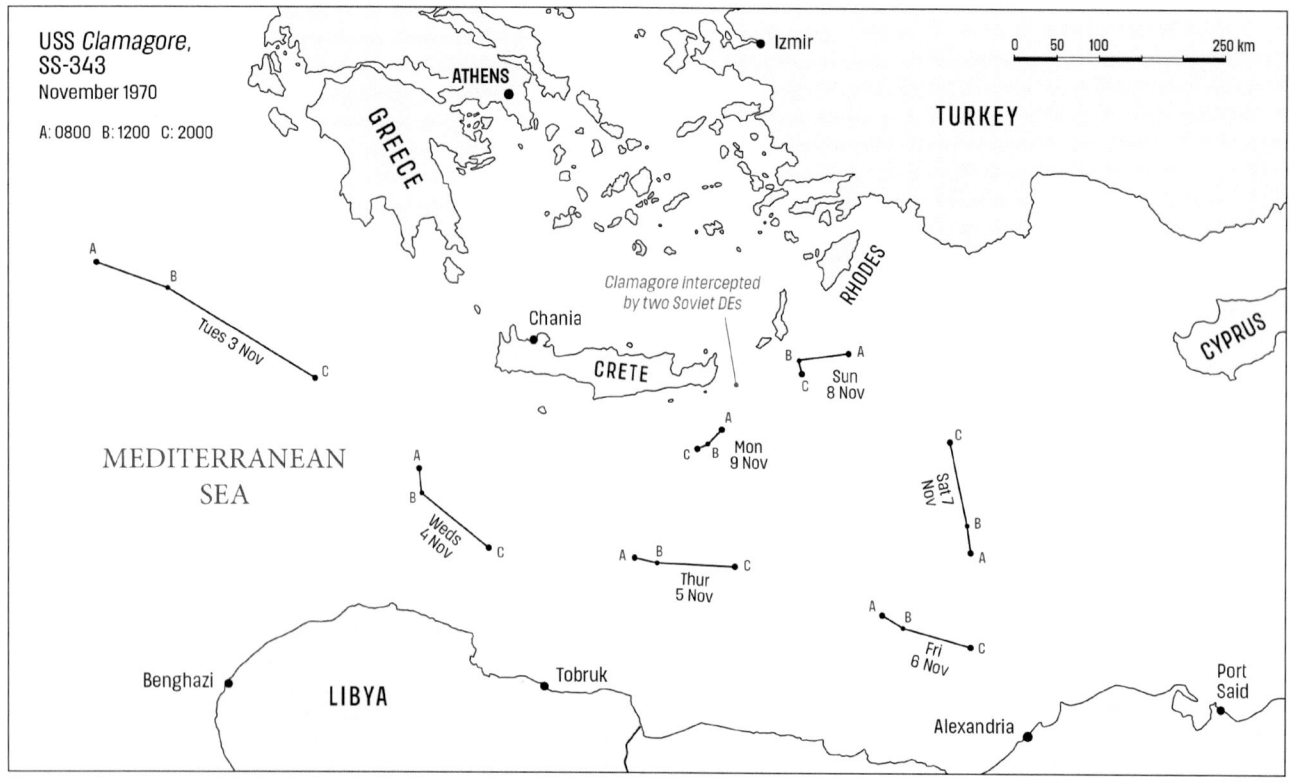

Clamagore's movements 3–9 November 1970. (Map by Paul Hewitt based on Clamagore November 1970 Deck Log Book)

together or alternating them. This activity continued uninterrupted until the 5th, when a fire in the forward engine room forced it to surface and come to a stop. Fortunately, the fire was quickly extinguished and electrical power was restored. Nevertheless, Clamagore continued on the surface for the rest of the day, resuming its role as a target just after midnight on 6 November.[29]

Meanwhile, Reimann took Courtney back to sea, departing Soudha Bay on 5 November. Having rounded Crete's east coast and passed through the Kasos Strait, Reimann headed his tailship south to resume special operations with Van Voorhis.

On 6 November, Courtney had crossed both Van Voorhis' and Clamagore's track to deploy its ITASS array 85nm north of the port of Marsa Matruh in Egypt. With the tail deployed, Reimann steered his tailship on a south-east course, paralleling Van Voorhis' and Clamagore's tracks. Both tailships continued streaming their arrays on parallel tracks with occasional slight course alterations, which was indicative of trying to obtain a true bearing on the submarine. At the time Courtney began streaming its array, Clamagore was less than 40nm north of Courtney's track, while Van Voorhis was over 65nm north of the submarine. This continued throughout the 6th, when Courtney changed course and began to close on Van Voorhis' track and cross astern of Clamagore's track.

During the time the tailships operated as a tactical pair, they made numerous minor course changes to finalise the bearing to the acoustic signatures of Clamagore and other targets of interest. As mentioned previously, this posed a challenge for the OTs on both tailships, as ITASS was operating in heavily trafficked waters, with numerous merchant ships and other craft transiting east–west and north–south:

Established contacts were almost always merchant ships, churning noisily through the busy Mediterranean. They were given contact numbers, logged onto a target sheet form, and tracked for hours

until their signal finally faded. A straight edge calibration bar on the AQA-5 allowed us to mark on the electrostatic paper with a flair [sic] pen the contact number, the observed primary rotation frequency of the vessel's propeller, and any other audio signals that seemed to track with the contact. Most times an interesting phenomenon prevailed with close range contacts and a second, third and sometimes fourth audio harmonic of the propeller were detected with decreasing amplitude or signal strength.[30]

Courtney continued to close on Van Voorhis' track through the remaining hours of 6 November and by the 7th, both tailships were on a westerly course and parallel to one another. On this day, the tailships exhibited very little westward movement because they were constantly changing course in order for the OTs to obtain and maintain contact on Clamagore.[31] Later that night, the distance between the two tailships had closed to 60nm, while Clamagore turned northward and east of both tailships.

By midnight on 7 November, all three had turned north, with only Courtney in a position to detect and track Clamagore. It maintained a parallel course to the west of Clamagore's track and maintained a distance inside of 35nm up until 0800 hours on the 8th, when Reimann steered his tailship westward. Midday found Courtney over 100nm west of Clamagore's track, while Hunt had taken Van Voorhis further north and opened the distance to the submarine as well. It appears that both captains were repositioning their commands to pick up Clamagore as the submarine headed north toward the Greek island of Kárpathos.

By midday on 8 November, Hine's submarine closed within 30nm of the island, heading on a west by south-west course. Van Voorhis closed on Clamagore's track, while Courtney headed south and at one point was over 100nm south of the submarine.

The 9th would be the final day of the operation, but it would be a day to remember for those aboard Clamagore. Earlier, Hine changed

USS *Van Voorhis* anchored in Soudha Bay, Crete, 10 November 1970. Note the ITASS gear visible on its stern. (Photograph by STG2 Nick Vidnanski)

USS *Grand Canyon*, AD-28. (NHHC 1147736)

course north-westward toward the Kasos Strait and continued to operate the boat's snorkel whilst mostly submerged. He was heading toward what was the Soviet Fifth *Eskadra*'s fair weather anchorage, known by US and NATO as the East of Crete Anchorage. The anchorage was situated in the Kasos Strait and over a relative shallow sea mound approximately 200ft below the surface. As *Clamagore* approached the anchorage, the Soviets reacted.

Just before sunrise, whilst still submerged, *Clamagore* stopped snorkelling and Hine ordered "battle stations torpedo". Although not indicated in the submarine's log, Hine probably ordered his crew to battle stations because the Soviets were harassing his submarine, possibly with their sonars. Hine then ordered *Clamagore* to surface, and the boat did so in the midst of "three Soviet combat vessels".[32]

For the next three hours, *Clamagore* remained at battle stations torpedo, while being harassed by the Soviets. Hine ordered various courses and speed changes, including all stop … all back 5 knots … all ahead 11 knots, and finally he slowed his boat to 6 knots".[33]

The Soviet warships continued to shadow *Clamagore* for two more hours. Shortly after 0800 hours, Hine recorded in his log: "Soviet DE-897 and DE-874 departed on course 008, speed 15." Seeing them departing, Hine "secured battle stations torpedo". He then ordered his boat to submerge and continue with the "special oceanographic operation".[34] By the course written in *Clamagore*'s log, the Soviet DEs were heading back to the East of Crete Anchorage.

With the conclusion of the operation, *Clamagore* rendezvoused with *Van Voorhis* to transfer two of *Clamagore*'s enginemen, who had been aboard the tailship during the operation.[35] With the transfer completed, *Van Voorhis* headed north to rendezvous with *Courtney* and they proceeded together to Soudha Bay to refuel. They returned to Naples on 12 November.

When *Van Voorhis* returned to Naples on the 12th, it secured alongside the destroyer tender USS *Grand Canyon*, AD-28, to have its ITASS gear transferred to *Lester*. The transfer took place on Tuesday, 17 November, when *Grand Canyon*'s Mike boat (LCM) came alongside, off *Van Voorhis*' stern. Its OTs and boatswain mates began to unwind the ITASS cable minus the sensor modules into the well deck of the LCM. Once the cable was secured on the Mike boat, it moved alongside *Lester*, and *Lester*'s OTs and boatswain mates reeled the cable onto their vessel's spool. After lunch, a civilian-manned floating crane was towed into position to lift the ITASS van from *Van Voorhis* onto *Lester*. With the transfer completed, *Van Voorhis* officially turned over its ITASS responsibilities to *Lester*; just after sunset, *Van Voorhis* departed Naples to return to the United States.[36]

Inside the ITASS Van: Equipment and Operations

Inside the ITASS 'van' room were several systems. Top left and top right was the AN/AQA-5 Acoustic Multichannel Charts Recorder Processing System. This system was an off-the-shelf system manufactured by Emerson and used in the P-3 Orion and P-2 Neptune MPA/ASW aircraft.

The following description is from an OT who served aboard the *Courtney*:

The AN/AQA-5 had four displays which corresponded to a relative bearing to the ship's heading. … Each display corresponded to a bearing 'wedge' relative to the ship's heading. Those bearing wedges added up to 180 degrees in relative coverage. But, the wedges differed in width. The midships relative bearings (90 and 180 degrees) had a very narrow bearing wedge and as such,

ITASS van interior equipment configuration. (Stanley G. Lemon IEEE Journal of Oceanic Engineering, 19 July 2004)

the data processing unit could capture a large percentage of the acoustic signal yielding a much stronger signal on the AQA-5 display. As you move away from midship bearing, the bearing wedge would increase. This would mean the data processing would capture more ambient noise along with the same acoustic signal yielding a lower signal to noise ratio and thus, a weaker signal on the AQA-5 display. So … when one would determine the true bearing of the contact, the ship would maneuver to place the contact as close as possible to midship bearing (90 or 180 degrees).

The hydrophones were omni directional, so the displays covered 180 degrees of azimuth on the port and starboard side of the hydrophone array. On the vertical axis was the time stamp and on the horizontal was the acoustic signal frequency in Hertz (Hz).

When a contact was obtained on a display, it could be on either the starboard or port side of the array. To determine which side of the array was the acoustic signal from the contact, the ship's OOD would alter course by a few degrees and the reaction to the change in relative bearing would determine whether the acoustic signal was on the port or starboard side of the array. One side would be determined the actual bearing whilst the other was considered a mirror bearing.

Maneuvering the ship was not as easy as it sounds. The array length, including the tow cable, would, often times, yield a scope of thousands of feet of deployed gear meaning that when the ship made a turn, it could take some period of time (30 minutes in some cases) before the array would become stable and produce usable data. I lost a lot of contacts during the ship's maneuvering.

With the bearing determined, the OTs would resolve the relative bearing with the ship's true heading and calculate the true bearing of the contact. For example, if the relative contact was determined to be 090 degrees and the ship was heading on a course of 040 degrees true, the contact's true bearing from the array and the ship was 130 degrees true.[37]

For the next three weeks, *Lester*'s OTs and civilian technicians worked to make their newly acquired ITASS operational. On Wednesday, 9 December, Edwards took his tailship out into the Tyrrhenian Sea to 'shake down' the system. After two days at sea, Edwards brought his ship back to Naples. Three days later, *Lester* got underway for its first special hydrographic operation. It was preceded by the USS *Cutlass*, commanded by CDR D.R. Lundquist, USN. Arriving at their respective positions after nightfall, *Lester* deployed the array and *Cutlass* submerged and began to alternate snorkelling and running silent, then surfacing whilst snorkelling, diving back again to PD.[38]

USS *Cutlass*, SS-478, K-1107442. (NHHC)

USS *Lapon*, SSN-661, K-77033. (NHHC)

Unlike the special hydrographic operation involving its sister ships, *Lester*'s track took it toward Cape Spartivento, Sardinia, and away from *Cutlass*, which remained approximately 90nm south-west of the Isle of Capri. However, Edwards reversed *Lester*'s course on 15 December, steered his tailship back into the Tyrrhenian and closed on *Cutlass*' position. At that time, Lundquist had surfaced his submarine and had begun heading toward *Lester*.

Wednesday, 16 December found *Lester* 35nm south of Cape Spartivento again, while *Cutlass* had continued travelling south and was on the surface just 10nm west of Isola Marettimo, an island west of Sicily and north of the Strait of Sicily. That night, *Cutlass* entered the shallow waters of the Strait of Sicily and was 10nm west of the Italian island of Pantelleria. *Lester* was operating south of Sardinia's Capo Carbonara,[39] whilst *Cutlass* was running its snorkel at PD in shallow waters, which depth averaged 300ft, and within the major east–west shipping lanes. The distance between the two remained just over 120nm. With that distance, together with the combined ambient and shipping noises, detecting *Cutlass* would have been a challenge for *Lester*'s ITASS. The special hydrographic operation

concluded just before sunrise on 17 December. Interestingly, and what may not be a coincidence, the Sturgeon-class SSN, the USS *Lapon*, SSN-661, under command of CDR G.E. Green, USN, departed Naples on Sunday, 13 December, one day before both *Lester* and *Cutlass* departed. *Lapon*'s log stated that it "commenced special log entries as directed by the Chief of Naval Operations". The boat's deck log book picks up the submarine's operations on Saturday, 19 December, "From Special Operations to Naples, Italy". *Lapon* arrived at Naples that morning.[40] Although it cannot be confirmed, it is possible that *Lapon* was also acting as a cooperative target for *Lester*'s ITASS.

With the conclusion of special hydrographic operations, the Christmas/New Year holiday found the tailships moored at their new homeport; the first of three Christmas/New Year holidays in which the men would be away from their homes in the US. Some had their families with them, and that certainly made a difference. The following year, 1971, would be the first year of intense ITASS operations.

8

1971: THE FIRST FULL YEAR OF ITASS OPERATIONS

The Soviets are not nine feet tall by a long shot; but they are good.[1]

The following intelligence summary, taken from the 1971 Sixth Fleet Command History, gives an indication of Soviet naval activity and OOB confronting the Sixth Fleet and NATO. It serves as a backdrop to tailship operations.

Intelligence Situation

"The Soviet Navy's concentration in the Mediterranean had increased, with the average number of ships present rising ... to a total of 52."[2] Of that number, only 28 were combatants. The remaining were auxiliaries, to include nine intelligence collection ships.[3]

Surface ship activity during the first five months of the year centred around the presence of the hybrid helicopter carrier/missile cruiser (*Protivolodochnyy Kreysert, PKR*) the *Leningrad* and the modified Sverdlov-class cruiser *Dzerzhinskiy*.[4]

The Soviet naval air OOB was similarly increased, most notably with 10 missile-carrying Tu-16 Badger medium bombers. The

Badgers were capable of carrying the Raduga KSR-2 (NATO AS-5 KELT) ASM. "This gave the Soviets a credible air-strike capability ... for the first time. The ASW inventory was modernized ... [with] the IL-38 MAY."[5]

"The Soviet submarine level continues to average slightly over eleven deployed units ... and the number one threat in the Mediterranean is the Soviet submarine force."[6] At the start of the year, the Fifth *Eskadra*'s submarine OOB consisted of two Juliett SSGs, two Victor I SSNs and 12 Foxtrots, with one under repair in Egypt. The chart below shows the OOB from January–December 1971.[7]

During the year, the Soviets conducted three conventional submarine turnovers. Six Zulu SS-class diesel submarines and one Juliett were replaced by five Foxtrot submarines and one Juliett. In December, a similar turnover occurred.[8] These turnovers provided a splendid opportunity for the tailships to detect, identify and track these submarines.

The *Protivolodochnyy Kreysert* (*PKR*) *Leningrad*. (Author's collection)

information transmitted up the coaxial cable to the racks of AQA-5 monitors in the van. The AGA-5 monitors transferred realtime hydrophone audio electric signals to electrostatic paper with a horizontally traversing stylus … In our van the AQA-5s were arranged along three interior sides to reflect the front of the array to the end of the array, or 0 degrees to 180 degrees in line with the axis of the ship.[10]

The IL-38 MAY. (US Department of Defense)

On 10 January, *Courtney* and *Hammerberg* were heading northward, entering the Gulfe Du Lion.[11] Both tailships were running parallel with the north–south shipping lane and heading toward Marseille, with *Hammerberg* to the east of *Courtney*. Of interest, *Courtney*'s log emphasised that it was "in the Rhone Fan".[12]

Until midday on Wednesday, 13 January, both tailships continued streaming their arrays over the Rhone Fan. But that afternoon, ITASS operations ended prematurely; *Hammerberg*'s condensers were no longer producing fresh water for its boilers. *Courtney* rendezvoused with *Hammerberg* and transferred fresh water to enable *Hammerberg* to continue.

Off They Go

The Christmas and New Year period in port for the tailships ended when *Courtney* and *Hammerberg* departed on the morning of Thursday, 7 January. Heading west, they passed through the Strait of Bonifacio between Corsica and Sardinia just after midnight on 8 January. With daylight, Reimann's *Courtney* and Anderson's *Hammerberg* began their ITASS operations in waters that were not known to be frequented by Soviet submarines.[9]

As shown in the map based on the January Deck Log Books of *Courtney* and *Hammerberg* both ships were streaming their arrays north-east into the Ligurian Sea and on a parallel course to one another, separated by 35nm. On Saturday, 9 January, they had doubled back down on their original tracks and were heading toward Menorca. By midnight, they had already turned north-west toward Barcelona and across the major Marseille to Gibraltar shipping lane.

Harry Jones, who served aboard the *Van Voorhis* and then transferred to *Lester*, recounts what it was like to work inside the ITASS van:

During the actual deployment of the towed array, two men were assigned to 4-hour watches in the van. We analyzed the acoustic

Together, they headed south and east toward the Strait of Sicily and Malta. Arrangements had been made for *Hammerberg* to affect repairs to its freshwater condensers in Malta.

Later on Thursday morning, and after refuelling from the USS *Caloosahatchee*, AO-98, the tailships parted company, with *Hammerberg* entering Malta and *Courtney* heading back to Naples, arriving early on 16 January. *Courtney* would remain in Naples until the 29th, While *Hammerberg* returned to Naples later in January.

In assessing the operation, one can see that the ITASS track moved anti-clockwise and at the edge of the operating box. This indicates the passive sonar was looking for acoustic signatures to the right of the track and centralised within the box. The track also shows the tailships moving into the centre of the box, which could indicate ITASS was tracking an underwater contact. During this period, *Cutlass* had been in port at Monaco through the Christmas/New Year holiday. Previously, *Cutlass* had been a cooperative target for the tailships. Although one cannot confirm *Cutlass* was involved, the Sixth Fleet Command History does state that *Cutlass* continued operating in the Mediterranean until 20 January.[13]

On Friday, 29 January, *Courtney* and *Hammerberg* departed Naples to participate in Exercise NATIONAL WEEK VIII. The

Table 2: Soviet Submarines assigned to Fifth *Eskadra* in 1971												
	Jan	Feb	Mar	Apr	May	Jun	Jul	Aug	Sept	Oct	Nov	Dec
Charlie I K-25				X	X							
Victor I K-69				X	X							
Victor I K-147	X	X										
Victor I K-323	X	X										
Juliett K-24								X	X	X	X	X
Juliett K-156					X	X	X	X	X	X	X	
Juliett K203								X	X	X	X	X
Juliett K-318										X	X	X
Juliett K-304												X
Foxtrot B-26	X											
Foxtrot B-107	X											
Foxtrot B-416	X											
Foxtrot B-103	X	X										
Foxtrot B-57	X	X	X									
Foxtrot B-34	X	X	X	X								
Foxtrot B-59	X	X	X	X								
Foxtrot B-153	X	X	X	X								
Foxtrot B-205	X	X	X	X								
Foxtrot B-29	X	X	X	X	X	X						
Foxtrot B-413	X	X	X	X	X	X						
Foxtrot B-839	X	X	X	X	X	X	X	X	X	X	X	
Foxtrot B-435					X	X	X	X	X			

object of this biannual exercise was to train the USS *John F. Kennedy*, CVA-67, and USS *Forrestal*, CVA-59, battle groups in Anti-Air Warfare, Anti-Surface Warfare and ASW operations and tactics. This type of exercise could be considered a war game, a "unilateral exercise which evaluates the fleet capability to locate and track units of a potentially hostile fleet in the Mediterranean".[14] The exercise was the tailships' first opportunity to demonstrate ITASS capabilities.

On 30 January, both tailships commenced ITASS operations in the Ionian Sea. *Courtney* began its patrol south-east of Cape Passero, Sicily, while *Hammerberg* deployed to the east of *Courtney*. For Reimann's tailship, the operation was interrupted as he sent his crew to man-overboard stations. Earlier that morning, the Sixth Fleet had lost one of its aircraft. *Courtney* "recovered an unmanned life raft and pilot ejection seat and commenced searching for a survivor". Fortunately, as *Courtney* continued looking for the pilot, it received a message "that the pilot had been previously recovered".[15] This accident was a reminder that life at sea cannot be taken for granted. *Courtney* returned to streaming its tail.

The next week had *Courtney* and *Hammerberg* operating their tails within the planned exercise area. Both tailships were streaming their tails to detect Soviet submarines that might enter the area. It was known that two Soviet Victor Is were in the Mediterranean.[16] The two tailships conducted their patrol with ASW Group 2 (ASWGRU 2), comprising the USS *Wasp*, CVS-19, its air group (S-2 Tracker aircraft and SH-3 Sea King helicopters) and escorting destroyers.[17]

On 7 February, CORTRON 8's commander, CDR D. Crawley, USN, was high-lined

Table 2: Soviet Submarines assigned to Fifth *Eskadra* in 1971 (*continued*)												
Foxtrot B-6	X	X	X	X	X	X	X	X	X	X	X	X
Foxtrot B-41							X	X	X	X	X	X
Foxtrot B-116							X	X	X	X	X	X
Foxtrot B-840							X	X	X	X	X	X
Foxtrot B-21										X	X	X
Foxttrot B-49												X
Foxtrot B-130												X
Foxtrot B-400												X
Foxtrot B-440												X
Foxtrot B-838												X
Total/ Month	14+1	12+1	8+1	9+1	8	6	7	9	9	10	10	14

operating in the Med. One was a Sturgeon-class nuclear attack submarine, the USS *Lapon*, SSN-661, while two were the conventional submarines, the Balao-class USS *Bang*, SS-365, and Tench-class USS *Quillback*, SS-424.[18]

NATIONAL WEEK VIII commenced on 10 February, concluding on the 18th. The exercise area was located in the central Ionian Sea. Coinciding with this exercise was a quarterly amphibious exercise, PHIBLEX 8-71. Its exercise area was off Argolikos Bay on the south-east coast of the Greek Peloponnese and near the port city of Nafplio. The objective of the exercises was for Sixth Fleet units to conduct offensive/defensive operations to neutralise opposition air, surface and submarine forces, while screening the amphibious forces to the objective area, and then support the Marines as they moved ashore with naval gunfire and carrier air strikes.

With the exercises completed, both tailships returned to Naples on 18 February. They moored alongside *Lester*, which had not participated in the exercise. For the rest of February and until 16 March, all three ships remained in Naples, receiving maintenance from *Grand Canyon*.[19]

from *Courtney* to *Wasp* to meet with the ASWGRU 2 commander and his staff. Crawley briefed them on ITASS capabilities and mapped out the tactics that the ITASS ships would use against the US submarines playing Soviet subs. At the time, three US subs were

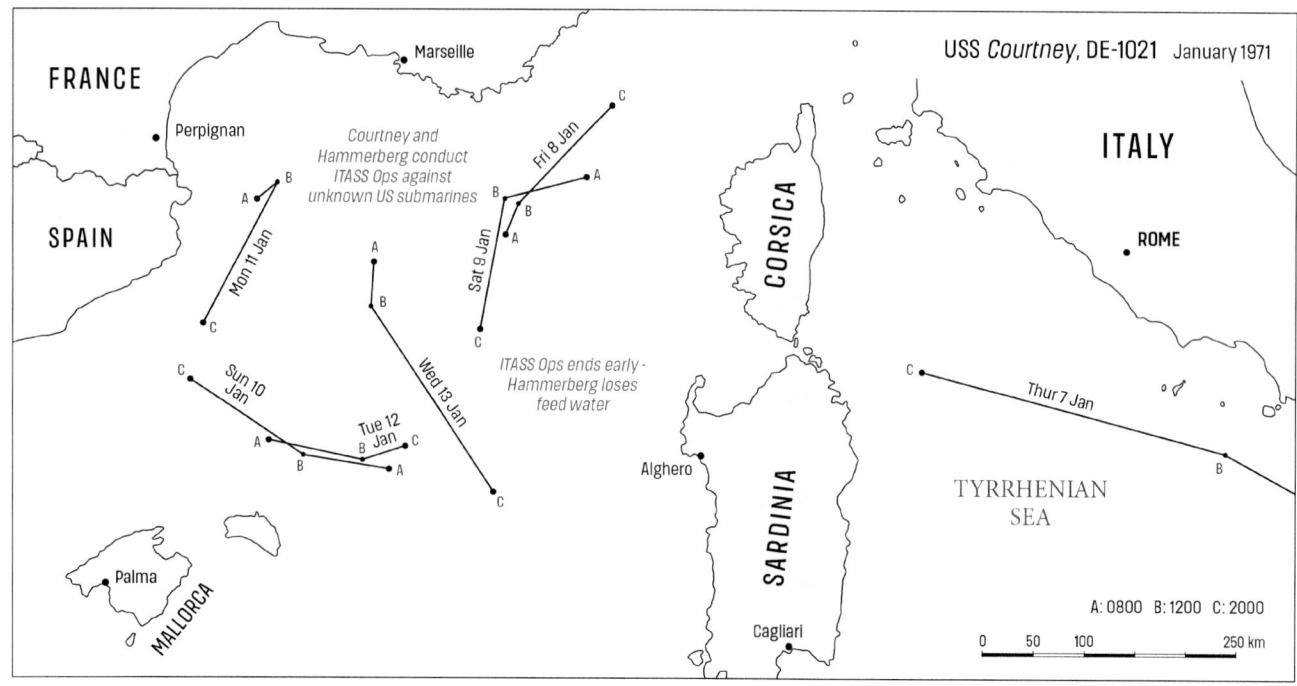

Courtney and *Hammerberg's* ITASS operations, 8–13 January 1971. (Map by Paul Hewitt based on *Courtney* and *Hammerberg* January 1971 Deck Log Books)

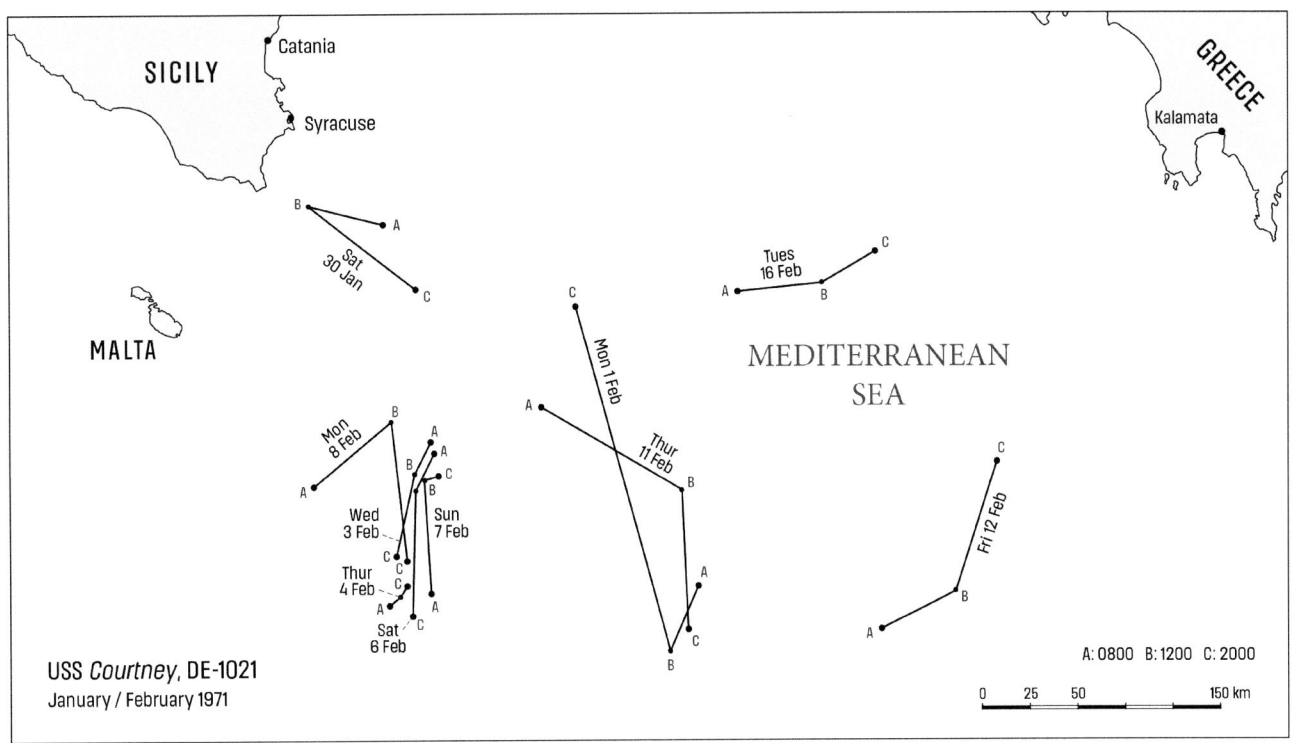

Courtney's ITASS tracks during National Week VIII, 30 January–17 February. (Map by Paul Hewitt based on *Courtney* and *Hammerberg* January 1971 Deck Log Books)

On 16 March, *Courtney* and *Hammerberg* departed Naples and proceeded through the Tyrrhenian Sea toward the western Mediterranean, between Sardinia and the Balearic Islands. Just after midnight on 18 March, both ships were streaming their tails.[20] Their deployment coincided with the departure of Task Group 60.2, whose ships had been ported at Palma and Barcelona. The *Roosevelt* and its escorts left on 17 March to operate east of the Balearic Islands and then in the Tyrrhenian prior to arriving at Naples on 25 March.[21]

Looking at the Mediterranean's geography, it is reasonable to deduce that at least one Soviet Foxtrot submarine would have positioned itself south of the Balearic Islands in order to observe the *Roosevelt* and its escorts as they sailed eastward from Palma and Barcelona. At the same time, other Foxtrots could be positioned between Sardinia and Algeria, and in the Tyrrhenian Sea, with another positioned in the Strait of Sicily.[22]

Admiral Kidd, Commander Sixth Fleet, COMSIXTHFLT, said as much:

I think that one additional reason the Soviets have so many submarines has to do with their choke point philosophy. They want to be sure that they have enough submarines to control the natural choke points in the Mediterranean. There are seven. Moving from west to east there is Gibraltar, the waters between Sardinia and the African coast, the Strait of Sicily, Strait of Messina, the area between Crete and Africa, and the two passages at each end of Crete leading into the Aegean Sea. If you and I are playing in the line of the Chicago Bears, and we want to stop that fella getting through the line, we line up shoulder to shoulder so he can't squeeze through. Line them up side by each so that nobody can get through … at least not undetected.[23]

Positioning *Courtney* and *Hammerberg* east of the Balearics provided an opportunity for the tailships to detect an awaiting submarine and provide tactical warning to the *Roosevelt* battle group. Comparing the tailship tracks, the *Roosevelt* battle group operated in the Balearic Sea during most of seven days before its Naples port visit. According to the Sixth Fleet Command History, there were no scheduled exercises during the period. It can be assumed that *Roosevelt* was carrying out normal flight operations, with its escorts screening its movements. Additionally, this time at sea provided an opportunity for the *Roosevelt*'s escorts to refuel and take on stores prior to the Naples port visit.

Courtney suspended ITASS operations on 20 March to refuel and water at Cagliari, Sardinia, returning to sea the following day. It continued operating with *Hammerberg* until the 26th. Then both tailships retrieved their arrays, arriving at Naples on 27 March. "The first quarter of the new year concluded with ASW operations in the Western Mediterranean."[24]

As this last operation showed, tailship operations were evolving: "The first few months in the Med were filled with collecting data, developing tactics and generally getting to know the low frequency acoustic environment … frequent changes to op-orders during the early stages as operational commanders tried to find the right niche for this new capability."[25]

ITASS operations continued apace from April through the summer and into the autumn months of 1971.[26] Three such operations involving *Courtney* are illustrative of the squadron's operational tempo during the year. Some involved follow-on exercises, such as another NATIONAL WEEK, as well as independent ITASS operations in the Ionian Sea.

On 21 June, *Courtney*, now commanded by LCDR Alfred Spruell, USN, departed Naples and headed south-west toward the Algerian coast, arriving on station on the 23rd. For the next six days, *Courtney* streamed its tail on an east–west track that paralleled the Algerian coast, whilst keeping outside of Algerian territorial waters.

During this time, the number of Soviet submarines operating in the Mediterranean had reached a low point. Prior to *Courtney*'s patrol, Victor I SSN K-25 and Charlie I SSGN K-69 had departed

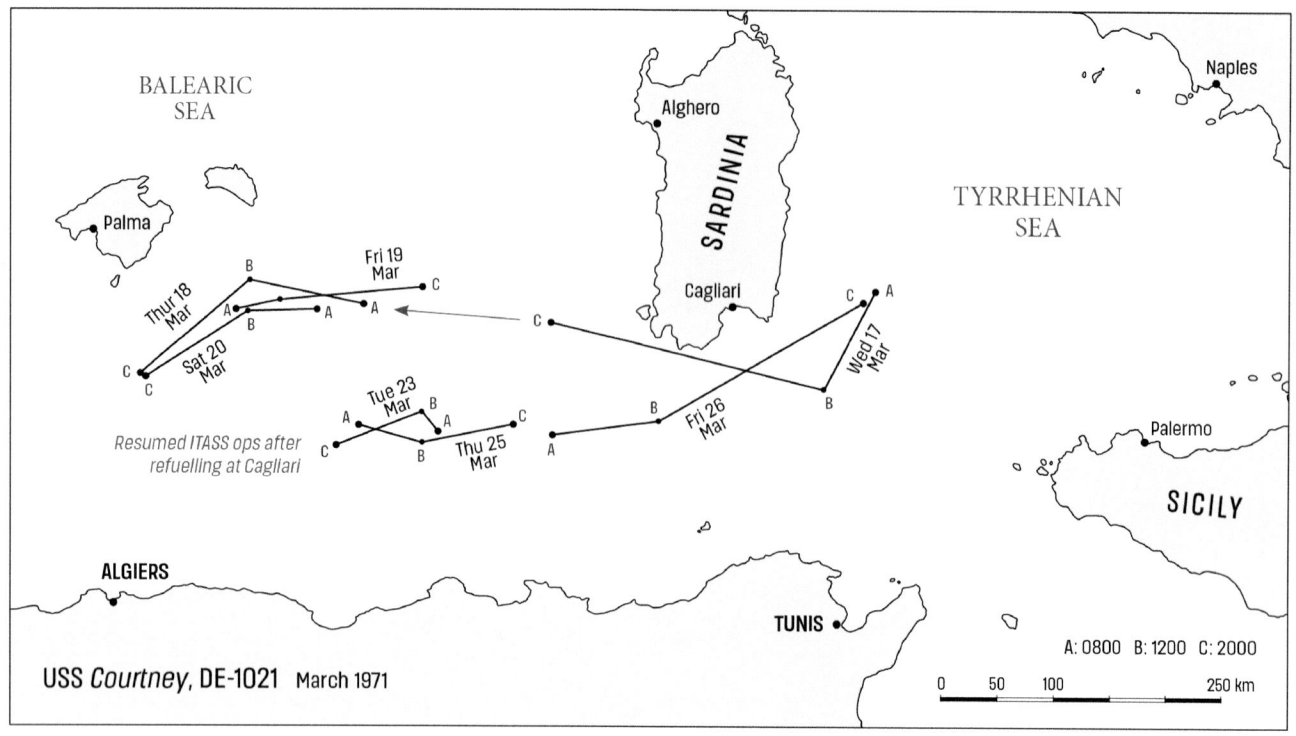

Courtney's ITASS patrol tracks, 17–26 March 1971. (Map by Paul Hewitt based on *Courtney* March 1971 Deck Log Book)

the Med at the end of May and returned to their Northern Fleet base. The only submarine missile shooter remaining in the Med was Juliett K-318; it was estimated this was in the eastern Med.

Additionally, Foxtrot B-34, B-59, B-153 and B-205 left the Med during April and May. The remaining Foxtrot operating in the Med was Foxtrot B-6, which had returned to operational status in May after being in the yards at Alexandria for nine months. B-6 joined Foxtrot B-839, B-435, B-29 and B-413; the last two were exiting the Mediterranean.[27]

The decision to position *Courtney* off the Algerian coast was due to the westward transit of B-29 and B-413. As mentioned previously, it was thought Soviet submarines would use the waters off the Moroccan and Algerian coast to help mask their east–west transit. Positioning the tailship along the Algerian littoral also increased the chances of detecting three Foxtrots – B-41, B-116 and B-840 – after they entered the Med from their North Fleet base at the end of June.

Courtney continued streaming its tail off the Algerian coast until the morning of 29 June. Then

Commander in Chief
U.S. Naval Forces, Europe

The Commander in Chief, U.S. Naval Forces, Europe takes pleasure in commending the officers and men of

ESCORT SQUADRON EIGHT

consisting of

Commander Escort Squadron EIGHT and Staff
USS HAMMERBERG (DE 1015)
USS COURTNEY (DE 1021)
USS LESTER (DE 1022)
USS VAN VOORHIS (DE 1028)

for service as set forth in the following

CITATION:

For meritorious service during the period 5 September 1970 through 29 July 1971 while conducting highly important and sensitive antisubmarine warfare operations in the Mediterranean Sea. Participating both in a comprehensive test program of special significance, and in Fleet-wide operational exercises, Escort Squadron EIGHT completed all assigned missions with outstanding success and professionalism. The officers and men of the Squadron displayed exceptional initiative and dedication throughout this period of arduous employment and, through skilled utilization of their special capabilities, contributed significantly to the strengthening of the United States Sixth Fleet's antisubmarine warfare posture. Escort Squadron EIGHT's performance throughout was in keeping with the highest traditions of the United States Naval Service.

W. F. BRINGLE
ADMIRAL, UNITED STATES NAVY
COMMANDER IN CHIEF, UNITED STATES NAVAL FORCES, EUROPE

Letter of commendation. (Author's collection)

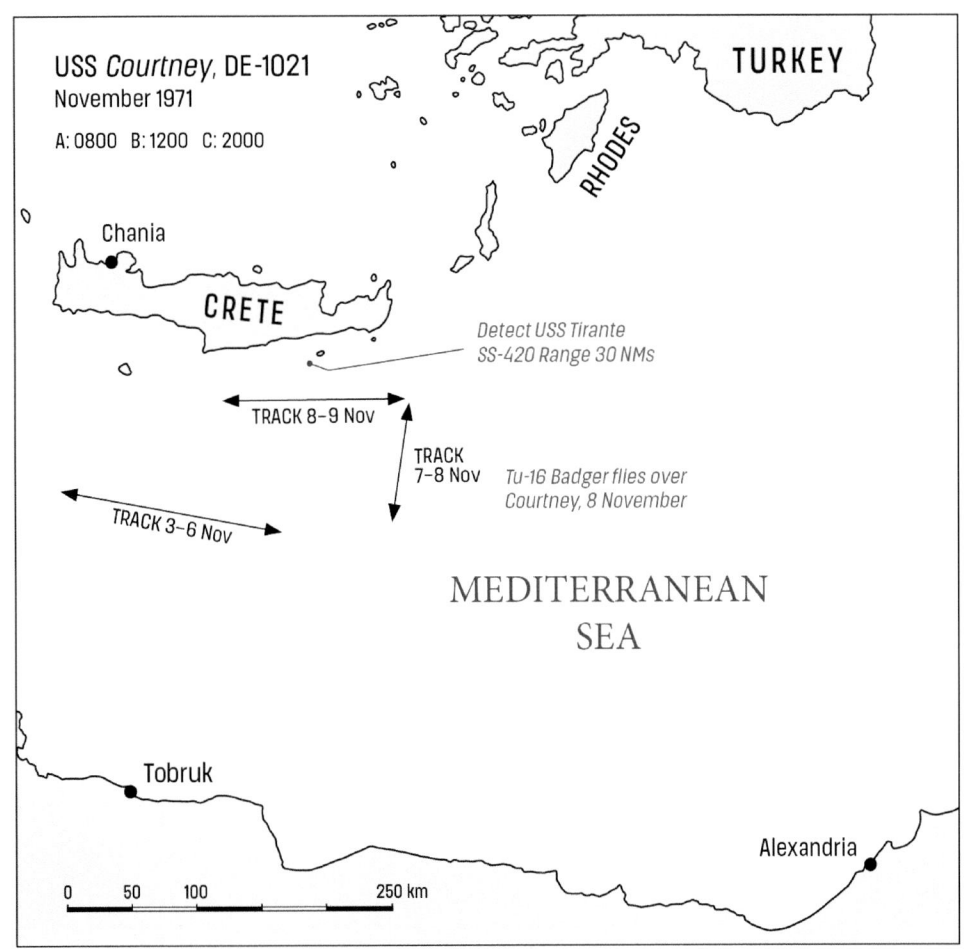

USS *Courtney*, DE-1021
November 1971

A: 0800 B: 1200 C: 2000

TURKEY

RHODES

Chania

CRETE

*Detect USS Tirante
SS-420 Range 30 NMs*

TRACK 8–9 Nov

TRACK
7–8 Nov *Tu-16 Badger flies over
Courtney, 8 November*

TRACK 3–6 Nov

MEDITERRANEAN
SEA

Tobruk

Alexandria

0   50   100   250 km

Exercise National Week XI, 2–10 November. (Map by Paul Hewitt based on *Courtney* November 1971 Deck Log Book)

Spruell took his tailship further north and began streaming the tail south of Mallorca on a west–east track that paralleled the more inshore track that his tailship had taken on 23 June. This lasted until the 30th, when Spruell retrieved the tail and headed back to Naples, returning to Naples on 1 July. *Courtney* remained there until the morning of 15 July.

Spruell took *Courtney* south for ITASS operations in the Ionian Sea, deploying its tail south of Messina on 16 July. Spruell headed *Courtney* south-east across the Ionian until reaching a position approximately 90nm west of Crete's Akra Krios lighthouse on the 18th. He then reversed course toward Messina, arriving at Taormina, Sicily, on 20 July for two days' shore leave for the crew. Back out again on the 22nd, Spruell steered *Courtney* on a south by south-east heading, streaming the tail for approximately 320nm until reaching a point 145nm west by south-west of Crete's Akra Krios lighthouse on 24 July. With the tail deployed, Spruell steered *Courtney* on an easterly heading and turned back on a reciprocal course when reaching 25nm south-west of Akra Krios lighthouse. Returning to a position 130nm west of the Akra Krios lighthouse, Spruell took his ship back on a course toward Messina and home, returning to Naples on the 28th.

This particular ITASS operation was unusual for the tailships, as it had one of them streaming its tail diagonally (north-west to south-east) on a steady course across the Ionian Sea. During this time, only one Juliett and six Foxtrots were operating in the Mediterranean. Additionally, when *Courtney* departed Taormina on 22 July, the USS *America* carrier battle group, TG 60.1, had departed ports "in Corfu, Greece and southern Italian ports" on the same

day. During the time *Courtney* was operating its tail, the units of TG 60.1 had rendezvoused in the central Ionian and commenced operations north of *Courtney's* tracks until they anchored in Soudha Bay on 29 July, a day after *Courtney's* return to Naples.[28]

In November, *Courtney* spent 18 days at sea. The first nine days saw it operating south of Crete participating in NATIONAL WEEK XI, which commenced on 2 November. The following eight days had Spruell's *Courtney* operating in the Ionian Sea.

During the exercise, there were nine Soviet submarines in the Mediterranean; six Foxtrots and an unusually high number of three Julietts.[29] Coincidentally, Sixth Fleet had a single SSN, the USS *Haddo*, SSN-604, and one conventional submarine, the USS *Tirante*, SS-420, in the Med.[30]

Courtney departed Naples on 1 November and arrived on station 85nm south of Crete's Akra Krios lighthouse on 3 November. With the tail deployed, Spruell set an east by south-east course until the 4th, when upon reaching a point halfway between Crete and Libya he reversed course. *Courtney* continued its east–west track until 6 November, when Spruell ordered the tail to be retrieved so that *Courtney* could refuel.

With refuelling completed, Spruell repositioned *Courtney* further east and south of Crete. For the rest of the exercise, Spruell had *Courtney* streaming its tail in an L-shape pattern. With *Courtney* and the ships of TG 60.1 moving into the eastern basin, the Fifth *Eskadra* responded by increasing its reconnaissance and surveillance operations. One such occurrence was *Courtney* being overflown by a Tu-16 Badger on 7 November.

During the exercise's last day, *Courtney* detected the USS *Tirante* whilst the submarine was hugging Crete's shoreline emulating what Soviet subs were known to do when transiting the Moroccan and Algerian coast. *Courtney* tracked *Tirante* during the night of 8/9 November. The submarine was on the surface, charging its batteries. With the OTs resolving the bearing ambiguity, the tailship's CIC directed a P-3 Orion to overfly it and fly out on the bearing provided by the OTs. *Tirante* was caught on the surface; the P-3 reported that it sighted the exercise sub and sank it. The aircraft provided *Courtney* with the coordinates and it was determined that ITASS had detected *Tirante* at a distance of 30nm; the submarine was trying to mask itself by using the island of Koufonísi as cover.

On 9 November, one day before the exercise ended, *Courtney* refuelled at Augusta Bay. Spruell took his tailship back out into the Ionian on 11 November to conduct independent operations. Heading south, *Courtney* deployed its tail when reaching a position

55nm east of Malta. The tailship continued south until it reached 34°00'N/16°25'E on 12 November. At this position, Spruell turned *Courtney* due east. With its tail streaming behind, *Courtney* continued east until reaching a position 100nm north-east of Tripoli, Libya, on 13 November. Spruell then changed course to 040 degrees to head toward Greece and *Courtney*'s next turning point on 14 November.

However, before *Courtney* could reach its next turning point, it picked up a shadower; a Mod Kotlin-class destroyer, hull number 388, which lingered long enough to close the tailship and determine what the American was doing.[31] With the Soviet moving off and heading north-east toward the Soviet fair weather anchorage off Kithra, Greece, *Courtney* continued its own north-east course, reaching its next turning point of 38°35'N/17°40'E on 14 November.

With *Courtney*'s tail still streaming behind it, Spruell ordered a turn to the north-west toward Italy. For the next two days, *Courtney* continued north-westward. The operation came to an abrupt end 35nm south-east of Capo Rizzuto, Italy, on 16 November, when the OTs reported the tail had broken down. Spruell brought *Courtney* back to Naples the following afternoon. Thus ended the 'experiment'.[32]

The tailships continued ITASS operations for the next 30 days until mid-December, when the squadron stood down for the Christmas/New Year holiday. As a testament to how successful the tailships were, the squadron received a congratulatory message from Commander in Chief US Naval Forces, Europe.

What would the next two years bring for the tailships of Escort Squadron 8?

9

1972–1973: FROM ZENITH TO NADIR

Intelligence Situation

The Soviet naval presence in the eastern Mediterranean saw a significant reduction in capability: "[T]he return of the Soviet Mediterranean Air Squadron to the USSR substantially reduced the Soviet capability to conduct ASW operations, terminated collection against Sixth Fleet units by reconnaissance/ELINT configured aircraft … and eliminated Soviet ASM strike threat by TU-16s."[1]

The number of Soviet naval and auxiliary units reached its highest level in January, with 65 units. However, the number of Soviet surface and submarine units never reached those levels in January, even when a number of combatants transited into the Mediterranean from the Black Sea, as a result of heightened tensions between the Arab states and Israel in the late summer.

This buildup was in reaction to the Palestinian terrorist group Black September's attack on the Israeli Olympic team in West Germany on 6 September. During the last week in September, 17 ships transited from the Black Sea and took up station off Syria. This concentration was also in reaction to the USS *Forrestal* CV-59 BG entering the eastern Mediterranean basin.

In 1972, two semi-annual submarine turnovers occurred. In January, seven Foxtrots and one Juliett arrived; after entering the Med, they broke up into three groups and proceeded to their patrol areas. This was a tactic to complicate the ability of Sixth Fleet ASW assets to track the Foxtrots. As for the Juliett, "Inchopping Juliett had material problems and had to be escorted to Alexandria."[2]

On 3 November, three Foxtrots entered the Mediterranean from North Fleet bases. They were accompanied by a Kresta I and Kresta II missile cruiser and a Sverdlov-class light cruiser. At the same time, six Foxtrots, a Juliett SSG, a Kashin-class DDG and two Krivak-class missile frigates exited via the Straits of Gibraltar and returned to their North and Baltic Fleet homeports. Then in December, a Charlie I entered the Mediterranean. Additionally, the Soviets transferred two of their obsolescent Whiskey-class diesel-electric submarines to the Egyptian Navy. These movements had the potential of complicating Sixth Fleet's ASW operations.[3]

The transit and subsequent deployment of these Soviet submarines to their operational areas presented opportunities for the tailships to detect and track their movement. As recorded by the Sixth Fleet:

ASW continued as top priority throughout the year. The Soviet submarine level remained at an average of slightly over eleven units in the Mediterranean. Sixth Fleet ASW forces remained at the same level as in the past with two exceptions. Because of the deployment of a submarine tender in July 1972, the submarine force increased to a level of six SSNs and subsequently levelled off at four when the tender returned to CONUS in November. In addition, USS *Intrepid*, CVS-11 deployed in December with an ASW air group composed of squadrons of fixed wing and help ASW aircraft.[4]

New Year 1972 would become the zenith – the highpoint for ITASS operations.

Off They Go Again

After the Christmas/New Year stand-down, *Courtney* departed on 23 January for a two-day sea trial to shake things out and prepare for the first major Sixth Fleet exercise, NATIONAL WEEK XII. It and its sisters were showing wear after conducting extensive operations during the previous year. During the rest of the month, both *Hammerberg* and *Lester* spent time conducting sea trials to ensure they were also ready for NATIONAL WEEK XII.

All three tailships departed Naples on Thursday, 3 February, in order to be in position for the exercise. This would be the first time all three would participate. Entering the Ionian Sea on the 4th, all three ships were soon on station when the exercise commenced on Saturday, 5 February.[5]

Both CVBGs – TG 60.1, led by the USS *Independence*, CV-62, and TG 60.2, led by the USS *John F. Kennedy*, CV-67 – participated. Additionally, they were joined in the exercise by the USS *Sunfish*, SSN-649, and the diesel submarine *Cutlass*, SS-478. All were joined by COMSIXTHFLT, Vice Admiral Gerald Miller, USN, aboard the flagship, USS *Springfield*, CLG-7.[6]

Of course the carriers were not without their Soviet tattletales, two Kashin-class DDGs (hull numbers 533 and 527), to keep tabs on the Americans. With the deployment of the Kashins, the Soviets were also conducting an exercise of sorts; they routinely sent back positioning reports to the commander of the Fifth *Eskadra*, which

Table 3: Soviet submarines assigned to the Fifth Eskadra in 1972.

(Information derived from www.deepstorm.ru)

	Jan	Feb	Mar	Apr	May	Jun	Jul	Aug	Sep	Oct	Nov	Dec
Charlie I K-25				X	X	X						
Charlie I K-313			X	X	X							
Charlie I K-302						X	X	X				
Victor I K-323				X	X	X						
Victor I K-438												X
Juliett K-24	X	X										
Juliett K203	X	X										
Juliett K-304	X	X	X	X	X	X						
Foxtrot B-840	X	X										
Foxtrot B-116	X	X	X	X	X	X	X	X	X	X	X	
Foxtrot B-41	X	X	X	X	X	X	X	X	X	X	X	X
Foxtrot B-6	X	X	X	X	X							
Foxtrot B-57	X	X	X	X	X							
Foxtrot B-26					X	X	X	X	X	X	X	
Foxtrot B-31					X	X	X	X	X	X		
Foxtrot B-94					X	X	X	X	X	X	X	
Foxtrot B-98					X	X	X	X	X	X	X	
Foxtrot B-416					X	X	X	X	X	X	X	
Foxtrot B-21	X	X	X	X	X	X	X					
Foxtrot B-49	X	X	X	X	X	X						
Foxtrot B-130	X	X	X	X	X	X						
Foxtrot B-400	X	X	X	X	X	X						
Foxtrot B-440	X	X	X	X	X	X						
Foxtrot B-838	X	X	X	X	X	X						
Foxtrot B-435									X	X	X	X

gave him up-to-date targeting information for coordinating his strike assets.[7]

During the exercise's combat phase on 6/7 February, the tailships successfully detected and 'localised' two of the exercise submarines. With the conclusion of the exercise, they went to liberty ports for some R&R. *Courtney* spent four days in Athens before heading back out to operate off the Libyan coast. However, it suffered an ITASS mechanical failure and was subsequently tasked to conduct BYSTANDER operations – surveilling Soviet surface units. For the tailship sailors, this was an opportunity to play 'bumper cars' with the Soviets.

Courtney versus *Leningrad*

Periodically, the tailships were tasked to conduct surveillance (BYSTANDER) operations of Fifth *Eskadra* units. *Courtney* departed Athens on Monday, 14 February to resume ITASS operations in the Ionian Sea. Shortly after *Courtney*'s departure, it and other Sixth Fleet surface and air units were tasked to conduct BYSTANDER operations against Soviet units operating in the eastern Ionian Sea and west of Crete. The Soviet force consisted of the *Leningrad*, its escorts and a Foxtrot-class diesel submarine.

The Soviets had been conducting what Sixth Fleet assessed was an ASW exercise, with the submarine acting as a target for *Leningrad* and its escorts. The exercise included a live fire event which saw the *Leningrad* firing a salvo of its RBU-6000 ASW rockets.

While the Soviets were conducting their exercise, *Courtney* and other Sixth Fleet destroyers followed the Soviet units. For *Courtney*, Spruell tried to maintain a position off *Leningrad*'s starboard or port quarter, keeping a distance of 2,000 yards. At times this was

Table 3: Soviet submarines assigned to the Fifth Eskadra in 1972 (*continued*) (Information derived from www.deepstorm.ru)											
Foxtrot B-34									X	X	X
Foxtrot B-205									X	X	X
Total/ Month	14	14	12	13	19	17	8+1	8	8	10	8+1	4

difficult to do, as one of the *Leningrad*'s escorts, a Petya-class light frigate, would try to come between *Courtney* and *Leningrad*, forcing the tailship to veer away and stop. Collision was a constant concern,

As gas turbine ships, Petya frigates were much faster going from a dead stop to flank speed than the steam-powered US counterparts. Petya- and Mirka-class light frigates were the ships of choice when countering US ships trying to maintain a tattletale station against a high-value platform such as the *Leningrad*.

However, the tailships had an advantage: they could go into full reverse quicker than the Soviet gas turbine ships. Spruell would order "all back full" and shift *Courtney*'s twin rudders hard to port. Once *Courtney* fell behind the Soviet, he would shift the rudders to turn starboard and cut under the Soviet's stern, whilst ordering "all ahead flank". By this method, Spruell was able to keep station on *Leningrad*.[8]

With the completion of the exercise, the Soviets anchored at the fair weather anchorage off the Greek island of Kithira. Shortly upon arriving at the anchorage, *Leningrad* departed without its escorts and proceeded westward at high speed. The *Courtney* was directed to follow the Soviet ship at its best possible speed. The reason for *Leningrad*'s highly unusual departure was that it had been directed to leave the Mediterranean and go to the assistance of a stricken

Podvodnaya Lodka Atomnaya Raketnaya Ballisticheskaya (*PLARB*) type submarine.[9]

The submarine was a Project 658-class (NATO-designated Hotel II-class SSBN), the first generation of Soviet nuclear submarines to carry nuclear-armed ballistic missiles. The submarine was identified as K-19, and it carried three R-19 liquid-fuelled, single-stage missiles (NATO-designated SS-N-4 SARK). Each missile was equipped with a single nuclear warhead with explosive power approximating one megaton.[10]

Whilst on submerged patrol, the boat had suffered a major fire on 24 February. At the time, the submarine was approximately 600nm north-east of Newfoundland and 450nm south of Cape Farewell, Greenland. K-19 was on the surface and DIW. The crew was able to extinguish the fire but it left 28 of their number dead. Although dozens of Soviet ships were directed to assist the endangered submarine, including the *Leningrad*, another Soviet submarine met the stricken fleet ballistic missile submarine and took it in tow. It took 23 days for the K-19 to be towed back across the Atlantic to its North Fleet base on the Kola Peninsula.[11]

Courtney followed as best as it could, but the tailship could not match *Leningrad*'s speed. Slowly, the Soviet increased its distance from the venerable American, until the distance drastically changed.

At one point, *Courtney* lookouts spotted smoke pouring out of the helicopter cruiser's port side and under its flight deck. It appeared to be a hangar fire. The little American came up on the port side of the Soviet, and as it did, the size difference became obvious. All on *Courtney*'s starboard bridge wing had to crane their necks upward toward the *Leningrad*'s bridge. *Courtney*'s skipper, LCDR Spruell, signalled the Russian asking if it needed assistance. *Leningrad* replied courteously: "No thank you." *Courtney* pulled away and took up station astern.[12]

It did not take long for the Soviet to turn on the speed. Initially, *Courtney* matched the Russian's speed, but it reached a point where the Russian was just too fast, widening the distance from the American. *Courtney* broke off the chase and headed toward the Strait of Messina and home to Naples.

Sixth Fleet continued to follow *Leningrad* as it steamed toward Gibraltar and into the Atlantic. *Leningrad* was one of 30 ships and submarines that participated in the K-19 rescue operation.[13] However, it did not linger on the storm-

The *Leningrad* as seen from the *Courtney*. A Kresta II CG and a Foxtrot submarine can also be seen. (Author's collection)

A Petya-class light anti-submarine frigate. (NH 80295)

K-19 on the surface, disabled and drifting. (Norman Polmar, *Cold War Submarines*)

tossed North Atlantic, and quickly returned to the Mediterranean to resume its six-month deployment.

In April, both NATO and the Fifth *Eskadra* conducted ASW exercises. For the Soviets, a "Spring ASWEX exercise took place southwest of Kithira, 31 March to 5 April. *Leningrad*, six destroyers, IL-38 Mays and submarines conducted the exercise. Activity shifted to south of Crete during the final phase."[14]

With the completion of the exercise, the Soviets conducted the periodic submarine turnover. Seven Foxtrots and the single Juliett departed the Mediterranean on 27 May and headed north into the Atlantic toward their Northern and Baltic Fleet bases. Six Foxtrots and one Juliett entered the Med.[15]

As part of a Sixth Fleet/NATO response to the new arrivals, *Courtney* and *Hammerberg* sortied from Barcelona, Spain just after mid-day on the 27th. At 1730 on 28 May, *Courtney* began her ITASS patrol, approximately 40NMs north of Cape Bougaroun, Algeria.[16] *Courtney* proceeded westward and parallel to the Algerian coast. At the same time, LCDR Spruell keep his tailship north of what he estimated would be the Soviet submarines eastward transit. His decision was based on precedent; Soviet submarines were known to hug the Algerian coast whilst submerged, using the North African continental shelf to mask their movements.[17]

Courtney continued westward until late morning on the 29th. While approximately 60NMs north of Algers, Spruell reversed his tailship's course and headed eastward. He continued to sail parallel to the Algerian coast and north of the transiting Soviets. This continued until 2200 on 31 May when a VP aircraft reported that it had sighted a nearby Juliett SSG on the surface.[18]

Shortly after receiving the sighting report, Spruell altered course toward the submarine, commenced retrieving the array, turned off navigational lights, and activated his tailship's sonar. At 2212, the Juliett went sinker. Three minutes later, Spruell ordered the 1AS attack team into action. With the array on deck by 2220, the tailship, using its active sonar began prosecuting the Juliett's datum. This continued for the next hour, when the 1AS attack team was secured, and Spruell headed northward at 20 knots. Just before midnight, *Courtney* slowed to 10 knots and began streaming her array.[19]

Beginning on 1 June and lasting through the evening hours on 4 June, Spruell had altered *Courtney*'s ITASS track to a north/south orientation and perpendicular to the transiting Soviets. However, this movement stopped at 2251 on the 1st, when Spruell ordered the crew to retrieve the array and steer toward a radar contact which shortly went sinker. *Courtney* continued searching for the sub for the next four hours, until just before 0400 on the 2nd, *Courtney* resumed streaming her array and continued her north/south ITASS track.

During the late morning hours on 4 June, Spruell returned to an eastward course toward the Strait of Sicily, entering the strait during the early morning hours on the 5th. Prior to daylight, Spruell ordered the array to be retrieved, then steered *Courtney* toward the USS *Seattle*, AOE-3 to refuel. With *Courtney* refuelled, she resumed

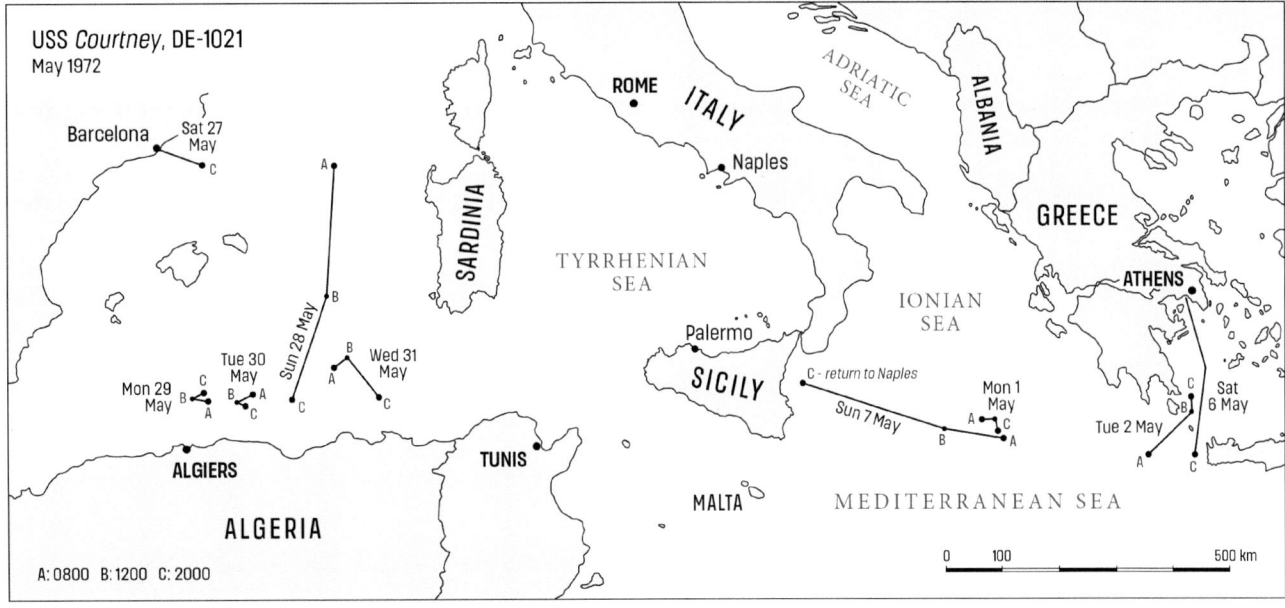

Courtney and *Hammerberg* conduct ITASS Ops against inchopping Soviet submarines, 27–31 May 1972. (Map by Paul Hewitt based on *Courtney* May 1972 Deck Log Book)

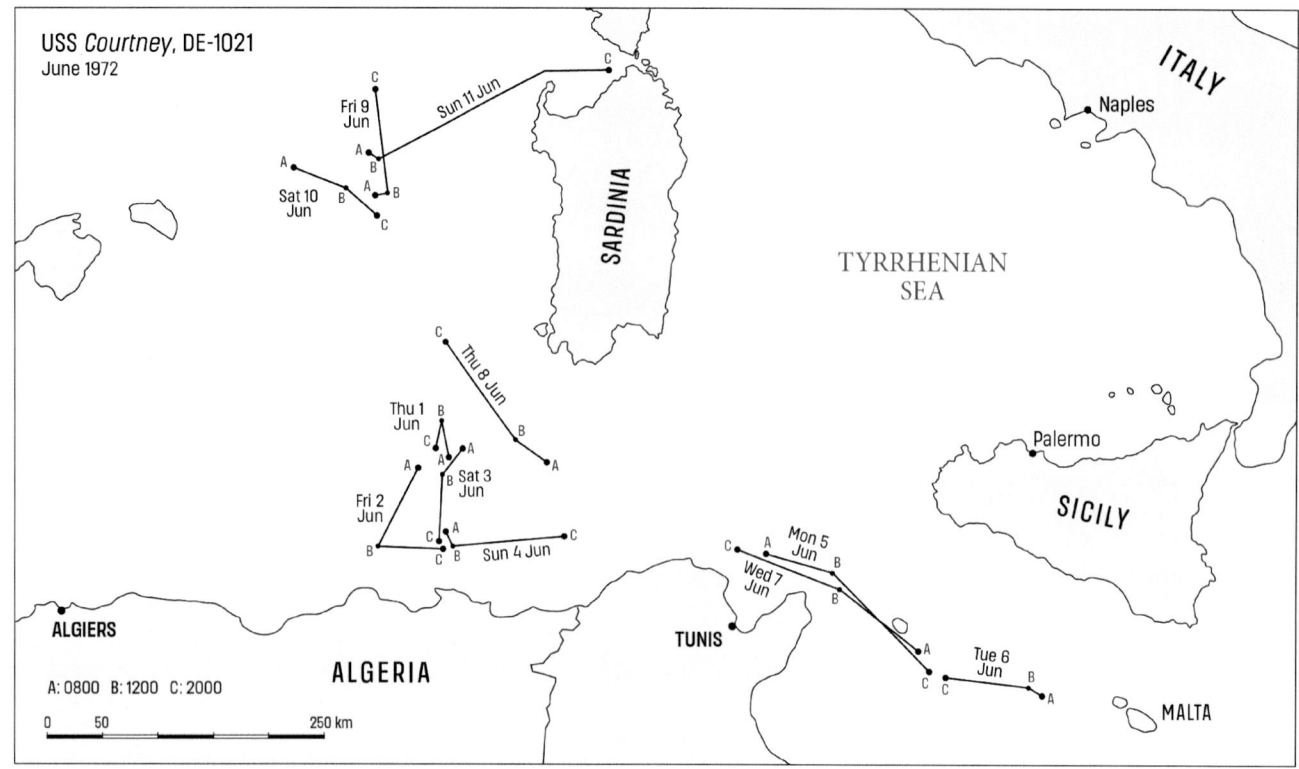

Courtney prosecuting inchopping Soviet subs with ITASS and active sonar. (Map by Paul Hewitt based on *Courtney* June 1972 Deck Log Book)

her ITASS track down through the Strait of Sicily, passing south of the Italian Island of Pantelleria and toward the Soviet Fifth *Eskadra*'s fair weather anchorage in the Gulf of Hammamet. Shortly after 0800 on the 6th, and approximately 40NMs west of Malta, Spruell reversed course and took his tailship back northward through the strait. While still streaming her array, *Courtney* exited the strait during the afternoon hours on the 7th, and proceeded westward toward Sardinia.

At 0800 on the 8th, *Courtney* was south of Sardinia's Capo Spartivento and heading north-westward. It was during the early morning hours on the 9th that the tailship acquired sonar contacts on two separate submarines. With each contact Spruell retrieved the array and actively prosecuted the contacts with *Courtney*'s sonar. For the next two days, *Courtney* continued streaming her array between the islands of Menorca and Sardinia. Her June deck long states the tailship was conducting a series of ASW exercises. It is possible she was exercising against the newly arrived Permit class SSN, the USS *Dace*, SSN-607. After 14 days of a successful ITASS patrol, *Courtney* and *Hammerberg* returned to Naples on 12 June.

Courtney remained inport Naples through the rest of June, whilst *Hammerberg* and *Lester* conducted their ITASS patrols. *Lester* returned on 28 June while *Hammerberg* returned on 2 July. All three tailships were present on 3 July when Commander R.F. Donnelly, USN was relieved by Commander V.C. Snyder, USN as COMCORTRON Eight. *Hammerberg* departed on her next ITASS patrol after the change of command.[20]

With *Hammerberg* still at sea, *Courtney* departed on 9 July to conduct a five-day ITASS bearing accuracy test in the Tyrrhenian with the USS *Tringa*, ASR-16. On Saturday, *Courtney* and *Hammerberg* rendezvoused to transfer CORTRON Eight to *Hammerberg*. Both ships returned to Naples and joined *Lester* which was already in port. But on 16 July, with *Lester* still in port, both *Courtney* and *Hammerberg* departed for the Algerian Basin and their next ITASS patrol. However, *Courtney*, with COMCORTRON

Eight aboard, was ordered by COMSIXTHFLT to head south to the Soviet fair weather anchorage at the Gulf of Hammamet, located approximately 15 miles off the Tunisian east coast. Leaving *Hammerberg* to continue on her ITASS patrol, *Courtney* proceeded to the Soviet anchorage to conduct Bystander Operations against a Foxtrot-class submarine, which had arrived at the anchorage. When *Courtney* arrived at 0130 on the 18th, a US Agile class minesweeper built for the Italian Navy, the ITS *Storione*, M-5431, was already on station, watching the Foxtrot.

Shortly after daylight, *Storione* departed, leaving *Courtney* to slowly manoeuvre to maintain a watchful eye on the submarine. Anchored near to the submarine was the *Aleksin*, an auxiliary oil tanker. Also at anchor was a Project 159; a *Storozhevoi Korabi* – Sentry Ship (NATO-designated Petya-class light frigate, *Petya DE-676*).

With *Courtney*'s Snoopy Detail set to record the Foxtrot's presence, Spruell ordered the Blue ASW Tracking Team to station,[21] when the Foxtrot got underway and went sinker. The submarine did not remain submerged for too long; it surfaced and tied up alongside the *Aleksin*'s starboard side. Through the rest of the day and into the night of the 18th, Spruell ensured *Courtney* maintained visual contact on the submarine as it was tied alongside the tanker.

Just 25 hours after *Courtney* had arrived at Hammamet, the Gearing-class destroyer, USS *Strong*, DD-758 'arrived to assist in Bystander Ops. CORTRON 8 OTC' [CDR Snyder Officer in Tactical Command].[22] Through the rest of 18th and into the late evening of the 19th, the two US ships operated as a tactical pair, maintaining surveillance on the submarine and her anchorage mates.

The routine of seeing the Foxtrot alongside the tanker was broken. At 2339 *Courtney* lookouts reported that they no longer saw the submarine alongside the tanker. Almost simultaneously, the ship's sonarmen reported that they heard sounds associated with a submarine submerging; 'Soviet submarine going sinker'. With the captain on the bridge, *Courtney* steered bow on toward the submarine and tanker. Spruell and the bridge watch, saw to their surprise, what

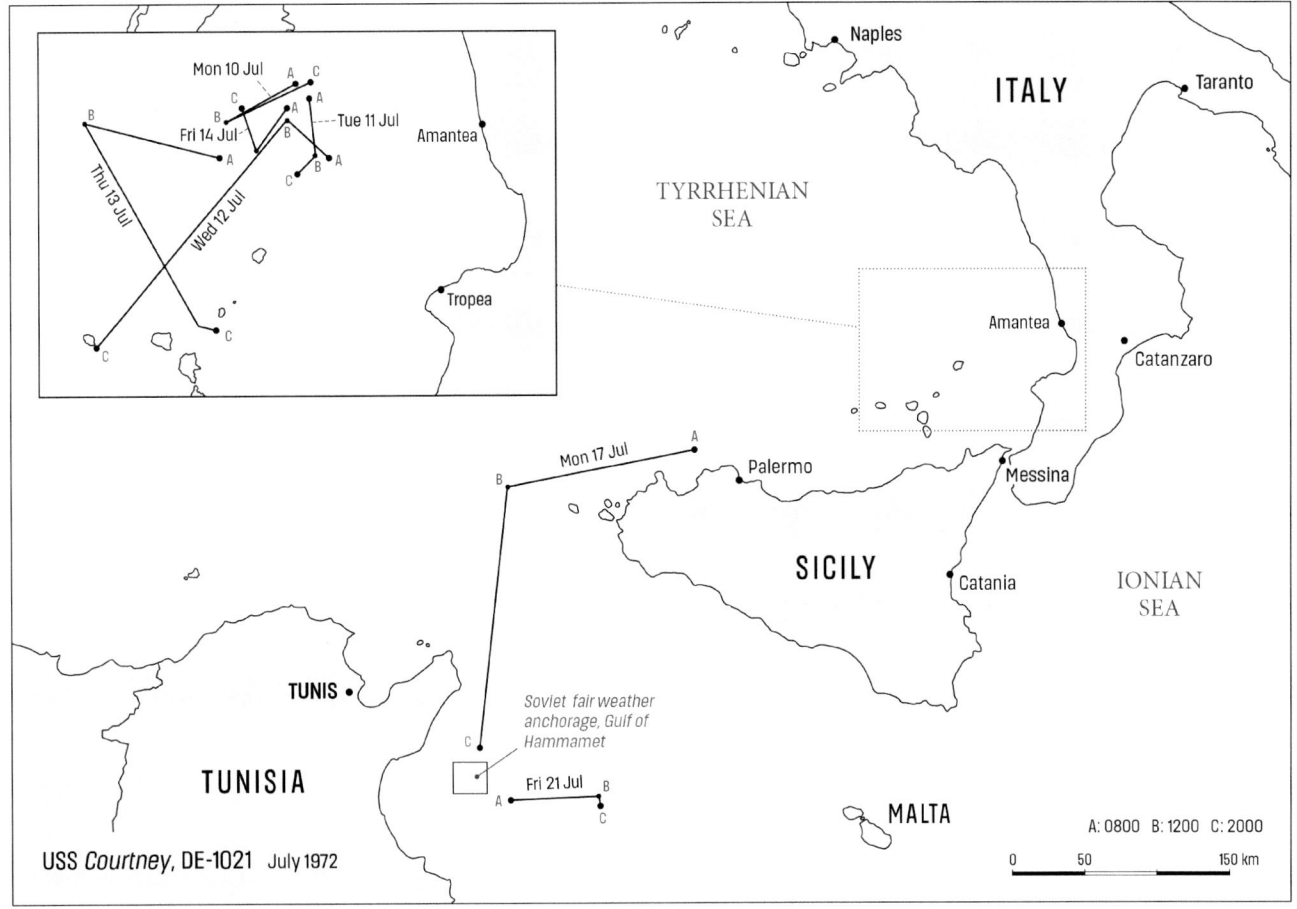

Courtney's operations in July 1972. (Map by Paul Hewitt based on *Courtney* July 1972 Deck Log Book)

would have been the submarine fore and aft anchor lights were, instead, two white lights dangling off the tanker's starboard side; between the lights was just water. Shortly, *Courtney*'s CIC informed the bridge that the ship's radar had detected a small reflective object on the port side of the tanker's own radar reflection.[23]

The Deck Log Book shows what next transpired. With CDR Snyder now on *Courtney*'s bridge, and LCDR Spruell calling away the Blue ASW Tracking Team, CDR Snyder ordered, via secure radio telephone voice, both ships to form an expanded square active sonar search based on the submarine's datum (the radar reflection last seen and plotted by *Courtney*'s radarmen).

With the Americans forming their expanded square sonar search, Petya *DE-676* got underway, and steered toward the Americans. As a gas turbine-powered ship, the Russian quickly increased speed, closing the American formation at 30 knots.[24]

The Russian closed on a reciprocal course toward the Americans. The relative speed as the ships closed on one another was plotted at 45 knots. According to the *Courtney*'s CIC officer, LTJG Mark D. Tabing, USN, the situation was becoming very dangerous:

I remember that I was requested to come to the [port] bridge wing with my camera…So, I ran up the ladder and was stunned at the Petya's speed and proximity – really fast, really close and really loud with the GT [gas turbine] engaged! Of course, there was no way Courtney could out perform the Petya. In my opinion, without risking a devastating collision, Courtney was unable to maneuver effectively…I'm sure the U/W acoustics severely impacted our sonar search capabilities as well.

[By the way] the submarine was long gone.[25]

With Tabing, Spruell and Snyder on the port bridge wing, watching the Russian closing, and CIC plotting the movements of all the ships, the Russian passed close aboard — a port to port pass. For CIC, the radar reflections displayed a 'merged plot' and CIC passed the information to the bridge. It was estimated the two ships passed by one another inside of 100 yards.[26]

As the two Americans came to the end of the first leg of the expanded square search pattern. The outboard ship (*Courtney*) was required to turn to port and cross the wake of the inboard ship (*Strong*), subsequently reversing their positions. By this time, the Russian had already reversed speed, and was closing from astern.

With the Americans on their second leg of the search pattern, the Russian had caught up with them. The Petya was now between the Americans. At some point, the Russian released into the water a noise maker, generating the sound of a propellor through the water. *Courtney*'s sonarmen reported a high-speed propeller to the bridge and CIC. The purpose of the 'noise maker' was to jam the American's sonar.[27]

With the release of the noise maker, the Russian backed off and the Americans continued their sonar search. *Courtney*'s Deck Log recorded: "000-06 ICW Strong, while conducting expending square sonar search to attempt to gain sonar contact. 06-12 attempting to gain sonar contact. At 1222, commenced streaming ITASS. At 1848 commenced retrieving ITASS. 1943 ITASS on deck. At 2026 commenced refuelling from USS Caloosahatchee AO-98. RTN Naples as directed of CTF67".[28]

Earlier in 1972, the US Navy had "to decide whether or not to implant the array [SOSUS] in the Eastern Atlantic; since they could not be sure that the array would help solve the submarine detection problem".[29] The eastern Atlantic acoustic environment was noted for

Table 4: Soviet submarines assigned to the Fifth *Eskadra* in 1973

(Information derived from www.deepstorm.ru)

	Jan	Feb	Mar	Apr	May	Jun	Jul	Aug	Sep	Oct	Nov	Dec
Charlie I K-302			X	X	X							
Charlie I K-429			X	X	X							
Victor I K-438	X	X	X									
Victor I K-323							X	X	X			
Victor I K-367									X	X	X	
Victor I K-370				X	X	X				X	X	X
Victor I K-398									X	X	X	
Foxtrot B-4	X											
Foxtrot B-34	X	X	X	X	X	X	X	X				
Foxtrot B-41	X	X	X	X	X	X	X	X	X	X		
Foxtrot B-205	X	X	X	X	X							
Foxtrot B-435	X	X	X	X	X							
Foxtrot B-2			X	X	X	X	X	X	X	X		
Foxtrot B-840			X	X	X	X	X	X	X	X		
Foxtrot B-169			X	X	X	X	X	X	X	X		
Foxtrot B-49				X	X	X	X	X	X	X	X	X
Foxtrot B-400				X	X	X	X	X	X	X	X	X
Foxtrot B-435	X	X	X	X	X							
Foxtrot B-839									X	X	X	
Foxtrot B-21										X	X	X
Total/ Month	7	6	11	13	13	8	8	8	10	11	7	4

its high ambient noise levels produced by the hundreds of surface ships/craft plying north and south from the British Isles through the Bay of Biscay and along the Iberian Peninsula. These noise levels made detecting lower frequencies generated by the 50Hz signals of Soviet submarines difficult. Complicating the ability to detect submarines through ambient noise was whether the noise was either omni-directional or directional; "the value of the S/N [signal to noise] ratio was critical to know and predict".[30]

Furthermore:

… [S]hip noise filled in the notch between blade rate (the frequency related to the whirling propeller, [which], of course, is related to the engine speed) … it was also felt that the ambient noise is that frequency band which would be continuous, but there were specific frequencies [lines on the LOFAR graphics] that were clearly present and due to surface ships.[31]

The decision to deploy SOSUS in the eastern Atlantic was critically important, because the US and NATO navies had considerable difficulty detecting and tracking Soviet submarines heading south to the Straits of Gibraltar once they passed the GIUK (Greenland, Iceland, United Kingdom) gap SOSUS arrays.

In August, *Courtney* and *Hammerberg* were directed to the eastern Atlantic to conduct the operation. Operation EASTLANT was a two-week experiment conducted over the adamant objections of Commander Sixth Fleet, who did not want to lose the valuable passive sonar systems.

To determine the true bearing of the ambient (ship) noise, scientists in the Long Range Acoustic Propagation Program (LRAPP) "invented the measurement technique to ascertain the directionality of the noise field using two towed arrays":[32] They:

… would tow their tails … at very low speeds (3–4 knots) in very specific patterns. The patterns were octagonal …

The use of this type of pattern approximated a circle. Additional patterns with 12 equal sides were also used. Supporting the two tailships, were P-3 Orion aircraft. When a surface ship was detected, the aircraft was vectored on the bearing determined by the array … The P-3 identified the vessel and determined its distance and course and speed from the tailship.[33]

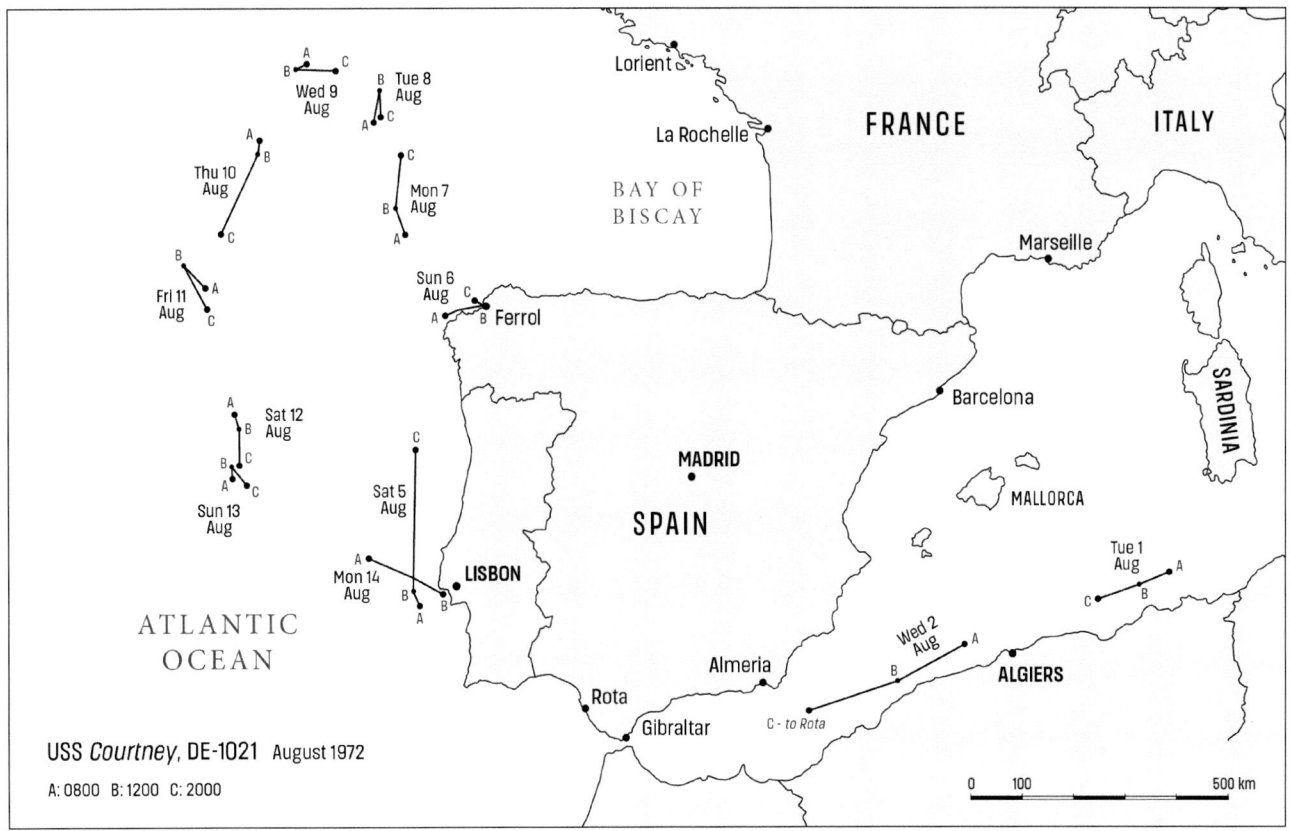

Courtney and *Hammerberg* EASTLANT experiment, August 1972. (Map by Paul Hewitt based on *Courtney* August 1972 Log Book)

The results of the exercise/experiment "showed an approximately 10-db azimuthal variation in the directional noise, which could be directly correlated to the nonuniform, but relatively static, shipping distribution".[34]

The results were presented to VADM Shear (Shear had replaced VADM Martel). The encouraging results changed how SOSUS would be used: "The SOSUS system went from detecting signals in an assumed omnidirectional ambient noise field to detecting signals by taking into account the directionality of the measured ambient noise."[35]

The success enjoyed by the tailships proved crucial in deciding where, from the Naval Facility at Brawdy, Wales, the SOSUS array(s) in the eastern Atlantic be positioned.[36] From 1973 through to the end of the Cold War at Sea, "Soviet submarines could be detected and continuously tracked from the GIUK Gap to the Straits of Gibraltar".[37]

Soviets kicked out of Egypt: Fifth *Eskadra* capability degraded

In July, Egyptian President Anwar Sadat ordered that all Soviet bases and equipment in Egypt were to be placed under direct control of Egyptian forces. In response, all Soviet aircraft squadrons departed, which represented a significant degradation in Fifth *Eskadra*'s aerial reconnaissance/surveillance and strike capabilities.

This forced Soviet surface combatants to depend on the modest logistics support facilities hosted by the Syrian government at Latakia and Tartus. From the last week in September to the first weeks in October, 17 Soviet ships concentrated their operations off the Syrian coast.[38]

This concentration and the corresponding movement into the eastern Mediterranean by the Sixth Fleet were influenced by the Palestinian Liberation Organization (PLO)-affiliated Black September terrorist group's attack against the Israeli Olympic team at the Munich Olympics: "The Munich massacre of Sept. 5 to 6, 1972, would have lasting repercussions on an international scale, waking up Western governments to the threat of terrorism."[39]

The months of September and October constituted an extremely busy time for the tailships. During the first six days in September, *Courtney* and *Lester* conducted joint ITASS operations in the Ionian Sea, using the Balao-class (Guppy-converted) submarine, USS *Tusk*, SS-426 as a cooperative target.[40] After a 17-day inport period, *Courtney* and *Lester* were back at conducting joint ITASS operations in the Ionian, which continued with a scheduled three day inport visit to Athens.

'At 2314 [11 October] entered Soviet anchorage. Soviet submarine alongside Don-984. 2325 steering various C/S while maneuvring to maintain station on submarine…Units at anchorage include Riga class DE-692 and DE-694…Maintaining station 1000-1500 yds from sub'. *Courtney* continued watching the Soviets through the late afternoon hours on 14 October, when the Foxtrot, together with the two Riga DEs and the Don AS-984 got underway. *Courtney* conducted an active sonar search when the Foxtrot submerged. She broke off the active sonar search during the 1100 hours on 15 October and headed back to Naples.[42]

In October, the Fifth *Eskadra* reacted to the *Forrestal* battle group's transit from the western into the eastern Mediterranean. Sixth Fleet estimated that the Soviet reaction entailed coordinated tracking and targeting exercises between their surface combatants and submarines.[43] This would have been the first operation the Fifth *Eskadra* conducted against the Sixth Fleet without their reconnaissance and strike airborne units.

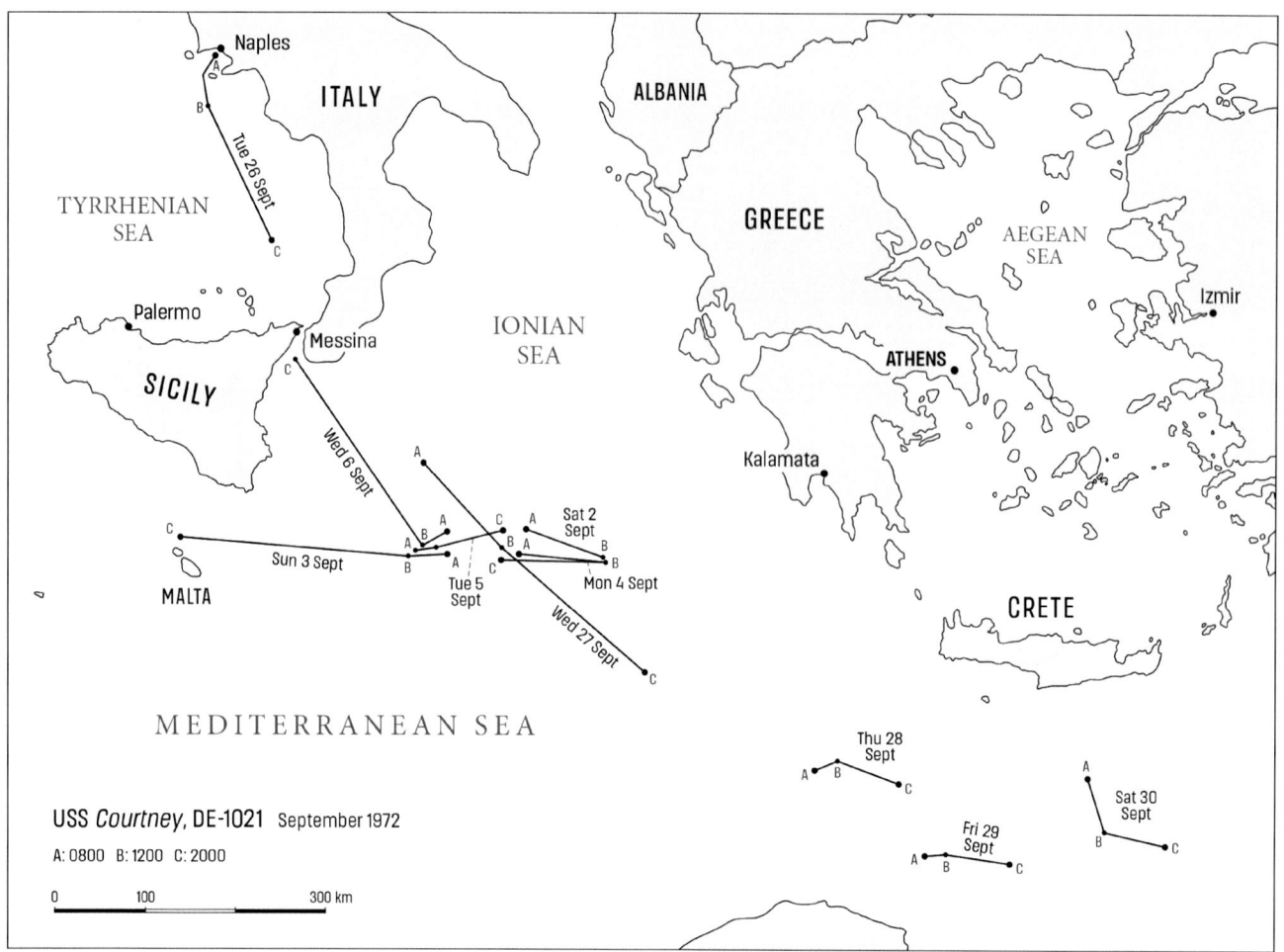

Back at sea on 9 October, Spruell had *Courtney* conducting a series of exercises to include a gunnery shoot and a simulated nuclear detonation (NUDET) drill before returning to Naples. However, *Courtney* was diverted by CTF67 to proceed to the Soviet fair weather anchorage, located northwest of Bizerte, Tunisia and east of the Tunisian, Galite Islands to conduct Bystander Operations. Reconnaissance had identified a Foxtrot submarine alongside the anchored Fifth *Eskadra* flagship, Project 310 *Batur*, (NATO designed Don-class submarine tender).[41] (Map by Paul Hewitt based on USS *Courtney* September 1972 Deck Log Book)

In November, Soviet naval activity in the Mediterranean was highlighted by the ritual turnover of deployed submarines:

Four Foxtrot submarines accompanied by three large surface combatants (Kresta I, Kresta II, Sverdlov CLCP) entered the Mediterranean on 3 November. A new twist on this turnover was the departure of one of the inchopping 'F' class submarines on 9 November for a transit to Cuba. The remaining three Foxtrots were escorted on the surface to the Gulf of Sollum anchoring there on 11 November. The outchopping submarine group which included six Foxtrots, a Kashin, two Krivaks and a Juliett SSG departed the Mediterranean via Gibraltar on 12 November.[44]

Courtney and *Lester* responded to this 'ritual turnover' by departing Naples on 2 November. Both ships began ITASS operations in the Balearic Basin on 4 November. They continued streaming their arrays through mid-day on 12 November, when after retrieving their arrays, they rendezvoused with the Garcia-class USS *Koelsch*, DE-1049 and the Gearing-class USS *Brownson*, DD-868. With COMCORTRON 8 as OTC, the four ships conducted an active sonar search while proceeding eastward toward the Strait of Sicily. Passing east of the Malta Channel and into the Ionian Sea, the two tailships participated in Exercise National Week XIV.

During the exercise, both tailships deployed their respective arrays in support of the ASW phase of the exercise.[45] At the time,

there were six US SSNs operating in the Mediterranean; four Permit class SSNs and two Sturgeon-class SSNs. One cannot discount that one of the objectives of the exercise, for the tailships, was to see if they were able to detect and track those SSNs participating in the exercise.

In December, P-3 Orion aircraft detected a "Charlie/Victor SSGN/SSN which inchopped Mediterranean via Gibraltar 21 or 22 December. Submarine was tracked by PATRON [patrol squadron] from 22–24 December."[46] The tailships went out to track the intruder. All three would then stand down in mid-December for Christmas and New Year's Day.

The following year would be one of increased challenges for all three tailships. They were wearing out.

1973: Worn Out

"ITASS escorts were way down the priority list."[47]

Intelligence Situation

Sixth Fleet intelligence for 1973 shows the Soviets stopped depending on missile-equipped surface ships and chose primarily nuclear-powered submarines to counter US carriers. This caused changes in how Sixth Fleet approached ASW:

During January … numerous submarine contacts by US forces, and subsequent Soviet efforts to interfere with the prosecution of

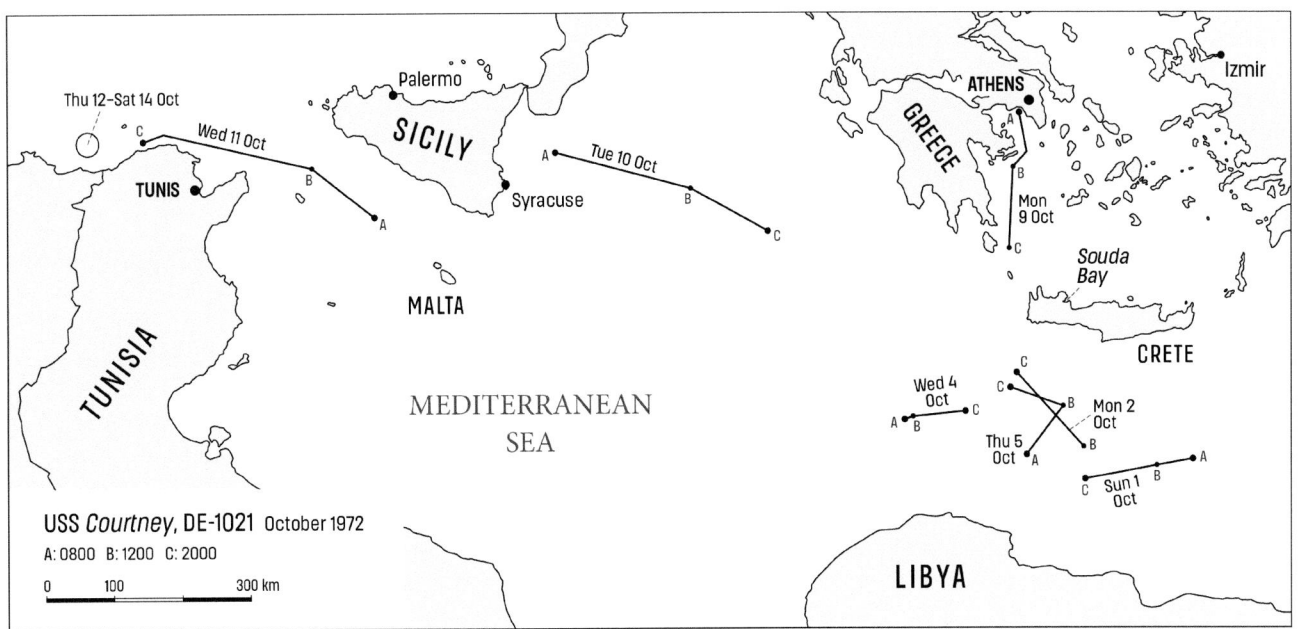

Courtney conducting Bystander Ops against a Foxtrot submarine. (Map by Paul Hewitt based on *Courtney* October 1972 Deck Log Book)

these contacts, highlighted the ASW exercise which lasted from 8 to 15 January … Other significant activity included the outchop of a 'V' SSN … the estimated presence of an additional 'C/V' SSGN/SSN during most of January, and the inchop of a 'C/V' in late January.

In February, the inchop of a probable 'V' class SSN on the 4th; the conformation of a second 'J' class SSG operating in the Mediterranean for most/all of February; possible anti-carrier warfare exercises conducted by a 'C' class SSGN against FORRESTAL on 5/6 February and against FORRESTAL and or INTREPID during 'NATIONAL WEEK XV'.

March was highlighted by a build-up of forces and subsequent ASW/ACW exercises … and by preparations for an impending diesel submarine turnover … Soviet ships and submarines began to gather in the central/western Mediterranean diesel submarine turnover.

April saw the diesel submarine turnover [that] began on 8/9 April, as four 'F' class SS and one 'J' class SSG entered the Mediterranean covertly. The number of inchopping submarines was raised to seven, as two more 'F's augmented the SOVMEDFLT [Soviet Mediterranean Fleet] later in the month. On 16 April, six incumbent … submarines (five 'F' class SS and one 'J' class SSG) made a westerly transit of the Strait of Gibraltar … The number of outchopping was raised to eight, as two more 'F's departed … late in April. Other significant activity … include the arrival in the Mediterranean of two 'C'/'V' class nuclear submarines.

SOVMEDFLT activity in May focused on surveillance of US carriers for each was a probable 'C' class SSGN. In the past, it has been normal for Soviet surface units to shadow US carriers east of the Strait of Sicily … The notable absence of these tattletale units … may indicate a shift in … surveillance tactics from … surface units to submarines, particularly SS-N-7 equipped 'C'

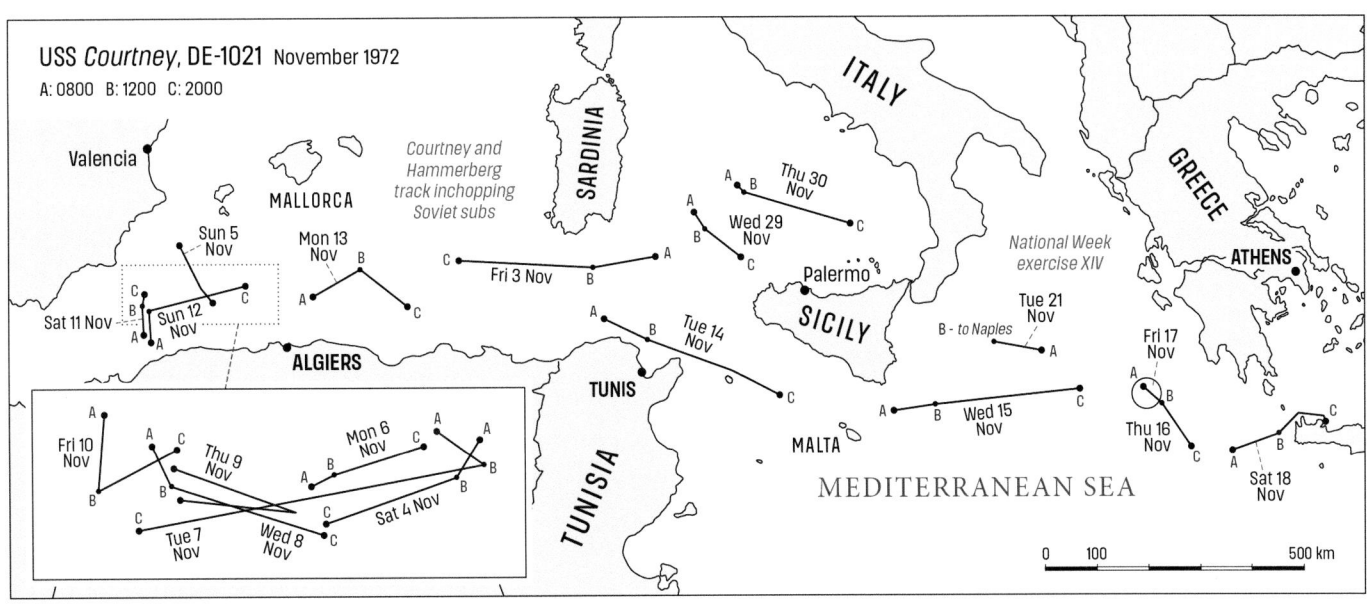

(Map by Paul Hewitt based on *Courtney* November 1972 Deck Log Book)

class SSGNs … For most of the month, four nuclear submarines, twice the normal number, engaged in Mediterranean operations.

Other significant SOVMEDFLT developments in June included continuation of the trend evidenced during May toward primary reliance on 'C' class [SSGNs] to shadow US carriers operating in the central Mediterranean.[48]

Off They Go For The Last Time

New Year's Day found the tailships at Naples. It was in 1973 that the US Navy publicly announced the presence of a significant number of overseas homeported ships:

The ships are: the destroyer tender USS *Cascade* (AD 16); the ocean escorts *Hammerberg* (DE 1015), *Courtney* (DE 1021) and *Lester* (DE 1022); the ocean patrol boats *Douglas* (PG 100), *Grand Rapids* (PG 98), *Antelope* (PG 86) and *Ready* (PG 87); and the patrol craft tender *Graham County* (AGP 1176). … Four afloat staffs also operate out of Naples – Escort Squadron Eight, Service Squadron Six, Patrol Division 21 and Submarine Flotilla Eight.[49]

By mid-January, the Sixth Fleet had returned to sea to conduct routine operations, including a major ASW exercise in the eastern Mediterranean. The tailships participated in the exercise, but ITASS operations were becoming increasingly difficult to conduct because of the deteriorating material condition of the ships. By the summer of 1973, the tailships were experiencing engineering, equipment and hull deficiencies, as Jack Flanagan, the *Lester*'s supply officer, remembers:

Dealey Class DEs were never designed to operate for extended periods without adequate support. In fact LESTER received regular overhauls every two years from her commissioning in 1957 up until her forward-basing in Naples. LESTER deployed from Newport to Naples in October 1970 for what would be a 3 year duration. Her Operating Schedule (OPSKED) was nominally 2 weeks underway then 2 weeks in port, then 2 weeks underway, then back to Naples for 2 weeks, then back out for 2 weeks, etc. It wasn't long before the actual time frames became increasingly erratic, more like a week or less in port, then nearly 3 weeks underway, then 10 days in Naples, then a week underway, then 2 weeks in Naples, etc. Keep in mind that in terms of actually getting any significant maintenance done while in Naples 10 calendar days in port could actually be 3 to 5 days of

actual maintenance and even that was unlikely given the other demands that might be made on the home-ported tender, USS CASCADE … The random lengths of time in Naples and frequent or short notice of schedule changes created any number of difficulties in handling both shipboard and personal logistics. The actual schedule simply ground both the ship itself and the crew (and their loved ones) into the ground.[50]

Jim Haddock, who reported aboard *Lester* in Naples in January 1972 as a newly minted ensign, served in the ship's Engineering Department as the Damage Control Assistant. This was his job until *Lester*'s decommissioning. Having seen at first-hand the material condition of his ship, his perspective is telling:

When I look back, it is hard to be kind to poor *Lester*. The surface navy was in pretty bad shape in 1972, and ITASS escorts were way down the priority list. *Lester* had almost no real war fighting capability and … was in terrible material condition. The preparations for moving the ship from Newport to Naples in 1971 did not address the major problems. The joint between the superstructure and the hull was deteriorated and sea water on the main deck would invade the mess decks, main deck passageways and some accommodations. On one occasion, water from the mess decks shorted out engine room ventilation controllers and stopped the ship. The engineering plant was unreliable and was held together with baling wire and hope. Major safety components in the engine room and fire room were bypassed or inoperative.

Courtney in a Naples dry dock. (David Silverthorn)

Returning home. (Author's collection)

Ensigns lowered for the last time. (Author's collection)

As a whole, the repairs were just enough to enable the ships to continue operating until they were scheduled to return to CONUS in October.

All three tailships did return to operational status during the summer, conducting ITASS patrols mostly in the Ionian Sea. They also participated in the INTERNATIONAL WEEK EXERCISE in July. September found the tailships preparing for their return to CONUS, and during the first week in October all three departed Naples for the last time.

Their departure coincided with the outbreak of the Yom Kippur War on 6 October. Tailship personnel thought their leaving would be held up because the Soviets reacted to the Arab-Israeli conflict by doubling the number of submarines operating in the Mediterranean to 23 units. Sixth Fleet's 1973 Command History noted that the "loss of the three ITASS ships without relief in early October reduced our ASW capability". Sixth Fleet noted that on "8 October HAMMERBERG (DE-1015), LESTER (DE-1022) and COURTNEY (DE-1021) departed Sixth Fleet".[53]

Upon arrival at the Norfolk Naval Base, and per the Inspection and Survey report recommendations, all three tailships were immediately decommissioned and then stricken from the Navy's list. They joined all but two of the Courtney/Dealey-class DEs in being scrapped by 1975. The two not scrapped would be transferred to the Uruguayan Navy (*Dealey*) and Columbian Navy (*Hartley*).

Also, I believe her overall condition improved over her last year and a half due to an infusion of good mid-level petty officers.[51]

Haddock remembers that in 1973, the Navy's Board of Inspection and Survey came to Naples to inspect all three tailships, "which prioritised (and demanded) correction of specific problems, adequate funding for repair parts".[52]

An inspection found a number of deficiencies that *Cascade*'s personnel could correct. However, *Courtney*'s deficiencies required the ship to be docked and serviced by a civilian Neapolitan shipyard.

10
CONTINUED DEVELOPMENT

The three tailships laid the foundation for the US Navy and its allies to effectively counter the Soviet Navy's submarine threat. Development of successive, passive, towed array sonar systems for surface ships, possessing improved accuracy, efficiency and reliability, continued into the twenty-first century.

The continued development took the US Navy in two interrelated directions. One addressed the Navy's strategic/surveillance ASW mission, augmenting SOSUS. The second was the fleet's operational/tactical ASW mission. Originally, the US Navy considered producing a single, towed array design that could be used for both missions. However, it was soon realised that the two mission requirements were different and a single system could not meet both.

SURTASS

For the surveillance mission, SURTASS was developed. SURTASS programme management came under the supervision of the Naval Electronics System Command. The system passed its first set of performance milestones in May 1973.

For the next seven years, SURTASS continued its development, and in March 1980 the system completed its technical evaluation. After that, the Navy awarded a contract for the construction of the first of 18 specially designed ocean surveillance ships – the Stalwart-class. The first to operate the AN/UQQ-2 SURTASS was the civilian-manned USNS *Stalwart*, T-AGOS-1, which deployed to the Mediterranean in 1984. It operated under Sixth Fleet's ASW Task Force, TF-66.

The Stalwarts were a mono-hull design. Each Stalwart could operate independently for up to 90 days at a time. However, it did not take long for the US Navy to realise the limitations of a mono-hull, operating at slow speeds in high sea states, especially during the winter months of the northern latitudes of the Atlantic and Pacific. The Navy thus decided to build twin-hulled ships that would provide greater buoyancy and stability.

The first Small Waterplane Area Twin Hull (SWATH) was delivered in August 1991 – the USNS *Victorious*, T-AGOS-19. *Victorious* demonstrated that a catamaran-type hull "provides a

USNS *Stalwart*, T-AGOS-1. (DNSC8607438)

Victorious' sister ship, USNS *Able*, T-AGOS-20. (VIRIN:090531-N-2638R-005)

highly stable platform under even the most adverse weather conditions, while providing a low self-noise profile".[1]

As designed, SURTASS acoustic data was uploaded via satellite communications to a Naval Operational Processing Facility (NOPF) for processing, analysis and integration into the Integrated Undersea Surveillance System (IUSS). Atlantic- and Mediterranean-deployed SURTASS ships sent their data to NOPF Norfolk, Virginia, while Pacific-deployed SURTASS ships sent it to NOPF Pacific, Pearl Harbor, Hawaii.

Overall, SURTASS operations proved to be highly effective in detecting and tracking Soviet submarines. However, during the 1960s, LFA mono operations. (Mark Thompson)

the Soviets "gained an intelligence source in the US Navy that could provide details of US submarine operations, war plans, communications and the SOSUS program. The source was John A. Walker, a Navy communications specialist".[2] Walker's treason provided the Soviets with sensitive materials relating to US submarines which "may well have accelerated Soviet interest in quieting their submarines".[3]

Coincidentally, the Soviets began to improve the design of their submarine propellers, which would reduce "two of the most important tonals in a submarine's signature … those modulated by the propeller at the rate at which its blades turned and those associated with particular items of rotating machinery".[4] Furthermore, in 1983, the Japanese firm Toshiba sold sophisticated milling machines to the Soviets, while a Norwegian company sold advanced computers to the Soviets for the milling machines. These sales "led to more efficient production of Soviet-designed submarine propellers".[5]

As a result of these compromises, the Soviets began deploying much quieter submarines. Additionally, Third World countries were procuring and deploying quiet, diesel-electric submarines, including

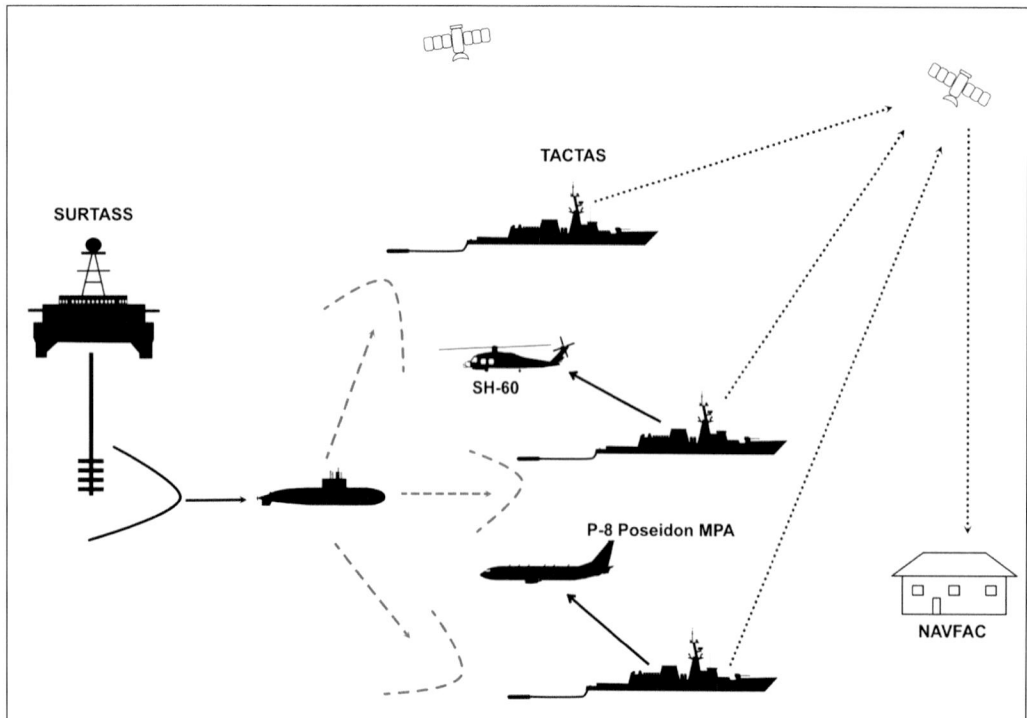

LFA bi-static operations. (Mark Thompson)

Notional Navy design for TAGOS-25. (Congressional Research Service)

receive array for active and passive sonar sensors that could operate in a mono-static or a bi-static mode.[6]

With the fall of the Soviet Union, the Soviet Navy submarine threat was greatly reduced. Consequently, the SURTASS programme was downsized. Through the 1990s and during the first decade of the twenty-first century, the SURTASS fleet of 23 ships was reduced to four US SWATH-designed ships. However, even with the changing ASW environment, SURTASS capability continued to evolve, especially to meet the growing nuclear and diesel/electric submarine threat from China.

For shallow water (littoral) operations, the SURTASS LFA system was reconfigured with smaller and lighter transducer modules and shorter receive arrays. Additionally, a second array was added to the system; two parallel (twin-lined) towed arrays gave the ship the ability to resolve bearing ambiguity without manoeuvring in order to obtain a true bearing. These arrays were shorter in length, which made the system suitable for placement on smaller ships.[7]

As of 2021, all five ageing SWATH-designed SURTASS ships were operating in the Pacific and stationed in Japan.[8] From Japan, these ships would deploy to the northern Pacific to surveil and track Russian submarines operating from bases on the Kamchatka Peninsula, and to the western Pacific to surveil and track Chinese submarines operating in the Yellow and South China Seas.

In 2021, the US Navy announced that it would procure the first of seven of a new class of TAGOS(X) ships, replacing the four US ships then operating in the Pacific. The Navy plan was to replace the current ships in response "to the submarine modernisation efforts of countries such as China and Russia".[9]

TACTAS
TACTAS evolved from the Towed Array Surveillance System – TASS

The success of ITASS brought "in 1972 six AN/SQR-15 systems [and] an improved AN/SQR-14 … ordered from CIC".[10] Two of the first TASS ships were the Pacific Fleet frigate USS *Bronstein*, FF-1037, and its Atlantic Fleet sister, USS *McCloy*, FF-1038.

As for *Bronstein*, it

… accomplished an extensive overhaul early in 1973, during which her aft 3-inch gun and captain's gig were removed and replaced with the AN/

the first generation of air independent propulsion submarines. The US Navy countered this trend by improving SURTASS.

In 1986, the US Navy established the Low Frequency Active (LFA) programme, which developed a low frequency active sonar system. The SURTASS LFA system was installed on the second SWATH ship, USNS *Able*, T-AGOS-20. The system was successfully demonstrated in 1994. The LFA system embodied a new digital

USS *McCloy*, DE/FF-1038, with TASS K-113390. (NHHC)

Victor III SSN *K-324* surfaced with USS *Peterson*, DD-969. The Moma-class AGI, *Nakhodka*, is between them. (NavSource)

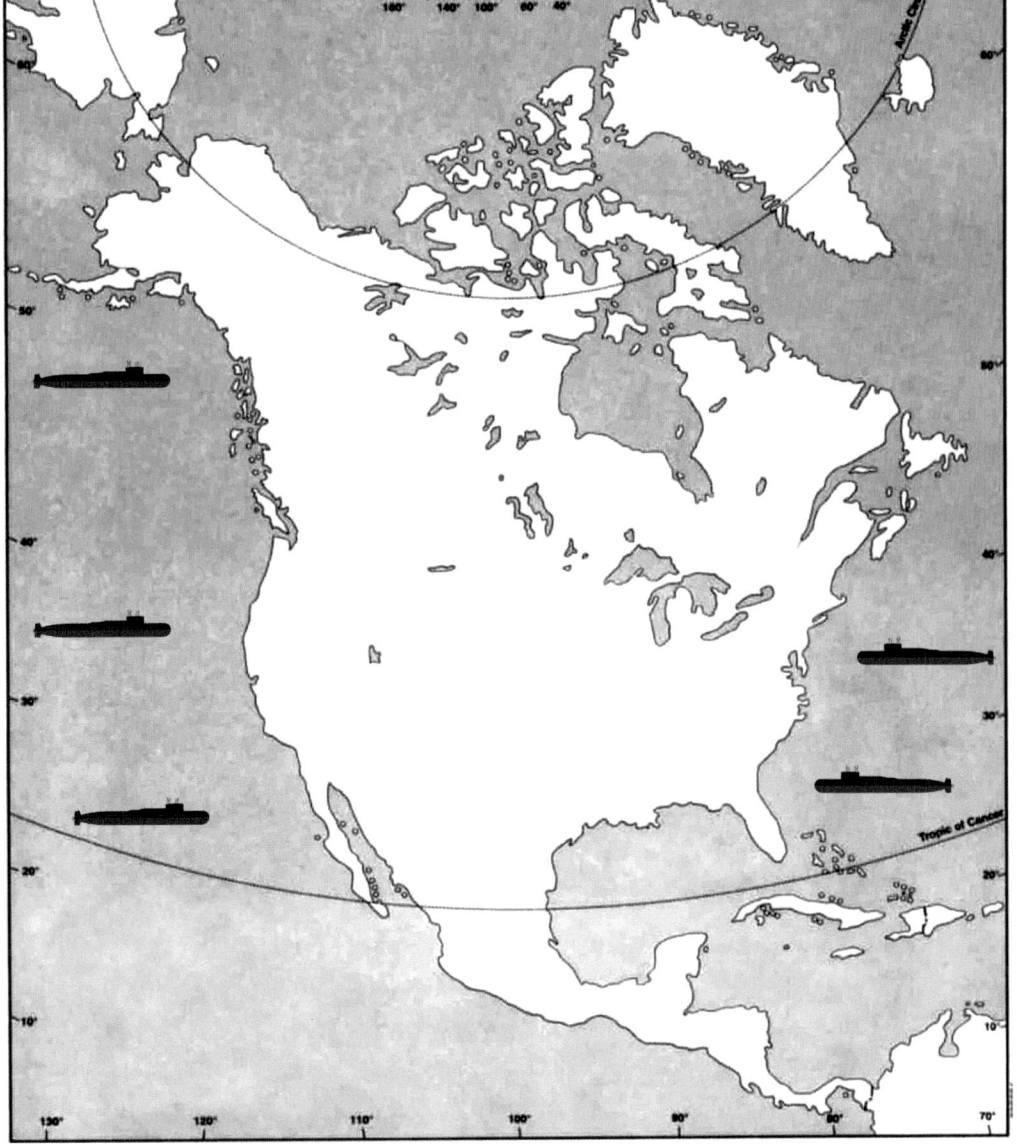

Yankee SSBN patrol areas. (Map by Tom Cooper based on Thomas B. Cochran et al., *Nuclear Weapons Databook Volume IV: Soviet Nuclear Weapons*)

SQR-15 … The experimental system comprised more than 6,000 feet of 1.25-inch coaxial cable and hydrophones that could be streamed from the fantail to allow for passive sonar operations. OTs operated a bank of AN/AQA-5 wide-band acoustic processors that processed the acoustic information from the TASS, from within a large equipment van installed into the hangar.[11]

Bronstein operated independently or with another TASS ship. The OTs became proficient in detecting Soviet submarines, specifically the Project 667A Yankee-class SSBNs, operating in the Yankee Eastern Missile Patrol Area (YEMPA) in the Pacific. "The ships' company largely viewed TASS … with pride, and referred to the system as 'The Tail'."[12] "TASS worked great for long range cueing when the host platform was operating far away from the Battle Group."[13]

McCloy received its TASS in 1974, operating its system in the Mediterranean and western Atlantic's Yankee SSBN patrol area. *McCloy* spent a considerable time in the Mediterranean. For all practicable purposes, it was one

USS Albert David, FF-1050, with TASS reel visible on the quarter deck. (NavSource)

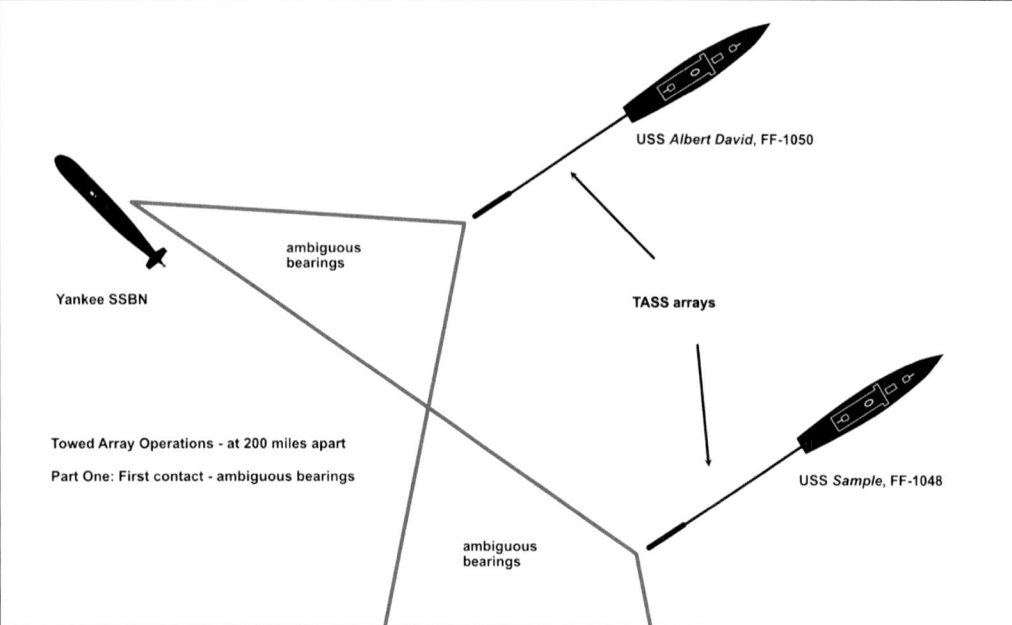

Towed array ASW tactics – ambiguous bearings. (Mark Thompson, based on Captain William Steagall, USN Ret)

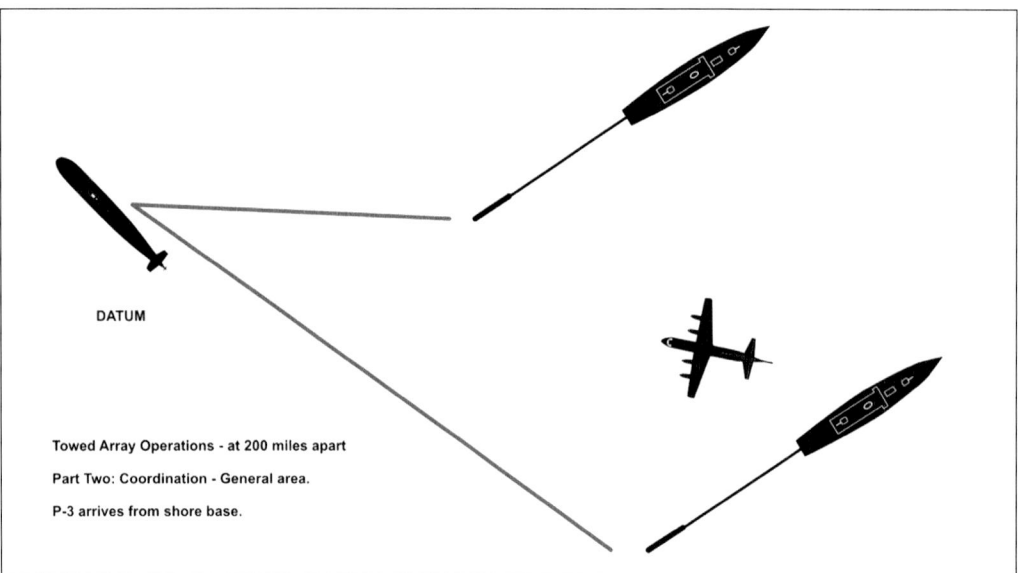

Towed array ASW tactics – bearing reconciled. (Mark Thompson, based on Captain William Steagall, USN Ret)

deploying to the Mediterranean would find and track Soviet subs. *McCloy* was a legendary ASW ship. Every time she went to the Med she came back with the 'Hook Em award' … the award given to the combatant in each battle group with the best ASW performance."

When *McCloy* was not deployed to the Mediterranean, it conducted TASS operations in the western Atlantic's Yankee SSBN patrol area, east and north of Bermuda: "The first Project 667A/Yankee SSBNs went on combat patrol in the Atlantic in June 1969. Sixteen months later, in October 1970, SSBNs of this class began patrols in the Pacific … By 1971 there were regularly two and on occasion up to four Project 667A SSBNs in that Western Atlantic."[14]

In October 1983, *McCloy* deployed to the Atlantic's Yankee SSBN patrol area, but was diverted westward "to go find a Soviet Victor III, a brand new Soviet nuclear submarine that we had never seen in the Western Atlantic".[15] As RADM (Rear Admiral) John L. Butts, USN, Director of Naval Intelligence, testified to the Senate Arms Service Committee in 1985, "These submarines often are assigned ASW missions off the US East Coast."[16]

The Victor III SSN *K-324*, a Project 671RTM, was based on the Victor II Project 671RT's design that included a technological feature (rafting) that significantly reduced the SL from the submarine's machinery: "The [turbine] gear assembly and

of the TASS ships that replaced the three CORTRON 8 tailships. For the next eight years, the ship would routinely deploy to the Mediterranean: "During the 1970s and 1980s, every battle group

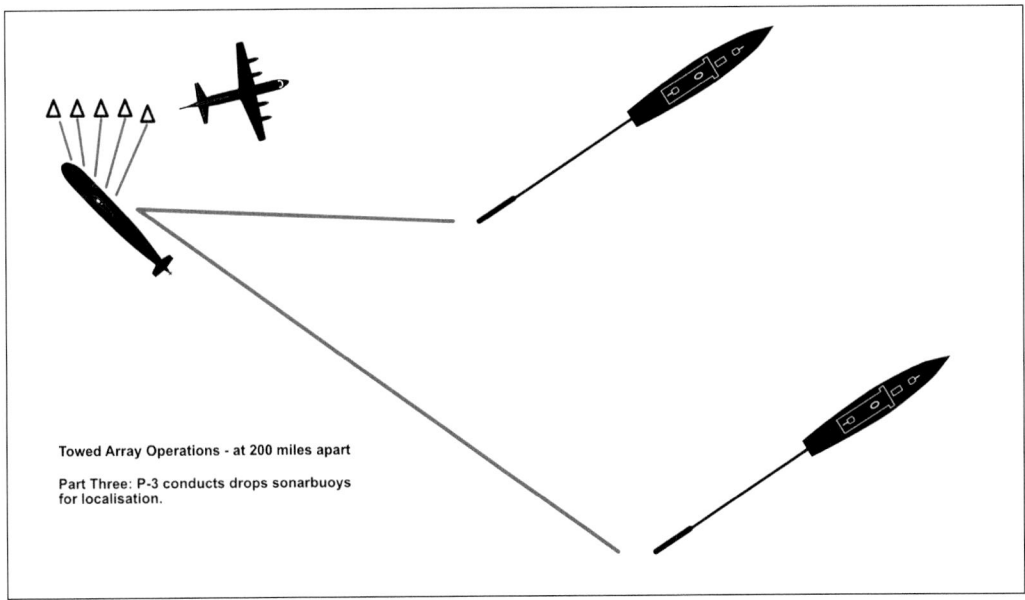

Towed array ASW tactics – localize contact. (Mark Thompson, based on Captain William Steagall, USN Ret)

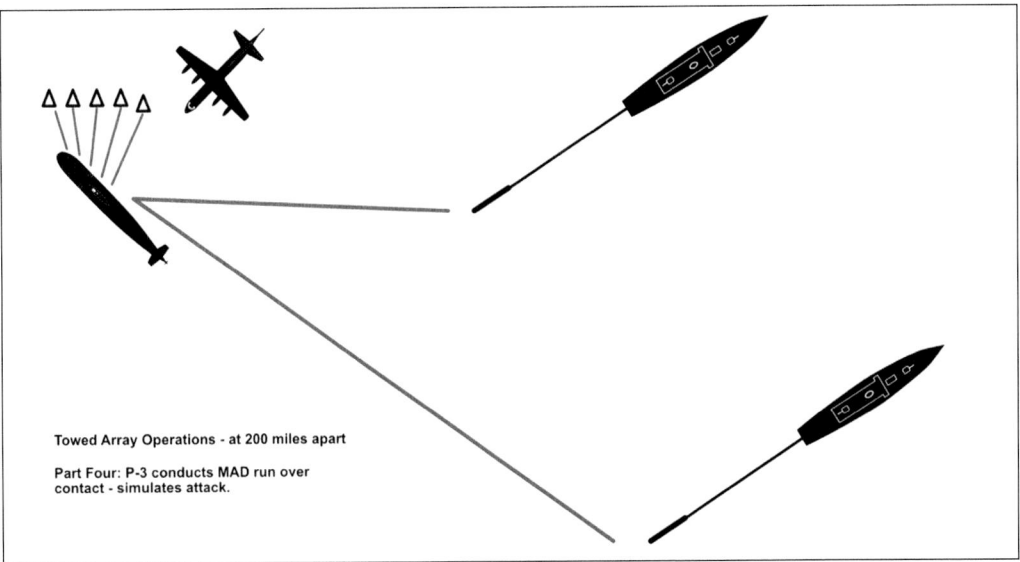

Towed array ASW tactics – simulates attack. (Mark Thompson, based on Captain William Steagall, USN Ret)

ship, the USS *Sample*, FF-1048, its sister ship.[19]

While operating in the YEMPA, the *Albert David* would operate with P-3 Orion aircraft flying out of any of three Pacific-based NASs – Adak, Alaska; Moffett Field, California; or Barbers Point, Hawaii. With the *Albert David* patrolling 1,200 miles from each NAS, it meant that the P3s would have four hours' transit to the patrol area and four hours back, leaving about four hours maximum time on station.

Working with P-3s, the *Albert David* and the *Sample* would be spaced as far as 200nm from one another. Upon receiving acoustics from a contact, the TASS from both ships would give two ambiguous bearings, one of which would be reconciled with the other to provide a datum. Supporting the reconciliation process, the P-3 would act as an ultra-high frequency (UHF) radio relay between the two ships. By using UHF communications and avoiding HF radio, the ships could not be detected by the submarine or shore-based HF/DF. With the submarine's datum determined, the P-3 would be vectored to the location. Once at the location, the aircraft would deploy sonobuoys and use its MAD system to tactically track the submarine.

turbogenerators with their mechanisms are mounted on one unit-frame support … shock-absorbing layout to reduce the acoustic field." This gave both Victors the same SL as the US Navy's Sturgeon-class SSNs.[17]

As proof of *McCloy*'s TASS and its OTs' skill, it "located the Victor III at extended range off Charleston". However, it was becoming increasingly difficult to maintain contact on the submarine, because of acoustic interference caused by heavy shipping traffic and degraded weather conditions. *McCloy* retrieved its tail and dashed to where it thought was a better location to pick up the Soviet submarine. On 31 October, after deploying its tail, *McCloy* quickly picked up *K-324*. The SL from the submarine was so strong that it was clear *McCloy* had positioned itself right on top of it. As *McCloy*'s CO said: "Just then we felt a shudder and we lost array power. The tail stretched, and then snapped like a whip." *K-324* had snared the array around its propellers. The next day, a US Navy P-3 Orion sighted the *K-324* "stopped on the surface 282 miles west of Bermuda and 470 miles east of Charleston, South Carolina. The *K-324* was towed to Cienfuegos, Cuba for repairs."[18]

One of the first Garcia-class FFs, the Pacific Fleet USS *Albert David*, FF-1050, received its TASS in 1974. This ship operated its TASS in the Pacific's YEMPA, either by itself or with another TASS

TASS proved to be an extremely effective, passive, narrowband ASW system, and it remained in the US Navy's inventory for many years. However, the Navy had a continued operational requirement for an improved capability that could be towed from cruisers, destroyers and frigates at high speed in seas up to sea state 4. As with the tailships of CORTRON 8, *Bronstein*, *McCloy* and *Albert David* had to slow down to barely steerage way so the OTs could properly analyse the acoustic data. However, depending on the sea state, the ship would roll as much as 40 degrees, which caused the crew considerable hardship.

The AN/SQR-18 and the follow-on AN/SQR-19 were developed during the 1980s. The design of the array was modular in its construction, comprising eight Very Low Frequency (VLF), four Low Frequency (LF), two Medium Frequency (MF) and two HF hydrophones. The array was towed approximately one mile from the ship in order to reduce noise interference radiating from the vessel. The AN/SQR-18 TACTAS began operations in the early 1980s, with the SQR-19 beginning in 1991. These two arrays were developed and deployed as a subsystem to the AN/SQQ-89 ASW combat system.

To pull together the data from TACTAS, active sonars and sonobuoys, the US Navy developed the AN/SQQ-89 ASW combat system, the first integrated ASW combat system for surface ships. Introduced in the late 1980s, it "provides surface warships with a seamlessly integrated USW/ASW detection, localization, classification and targeting capability. It correlates and manages acoustic sensor data from hull-mounted and towed array sonars to provide track data to the ship's combat information center (CIC)."[20] The system has evolved during the past 40 years, with its most recent upgrades requested by the Navy including integrating counter-mine systems in 2020.[21]

With the introduction of TACTAS, the US Navy's surface force evolved from an ASW sensor/weapon system centred on the active/ passive hull-mounted SQS-26 sonar, ASROC and the LAMPS-1 Kaman SH-2 Seasprite helicopter, to include towed passive sonar and the longer-range LAMPS III SH-60 Seahawk. This integrated ASW system gave the US Navy the tactical agility to detect and prosecute submarines at greater distances.

In 2008, the Multi-Function Towed Array (MFTA) AN/SQR-20, a passive and active sonar receiver, began to enter the fleet; the first of its kind in 20 years. It replaced the AN/SQR-19 TACTAS aboard US Navy warships. In 2015, the TB-37 MFTA (formerly the AN/SQR-20 TACTAS) contract was approved for seven systems, with the first entering the fleet in 2019. As with its predecessors, the TB-37 would be integrated into the improved AN/SQQ-89Av15 underwater combat system.[22]

11
LEGACY

Before the tailships, their men and families returned to the US from Naples, RADM Thomas R. Weschler, USN, visited each ship. At the time, Weschler was Commander Cruiser-Destroyer Force Atlantic Fleet. Jack Flanagan remembers Admiral Wechsler's visit to *Lester*:

Admiral Wechsler told those assembled on the flight deck that the folks whose idea of ASW was the typical DD/DE pinging on a sub, chasing it down and then pushing ash cans off the fantail or launching hedgehogs were stuck in the past. If you had to get that close to a sub to prosecute the contact you'd already have been sunk long before you got close enough. The ITASS Dealeys had done great work in proving the worth of towed arrays. You had much to be proud of.[1]

His tribute to Escort Squadron 8 was based upon his understanding of what passive towed array sonar systems could do. As commander of the Atlantic Fleet's cruiser-destroyer force, he pressed for the introduction of passive sonar into the fleet: "[P]assive sonar was essential. I pressed hard and got some experimental towed arrays for various ships of the force, worked on them, helped sell the concept."[2]

Prior to commanding the Atlantic Fleet's cruiser-destroyer force, Weschler commanded Cruiser-Destroyer Flotilla 2 in 1970 and oversaw "special ASW operations … a classified series of work that we were doing which involved nuclear submarines and surface ships with all our best ASW and patrol aircraft".[3] This included the ITASS conversion of Escort Squadron 8 DEs and their three-year deployment to the Mediterranean. He became intimately aware of ITASS as a system and its success and challenges.

Weschler explained his ASW philosophy:

[S]ubmarine warfare is not a single instrument playing; it's an orchestra. You've got to have the full orchestra if you really wanted to defeat submarines – passive for long-range detection; active, certainly, for localization and attack; active in certain phases like sortie from port or for purifying an area like an advance beachhead, that sort of thing. They all work together, and then ASW was heightened by what the aircraft and what the submarine could do.[4]

The April 2004 edition of the Institute of Electrical and Electronics Engineers' *Journal of Oceanic Engineering* acknowledged the accomplishments of the tailships of Escort Squadron 8:

Much to everyone's amazement, the systems worked well. During their stay in the Mediterranean, they accounted for over 50% of all submarine detections made by any method, including visual sighting.[5]

Bravo Zulu tailships!

BIBLIOGRAPHY

Books

Ball, Desmond and Tanter, Richard, *The Tools of Owatatsumi: Japan's Ocean Surveillance and Coastal Defence Capabilities* (Canberra, Australia: ANU Press, The Australian National University, 2015)

Blackman, Raymond V.B. (ed.), *Jane's Fighting Ships, 1971–1972* (New York: McGraw-Hill Book Company, 1971)

Ford, Christopher and Rosenberg, David, *The Admirals' Advantage: US Navy Operational Intelligence in World War II and the Cold War* (Annapolis, Maryland: US Naval Institute Press, 2005)

Friedman, Norman, *The Naval Institute's Guide to World Naval Weapons Systems* (Annapolis, Maryland: US Naval Institute Press, 1989)

Herrick, Robert Waring, *Soviet Naval Strategy: Fifty Years of Theory and Practice* (Annapolis, Maryland: US Naval Institute Press, 1968)

Johnson, Dominic and Tierney, Dominic, *Failing to Win: Perceptions of Victory and Defeat* (Boston: Harvard University Press, 2006)

McCammon, Captain Peter L., *Homeport Naples: USS Graham County (AGP 1176) in the Mediterranean, September 1972 to July 1974* (San Francisco: Blurb creative publishing service, second printing, 2008)

Polmar, Norman, *Guide to the Soviet Navy, Third Edition* (Annapolis, Maryland: US Naval Institute Press, 1983)

Polmar, Norman, *Guide to the Soviet Navy, Fourth Edition* (Annapolis, Maryland: US Naval Institute Press, 1986)

Polmar, Norman, *Guide to the Soviet Navy, Fifth Edition* (Annapolis, Maryland: US Naval Institute Press, 1986, 1991)

Polmar, Norman, *The Naval Institute Guide to The Ships and Aircraft of the US Fleet* (Annapolis, Maryland: US Naval Institute Press, 1997)

Polmar, Norman, *The Naval Institute Guide to the Ships and Aircraft of the US Fleet* (Annapolis, Maryland: US Naval Institute Press, 2013)

Polmar, Norman, Brooks, Thomas A. and Fedoroff, George E., *Admiral Gorshkov: The Man Who Challenged the US Navy* (Annapolis, Maryland: US Naval Institute Press, 2019)

Polmar, Norman and Moore, K.J., *Cold War Submarines: The Design and Construction of US and Soviet Submarines* (Potomac Books, 2004)

Polmar, Norman, Wertheim, Eric, Bahjat, Andrew and Watson, Bruce, *Chronology of the Cold War at Sea 1945–1991* (Annapolis, Maryland: US Naval Institute Press, 1998)

Polmar, Norman and Whitman, Edward, *Hunters and Killers Volume 2: Anti-Submarine Warfare from 1943* (Annapolis, Maryland: US Naval Institute Press, 2016)

Santore, John, *Modern Naples: A Documentary History, 1799–1999* (New York: Italica Press, 2001)

Solomon, Louis P., *Transparent Oceans: The Defeat of the Soviet Submarine Force* (Bethesda, Maryland: Pearl River Publishing, 2015)

Winkler, David F., *Cold War at Sea: High-Seas Confrontation between the United States and the Soviet Union* (Annapolis, Maryland: US Naval Institute Press, 2000)

US Government Papers

American Shipbuilding Technology and the Soviet Merchant Marine, A Staff Study, Permanent Subcommittee On Investigations of the Committee On Government Operations, United States Senate (Washington, DC: US Government Printing Office, 1975)

Central Intelligence Agency Memorandum for The Director of Central Intelligence, 'Military Thought (USSR): Reconnaissance Indications of Preparation for a Surprise Attack by US Naval Carrier Strike Large Units', 3 June 1977

CIA Memorandum for The Director of Central Intelligence, 'The Soviet Attack Submarine Force: Evolution and Operations', SR IM 71-11-S, September 1971

Cryptologic Almanac 50th Anniversary Series (U) The Widowmaker: SIGINT and Submarine K-19. Derived from: NSA/CSS Manual 123-2. Dated: 24 Feb 1998, DOCID: 4110868

National Photographic Interpretation Center imagery analysis report, Soviet Primorye-Class Intelligence Collection Ships, December 1984. CIA-RDP85T00840R000100200001-5, declassified on 17 November 2010

Reconnaissance Indications of Preparation for a Surprise Attack by US Naval Carrier Strike Large Units, 'Military Thought (USSR)'. Found in CIA Intelligence Information Special Report, 3 June 1977

The Soviet Space Program: National Intelligence Estimate, NIE 11-1-83S TS 833351, 19 July1983, CIA-RDP00B00369R000100050007-1

US Navy Command Histories

'Escort Squadron Eight Command History 1971', NHHC

OPNAV Report 5740-1, Command History of Commander Escort Squadron Eight, Commanding Officer, USS *Cascade*, AD-16, AD16/00/MIN:dbt 5750 Ser: 282, Mar 7 1974

United States Sixth Fleet, 'Sixth Fleet Command History 1970', 24 March 1971, NHHC

United States Sixth Fleet, 'Sixth Fleet Command History 1971', 1972, NHHC

US Sixth Fleet, 'Sixth Fleet Command History 1972', NHHC

'USS *Hammerberg* (DE-1015) Command History', Navy Department Office of the Chief of Naval Operation, Division of Naval History (OP-29), Ship's History Section

1970 Command History, USS *Lester*, DE-1022, 3 August 1971, NHHC

Research/Scientific Papers

Carey, W., 'Evolution of Passive Towed Array Systems', paper presented at conference titled 'How Did We Get Here?', sponsored by the Acoustical Society of America, December 2001

Massachusetts Institute of Technology, Project HARTWELL, 'A Report On Security of Overseas Transport', Vol 1 of 2. Contract No. N5 ora 07846, 21 September 1950

Normark, William R., Barnes, Neal E. and Coumes, Francis, 'Rhone Fan, Mediterranean'; Submarine Fans and Related Turbidite Systems', ed by Arnold H. Bouma, W.R. Normark and N.E. Barnes, *Frontiers in Sedimentary Geology* (New York: Springer-Verlag, 1985).

Magazines/Newspapers Articles

'At Home Abroad – Or Homeporting Overseas', *All Hands*, The Bureau of Naval Personnel Career Publication (May 1973), Nav-Per-O, Number 676

Bidgood, Jess, 'Newport, a City That Loves Its Mansions, Shudders at Its Newest Ones', *The New York Times*, 4 December 2016.

Cote, Owen R. Jr, 'The Third Battle: Innovation in the US Navy's Silent Cold War Struggle with Soviet Submarines', Naval War College, Newport Papers Number 16 (Newport, Rhode Island: Naval War College, 2003)

Eliot, George Fielding, 'Polaris in the Mediterranean', *The Army Times*, 23 February 1963

Goldstein, Lyle J. and Zhukov, Yuri M., 'A Tale of Two Fleets,' *Naval War College Review*, Newport, Rhode Island. This information was obtained from an article written by I.V. Kasatonov, '*Flot vyhodit v okean*' ('The fleet is going to the ocean') (St Petersburg: Astra-Lyuks, 1995)

Hightower, John M. (AP), 'NATO May Get Mediterranean Polaris Subs', *Washington Post*, Sunday, 3 Feb 1963, p. A10

Kucherov, Alex, interview with COMSIXTHFLT (Vice Admiral Isaac C. Kidd, Jr, USN), *US News and World Report*, 8 July 1971; United States Sixth Fleet, 'Sixth Fleet Command History 1971', Section VIII Public Affairs, Appendix VIII-A, NHHC

Raub, Patricia, 'Discover Beautiful Rhode Island': State Promotion of Tourism from 1927–2015, *Rhode Island History* (winter/spring 2017), Volume 75, Number 1

Stillwell, Paul, *The Reminiscences of Vice Admiral Thomas R. Weschler, USN (Retired)*, Volume II (Annapolis, Maryland: US Naval Institute Press, 1995)

Whitman, Edward C., 'SOSUS: The "Secret Weapon" of Undersea Surveillance', *Undersea Warfare Magazine* (Winter 2005), Vol 7, No 2

US Government Websites

https://www.state.gov/12957

US Department of State, Office of the Historian, 'NSC-68, 1950', https://history.state.gov/milestones/1945-1952/NSC68

Miscellaneous Websites

https://www.iusscaa.org/history.html

Wikipedia, 'Mark 24Mine', https://en.wikipedia.org/wiki/Mark_24_mine

Wikipedia, KS-1 Comet, https://en.m.wikipedia.org/wiki/KS-1_Komet

Wikipedia, 'Tupolev-Tu-42', https://en.m.wikipedia.org/wiki/Tupolev_Tu-142

http://www.destroyers.org/ShipboardEquipment/bathythermograph.htm, Tin Can Sailors: The National Association of Destroyer Veterans.

Columbia University's Field Station at St David's was co-located with the Bermuda Sound Fixing and Ranging SOFAR Station, www.sofarbda.org/index.html

The CNO at the time was Admiral Thomas H. Moorer, https://en.wikipedia.org/wiki/Chief_of_Naval_Operations

https://12metercharters.com/about-us/sailing-history/newport-sailing

http://www.hazegray.org/danfs/escorts/de1028.htm

Salah, Mostafa and Boxer, Baruch, 'Mediterranean Sea', *Encyclopaedia Britannica*, online ed (Chicago: *Encyclopaedia Britannica* Inc., 7 November 2016), https://www.britannica.com/place/Mediterranean-Sea

National Geographic, https://www.natgeomaps.com/hm-1982-mediterranean-seafloor-map

Haze Grey, https://www.hazegray.org/features/russia/ssg.htm

Wikipedia, 'RPK-2 Vyuga', https://en.wikipedia.org/wiki/RPK-2_Vyuga

Wikimedia, 'Victor I Class Submarine', ID DN-ST-91-00403. Date Shot: 18 Sept 1990, https://commons.wikimedia.org/wiki/File:Victor_I_class_submarine.jpg

Wikimedia, 'P-70 Ametist', https://commons.wikimedia.org/wiki/File:P-70_Ametist.svg

Wikimedia, 'Kresta II Class Cruiser', https://commons.wikimedia.org/wiki/File:MarshalTimoshenko1986.jpg

https://en.wikipedia.org/wiki/S-125_Neva/Pechora. Obtained 31 March 2023

http://www.navsource.org/archives/06/06021021.htm

SS-N-14 Silex, https://en.wikipedia.org/wiki/Metel_Anti-Ship_Complex

Wikipedia, 'Robert Carney', https://en.wikipedia.org/wiki/Robert_Carney

De Lorenzo, F., Manzillo, G., Soscia, M. and Balestrier, G.G., 'Epidemic Of Cholera El Tor In Naples, 1973', *The Lancet*, 13 April 1974, DOI: https://doi.org/10.1016/S0140-6736(74)93214-0

Wikipedia, 'Mediterranean Climate', https://en.wikipedia.org/wiki/Mediterranean_climate

Wikipedia, 'USS Wasp (CV-18) 1968–1970', https://en.wikipedia.org/wiki/USS_Wasp_(CV-18)#1968–1970

Lee II, S.P. (AGS-31), https://www.history.navy.mil/research/histories/ship-histories/danfs/s/s-p-lee-ags-31.html

Deep Storm website, www.deepstorm.ru

National Public Radio, Munich Olympics Massacre, https://www.npr.org/2022/09/04/1116641214/munich-olympics-massacre-hostage-terrorism-israel-germany

Congressional Research Service, TAGOS(X) Ocean Surveillance Shipbuilding Program: Background and Issues for Congress, https://crsreports.congress.gov/product/pdf/IF/IF11838/12. Obtained 1 March 2023

Lasky, M, Dolittle, R.D., Simmons, B.D. and Lemon, S.G., 'Recent progress in towed hydrophone array research', IEEE Journal of Oceanic Engineering, Volume 29, Issue 2 (April 2004)

Naval History and Heritage Command, 'Brontstein II *FF-10370', https://www.history.navy.mil/content/history/nhhc/research/histories/ship-histories/danfs/b/bronstein-ii.html

Lundquist, Edward H., 'Bronstein-class Escorts Introduced New Sensors and Weapons', Defense Media Network (30 November 2016), https://www.defensemedianetwork.com/stories/bronstein-class-escorts-introduced-new-sensors-and-weapons/

https://www.nukestrat.com/russia/subpatrols.htm

America's Navy, 'AN/SQQ-89(V) Undersea Warfare/Anti-Submarine Combat System', https://www.navy.mil/Resources/Fact-Files/Display-FactFiles/Article/2166784/ansqq-89v-undersea-warfare-anti-submarine-warfare-combat-system/

Military Aerospace Electronics, 'Navy Says Lockheed Martin to Build AN/SQQ-89 Shipboard Anti-Submarine Warfare (ASW) and counter-mine systems', https://www.militaryaerospace.com/sensors/article/14169960/shipboard-antisubmarine-warfare-asw-countermine

AN/SQQ-89A(V)15 Integrated Undersea Warfare (USW) Combat System Suite, https://www.dote.osd.mil/Portals/97/pub/reports/FY2013/navy/2013ansqq89a.pdf?ver=2019-08-22-111213-517

US Navy Ship Deck Logs

USS *Andrew Jackson*, October 1970 Deck Log Book, NARA

USS *Clamagore*, SS-343, November 1970 Deck Log, NARA

USS *Courtney*, June 1970 Deck Log Book, NARA

USS *Courtney*, August 1970 Deck Log Book, NARA

USS *Courtney*, September 1970 Deck Log Book, NARA

USS *Courtney*, November 1970 Deck Log Book, NARA

USS *Courtney*, January 1971 Deck Log Book, NARA

USS *Courtney*, February 1971 Deck Log Book, NARA

USS *Courtney*, March 1971 Deck Log Book, NARA

USS *Courtney*, January 1972, Deck Log Book, NARA

USS *Courtney*, February 1972, Deck Log Book, NARA

USS *Courtney*, March 1972, Deck Log Book, NARA

USS *Courtney*, April 1972, Deck Log Book, NARA

USS *Courtney*, May 1972, Deck Log Book, NARA

USS *Courtney*, June 1972, Deck Log Book, NARA

USS *Courtney*, July 1972, Deck Log Book, NARA

USS *Courtney*, August 1972, Deck Log Book, NARA

USS *Courtney*, September 1972, Deck Log Book, NARA

USS *Courtney*, October 1972, Deck Log Book, NARA

USS *Courtney*, November 1972, Deck Log Book, NARA

USS *Courtney*, December 1972, Deck Log Book, NARA

USS *Cutlass*, November 1970 Deck Log Book, NARA

USS *John F. Kennedy*, CVA-67, October 1970 Deck Log Book, NARA

USS *Lapon*, December 1970 Deck Log Book, NARA

USS *Lester*, November 1970 Deck Log Book, NARA

USS *Springfield*, April 1971 Deck Log Book, NARA

USS *Threadfin*, October 1970 Deck Log Book, NARA

USS *Van Voorhis*, October 1970 Deck Log Book, NARA

USS *Van Voorhis*, November 1970 Deck Log Books, NARA

NOTES

Author's Introduction

1   The Incident at Sea Agreement between the Government of the United States and the Government of the Soviet Union Socialist Republics on the Prevention of Incidents on and over the High Seas was signed on 25 May 1972. See State Department website for specifics, https://www.state.gov/12957. Obtained 23 June 2020.

2   Norman Polmar, *The Naval Institute Guide to The Ships and Aircraft of the US Fleet* (Annapolis, Maryland: US Naval Institute Press, 2013), pp. 249–51.

3   Polmar, *The Ships and Aircraft of the US Fleet* (1997), pp. 488–89.

4   For fuller details of the ongoing confrontation and conflict between Israel and the Arab states following the 1967 war, see the Middle East@War *War of Attrition* mini-series.

5   *All Hands*, May 1973, Nav-Per O, Number 676, The Bureau of Naval Personnel Career Publication, p. 2.

6   In 1974, Naval Facility (NavFac) Brawdy, Wales was established. C.G. Jefford, *RAF Squadrons, A Comprehensive Record of the Movement and Equipment of all RAF Squadrons and their Antecedents since 1912* (Shrewsbury, Shropshire, UK: Airlife Publishing, 1988), p. 32; also, see IUSS Caesar Alumni Association, 'The Integrated Undersea Surveillance System (IUSS) History 1950–2010', https://www.iusscaa.org/history.html. Obtained 30 June 2022.

Chapter 1

1   Norman Polmar, Eric Wertheim, Andrew Bahjat, and Bruce Watson, *Chronology of the Cold War at Sea 1945–1991* (Annapolis, Maryland: US Naval Institute Press, 1998)

2   US Department of State, Office of the Historian, 'NSC-68, 1950' https://history.state.gov/milestones/1945-1952/NSC68

3   US Department of State, 'NSC-68, 1950'

4   'NSC-68'.

5   David F. Winkler, *Cold War at Sea: High-Seas Confrontation between the United States and the Soviet Union* (Annapolis, Maryland: US Naval Institute Press, 2000), p. 8.

6   Norman Polmar, Thomas A. Brooks, and George E. Fedoroff, *Admiral Gorshkov: The Man Who Challenged the US Navy* (Annapolis, Maryland: US Naval Institute Press, 2019), p. 110.

7   Polmar, et al., *Admiral Gorshkov*, p. 112.

8   Central Intelligence Agency Memorandum for The Director of Central Intelligence, 'Military Thought (USSR): Reconnaissance Indications of Preparation for a Surprise Attack by US Naval Carrier Strike Large Units', 3 June 1977, p. 4.

9   CIA Memorandum, 'Military Thought (USSR)', p. 4.

10 Polmar, et al., *Admiral Gorshkov*, p. 111.

11 CIA Memorandum for The Director of Central Intelligence, 'The Soviet Attack Submarine Force: Evolution and Operations', SR IM 71-11-S, September 1971, p. 1.

12 The 'SS' designator is NATO's shorthand for surface-to-surface, with the letter 'N' designating it is a naval SS missile.

13 Norman Friedman, *The Naval Institute's Guide to World Naval Weapons Systems* (Annapolis, Maryland: US Naval Institute Press, 1989), pp. 90–91.

14 Wikipedia, KS-1 Comet, https://en.m.wikipedia.org/wiki/KS-1_Komet. Obtained 31 March 2023.

15 'Reconnaissance Indications of Preparation for a Surprise Attack by US Naval Carrier Strike Large Units', *Military Thought (USSR)*. Found in CIA Intelligence Information Special Report, 3 June 1977, p. 14

16 *Military Thought (USSR)*, pp. 9–11.

17 The Soviet Space Program: National Intelligence Estimate, NIE 11-1-83S TS 833351, 19 July1983, CIA-RDP00B00369R000100050007-1, p. 13.

18 The Soviet Space Program, p. 13.

19 The US also had film-based space-based orbital systems that imaged Soviet naval facilities.

20 During his years in US Naval Intelligence, the author was well aware of Soviet RORSAT capabilities and limitations; The Soviet Space Program.

21 Wikipedia, 'Tupolev-Tu-42', https://en.m.wikipedia.org/wiki/Tupolev_Tu-142. Obtained 31 March 2023.

22 'American Shipbuilding Technology and the Soviet Merchant Marine, A Staff Study, Permanent Subcommittee On Investigations of the Committee On Government Operations, United States Senate' (Washington, DC: US Government Printing Office, 1975), p. 1.

23 Mr George Fedoroff's email to the author, 29 June 2020.

24 Fedoroff, 29 June 2020.

25 *Military Thought (USSR)*, p. 6.

26 Polmar, et al., *Admiral Gorshkov*, p. 112.

27 Robert Waring Herrick, *Soviet Naval Strategy: Fifty Years of Theory and Practice* (Annapolis, Maryland: US Naval Institute Press, 1968), pp. xxxii – xxxiii.

28 Norman Polmar and Edward Whitman, *Hunters and Killers Volume 2: Anti-Submarine Warfare from 1943* (Annapolis, Maryland: US Naval Institute Press, 2016), p. 88.

29 Owen R. Cote, Jr, *The Third Battle: Innovation in the US Navy's Silent Cold War Struggle with Soviet Submarines*, Naval War College, Newport Papers Number 16 (Newport, Rhode Island: Naval War College, 2003), p. 2.

30 Raymond V.B. Blackman (ed.), *Jane's Fighting Ships, 1971–1972* (New York: McGraw-Hill Book Company, 1971), p. 441. The Midway-class carriers were the first carriers, starting in 1949, to be modified as the first warships possessing a nuclear strike capability.

31 Polmar and Whitman, *Hunters and Killers*, p. 89.

32 The homing torpedo, using hydrophones to listen for a submarine's engines, was known as FIDO. For security purposes it was identified as the Mk 24 mine. 'FIDO', Wikipedia, 'Mark 24 Mine', https://en.wikipedia.org/wiki/Mark_24_mine. Obtained 2 July 2020.

Chapter 2

1 W. Carey, 'Evolution of Passive Towed Array Systems'. His paper was presented at a conference titled 'How Did We Get Here?', sponsored by the Acoustical Society of America, December 2001.

2 Carey, 'Evolution of Passive Towed Array Systems'.

3 Edward C. Whitman, 'SOSUS: The "Secret Weapon" of Undersea Surveillance', *Undersea Warfare Magazine*, Winter 2005, Vol. 7, No. 2.

4 Whitman, 'SOSUS'.

5 Whitman, 'SOSUS'.

6 Whitman, 'SOSUS'.

7 Whitman, 'SOSUS'.

8 Massachusetts Institute of Technology, Project HARTWELL, *A Report On Security of Overseas Transport*, Vol. 1 of 2. Contract No. N5 ora 07846, 21 September 1950, p. ii.

9 Massachusetts Institute of Technology, Project HARTWELL, p. 141.

10 Massachusetts Institute of Technology, Project HARTWELL, pp. 146–47.

11 Whitman, 'SOSUS'.

12 Whitman, 'SOSUS'.

13 AT&T's partners included Woods Hole, Scripps Institution and Columbia University's Hudson Laboratory; Whitman, 'SOSUS'.

14 Polmar and Whitman, *Hunters and Killers*, p. 125.

15 Polmar and Whitman, *Hunters and Killers*, p. 127.

16 Carey, 'Evolution of Passive Towed Array Systems'.

17 Carey, 'Evolution of Passive Towed Array Systems'.

18 Columbia University's Field Station at St David's was co-located with the Bermuda Sound Fixing and Ranging SOFAR Station, www.sofarbda.org/index.html. Obtained 23 July 2020.

19 Carey, 'Evolution of Passive Towed Array Systems'.

20 Carey, 'Evolution of Passive Towed Array Systems'.

21 Carey, 'Evolution of Passive Towed Array Systems'.

22 Carey, 'Evolution of Passive Towed Array Systems'.

23 The CNO at the time was Admiral Thomas H. Moorer, https://en.wikipedia.org/wiki/Chief_of_Naval_Operations. Obtained 25 July 2020.

24 Carey, 'Evolution of Passive Towed Array Systems'.

25 Carey, 'Evolution of Passive Towed Array Systems'.

Chapter 3

1 Dr Dudley's recollections from his email to the author, dated 18 May 2020.

2 Joseph Szep's recollections from his email to the author, dated 11 July 2022. Mr Szep served aboard the *Courtney* when it was homeported in Newport and prior to the DE's deployment to the Mediterranean.

3 Joseph Szep's email sent to the author, 15 July 2022.

4 Patricia Raub, 'Discover Beautiful Rhode Island': State Promotion of Tourism from 1927–2015, *Rhode Island History*, winter/spring 2017, Volume 75, Number 1, p. 4.

5 Jess Bidgood, 'Newport, a City That Loves Its Mansions, Shudders at Its Newest Ones', *The New York Times*, 4 December 2016.

6 https://12metercharters.com/about-us/sailing-history/newport-sailing

7 Raub, p. 9.

8 Joseph Szep's email sent to the author, 18 July 2022.

9 In the History of USS *Hammerberg* (DE-1015), Command History, Navy Department Office of the Chief of Naval Operation, Division of Naval History (OP-29), Ship's History Section, the DE "spent two and a half months in Newport while completing major repairs to her boilers".

10 Mr Edward Kerins, who as a young ensign straight from the Naval Academy, Class of 1967, was the *Hammerberg*'s Main Propulsion Assistant. He remembers that in the yard a large hole was cut in the DE's hull to pull out and replace what he remembers were the ship's evaporators. Telephone interview, 11 March 2021.

11 http://www.hazegray.org/danfs/escorts/de1028.htm

12 USS *Courtney* June 1970, Deck Log Book, NARA.

13 OPNAV Report 5740-1, Command History of Commander Escort Squadron Eight, Commanding Officer, USS *Cascade*, AD-16, AD16/00/MIN:dbt 5750 Ser: 282, Mar 7 1974.

14 USS *Courtney*, August 1970, Deck Log Book, NARA.

15 USS *Courtney*, 18 June 1970, Deck Log Book, NARA.

16 1970 Command History, USS *Lester*, DE-1022, 3 August 1971, NHHC.

17 1970 Command History, USS *Lester*.

18 'Sixth Fleet Command History 1970', Chronology Section, NARA; 1970 Command History, USS *Lester*, DE-1022, 3 August 1971, NHHC.

Chapter 4

1 United States Sixth Fleet, 'Sixth Fleet Command History 1970', Intelligence Section D-2-b, 24 March 1971.

2 Mostafa Salah and Baruch Boxer, 'Mediterranean Sea', *Encyclopaedia Britannica*, online edn (Chicago: Encyclopaedia Britannica Inc., 7 November 2016), https://www.britannica.com/place/Mediterranean-Sea. Obtained 28 January 2020.

3 Salah and Boxer, 'Mediterranean Sea'.

4 National Geographic, https://www.natgeomaps.com/hm-1982-mediterranean-seafloor-map. Obtained August 2020.

5 Salah and Boxer, 'Mediterranean Sea'.

6 Salah and Boxer, 'Mediterranean Sea'.

7 CIA Memorandum for Director of Central Intelligence, 'The Soviet Attack Submarine Force: Evolution and Operations'.

8 'Out-of-Area' is a term used by the US Navy describing those Soviet air, naval and naval auxiliaries operating beyond their home waters.

9 United States Sixth Fleet, 'Sixth Fleet Command History 1971', Section III-B-3, Anti-Submarine Warfare, NHHC.

10 Norman Polmar, *Guide to the Soviet Navy, Third Edition* (Annapolis, Maryland: US Naval Institute Press, 1983), p. 6.

11 Gaeta continues to be the homeport for Sixth Fleet's flagship. Maddalena was the port where a US Navy submarine tender was moored and provided support to deployed USN SSNs.

12 Polmar, *Guide to the Soviet Navy, Third Edition*, p. 6.

13 Polmar, *Guide to the Soviet Navy, Third Edition*, p. 102.

14 Polmar, *Guide to the Soviet Navy Fifth Edition*, p. 401.

15 The Juliett had to surface in order to activate its radar and fire its missiles.

16 Wikipedia, 'RPK-2 Vyuga', https://en.wikipedia.org/wiki/RPK-2_Vyuga. Obtained 14 August 2020.

17 Not included are the auxiliary ships – tankers, repair, submarine rescue and fresh water ships.

18 Norman Polmar, *Guide to the Soviet Navy, Fourth Edition* (Annapolis, Maryland: US Naval Institute Press, 1986), pp. 183–87.

19 Polmar, *Guide to the Soviet Navy Fourth Edition*, p. 450.

20 It was correctly assumed the NATO-designated SS-N-14 Silex was capable of striking surface ships as well as submarines with either a shape charged warhead for ships or a torpedo slung underneath its fuselage for either surface or submerged targets; https://en.wikipedia.org/wiki/Metel_Anti-Ship_Complex. Obtained 15 August 2020.

21 Wikipedia, 'S-125 Neva/Perchora'. The NATO-designated SA-N-1B Goa was a radar-guided SAM, possessing an effective range out to 14 miles. As with SAMs, the Goa could be targeted against surface ships. https://en.wikipedia.org/wiki/S-125_Neva/Pechora. Obtained 31 March 2023.

22 National Photographic Interpretation Center imagery analysis report, 'Soviet Primorye-Class Intelligence Collection Ships', December 1984. CIA-RDP85T00840R000100200001-5, declassified on 17 November 2010, p. 3.

23 The 'first salvo' assumes the fleet attacking first has the greatest chance of victory in any given tactical action. However, this requires the attacking force to possess superior operational intelligence capability through its organic and non-organic surveillance and reconnaissance sensors.

Chapter 5

1 USS *Courtney*, September 1970, Deck Log Book, NARA.

2 Image found in NavSource Naval History, http://www.navsource.org/archives/06/06021021.htm. Obtained 19 June 2021.

3 CDR Jack Flanagan, SC, USN Ret, wrote a paper to the author, titled 'USS *Lester*, DE-1022, 1 September 2020'. As supply officer to his DE, Jack provided a unique understanding of the logistic challenges facing CORTRON 8 ships while homeported in Naples.

4 'At Home Abroad – Or Homeporting Overseas', *All Hands*, The Bureau of Naval Personnel Career Publication (May 1973), Nav-Per-O, Number 676, pp. 8–9.

5 The DEs also received UNREP from Sixth Fleet oilers or they pulled into Augusta Bay, Sicily, to take on fuel.

6 The tailships were never designed to accommodate such capabilities.

7 Flanagan's paper to the author.

8 In addition to the DEs and *Cascade* homeported in Naples, there were four patrol gunboats (PGs) of the Asheville class, together with their tender, the converted Landing Ship Tank (LST) USS *Graham County*, AGP-1176, in September 1972. Captain Peter L. McCammon, USN Ret, *Homeport Naples: USS Graham County (AGP 1176) in the Mediterranean, September 1972 to July 1974* (San Francisco: Blurb creative publishing service, second printing, 2008).

9 United States Sixth Fleet, 'Sixth Fleet Command History 1971', Section IV Logistics, Section G, Maintenance of Forward Deployed Ships, paragraph 4, NHHC.

10 The author had an apartment overlooking the NSA compound and would take a local bus first thing in the morning, arriving at Fleet Landing just before 0700 hours. On the way back in the afternoon, travel would often take 60 minutes or more.

11 The park was named after Vice Admiral Robert Carney, USN, who was CinC, Allied Forces Southern Europe (AFSOUTH) 1951–53. He later became Chief of Naval Operations. Carney Park continues to be a recreational park for US service personnel and families living in Naples. Wikipedia, 'Robert Carney', https://en.wikipedia.org/wiki/Robert_Carney. Obtained 20 April 2021.

12 A few CORTRON 8 families had children born at the hospital.

13 'At Home Abroad – Or Homeporting Overseas', *All Hands*, pp. 8–9.

14 Santore, John, *Modern Naples: A Documentary History, 1799–1999* (New York: Italica Press, 2001), p. XXXII.

15 Santore, *Modern Naples*, p. 245.

16 Sanatore, *Modern Naples*, p. 261.

17 CDR Jack Flanagan, USN SC Ret, *Recollection of some significant moments as supply officer USS Lester (DE-1022), March 1972 to December 1973*, 1 December 2020. According to Flanagan, the NSA Housing Assistance Office suffered periodic problems of employees being 'on the take' to steer Americans to favoured landlords. Likewise, you might find that a seemingly inexpensive or 'great for the price' residence that was being recommended was in either a high-crime area or an area that was openly hostile to Americans.

18 Flanagan remembers: "On *Lester*, officers and crew that had residences ashore were scattered all over the metropolitan area of Naples. This made for great difficulties communicating among dependents. Remember, this was the time of no terrestrial phone lines in these residences, no cell phones, no internet, etc."

19 David Silverthorn, email sent to the author from a former *Courtney* sailor, 6 July 2020.

20 Electronics Technician First Class (ET1) Richard Eriksson, USN email dated 5 December 2009. Eriksson prolonged his stay in Naples because he obtained a transfer to the *Lester* prior to *Van Voorhis*' return to the US.

21 Steve Magistro wrote to the author in an email dated 2 May 2021.

22 Steve Kendall's email to the author, dated 2 May 2021.

23 Jack Flanagan, SC USN Ret; remembrances of his time as the supply officer onboard USS *Lester*, DE-1022.

24 Stephen Edwards' email sent to the author on 29 December 2020.

25 Claire Kelso, 'Thoughts on Naples, Italy, June 1971', 28 July 2022.

26 Jim Haddock, Captain, USN Ret., Monograph 'My take on USS *Lester* and Cortron 8', 12 December 2020.

27 Haddock, Monograph.

28 OT3 Jim Whyte, 'Memories from time onboard USS *Lester* (March 1972 – December 1973', 28 March 2021.

29 OT3 Jim Whyte, 'Memories from time onboard USS *Lester* (March 1972 – December 1973', 28 March 2021.

30 McCammon, *Homeport Naples: USS Graham County (AGP 1176) in the Mediterranean, September 1972 to July 1974*, p. 25.

31 McCammon, *Homeport Naples: USS Graham County*, p. 25.

32 F. De Lorenzo, G. Manzillo, M. Soscia, and G.G. Balestrier, 'Epidemic Of Cholera El Tor In Naples, 1973', *The Lancet*, 13 April 1974, DOI: https//doi.org/10.1016/S0140-6736(74)93214-0.

33 Edwards' email sent to the author, 29 December 2020.

34 Kelso, 'Thoughts on Naples, Italy'.

35 Kelso, 'Thoughts on Naples, Italy'.

Chapter 6

1   Comments by VADM Wendt at his change of command, 28 August 1970, as reported by Michael McGuire, *Chicago Tribune*, 29 August 1970; United States Sixth Fleet, 'Sixth Fleet Command History 1970', Section E, Public Affairs, NHHC.

2   United States Sixth Fleet, 'Sixth Fleet Command History 1970', Section D, Intelligence, D-1, 24 March 1971, NHHC.

3   The force level increase was due to the largest Soviet Navy peacetime fleet exercise, called *Okean* (Ocean), which occurred in April and May 1970. As a global exercise, it involved 84 warships, approximately 80 submarines (15 nuclear) and 45 naval auxiliaries, including intelligence collection ships. Additionally, it involved hundreds of aircraft. See US Naval Institute, Proceedings, 'Okean Massive Soviet Exercise: 50 Years Later', https://www.usni.org/magazines/proceedings/2020/april/okean-massive-soviet-exercise-50-years-later. Obtained 31 March 2023.

4   United States Sixth Fleet, 'Sixth Fleet Command History 1970', Section D Intelligence, D-2-b, 24 March 1971, NHHC.

5   US Sixth Fleet, 'Sixth Fleet Command History', Section D, 1970.

6   US Sixth Fleet, 'Sixth Fleet Command History 1970'.

7   United States Sixth Fleet, 'Sixth Fleet Command History 1970', Intelligence Section D-2-i, March 1971, NHHC.

8   Deep Storm website.

9   Deep Storm.

10 United States Sixth Fleet, 'Sixth Fleet Command History 1970', Intelligence Section D-5-a, March 1971, NARA.

11 Ford, Christopher Ford and Rosenberg, David, *The Admirals' Advantage: US Navy Operational Intelligence in World War II and the Cold War* (Annapolis, Maryland: US Naval Institute Press, 2005), p. 56.

12 Ford and Rosenberg, *The Admirals' Advantage*.

13 Ford and Rosenberg, *The Admirals' Advantage*.

14 Classic Bullseye was the name for the DoD worldwide HF/DF stations consisting of an AN/FRD-10 circularly arranged antenna array. They detected RF signals emitting from aircraft, surface ships and surfaced submarines. With more than one station detecting a signal, it was possible to determine a line of bearing and triangulate the location of the emitter. One such station was located at the US Naval Base, Rota, Spain.

15 Desmond Ball and Richard Tanter, *The Tools of Owatatsumi: Japan's Ocean Surveillance and Coastal Defence capabilities* (Canberra, Australia: ANU Press, The Australian National University 2015).

16 Ford and Rosenberg, *The Admirals' Advantage*, pp. 56–57.

17 Ford and Rosenberg, *The Admirals' Advantage*, p. 57.

18 United States Sixth Fleet, 'Sixth Fleet Command History 1970', Intelligence Section D-2-a, 24 March 1971, NHHC.

19 Wikipedia, 'Mediterranean Climate', https://en.wikipedia.org/wiki/Mediterranean_climate.

20 Alex Kucherov, interview with COMSIXTHFLT (Vice Admiral Isaac C. Kidd, Jr, USN), *U.S. News and World Report*, 8 July 1971; United States Sixth Fleet, 'Sixth Fleet Command History 1971', Section VIII Public Affairs, Appendix VIII-A, NHHC.

21 US Sixth Fleet, 'Sixth Fleet Command History 1971', Section VIII Public Affairs, Appendix VIII-A.

22 US Sixth Fleet, 'Sixth Fleet Command History 1971', Section VIII Public Affairs, Appendix VIII-A.

23 US Sixth Fleet, 'Sixth Fleet Command History 1971', Section VIII Public Affairs, Appendix VIII-A.

24 *Courtney* Oceanographic Technician Chief Senior Ralph Rooney, email to the author, dated 18 September 2004. He wrote: "The ITASS suite definitely had reliability problems."

25 Wikipedia, 'Mediterranean Climate'.

26 Lyle J. Goldstein and Yuri M. Zhukov, 'A Tale of Two Fleets', *Naval War College Review*, Newport, Rhode Island. This information was obtained from an article written by I.V. Kasatonov, *Flot vyhodit v okean* (*The fleet is going to the ocean*) (St Petersburg: Astra-Lyuks, 1995), p. 269.

27 Captain Eugene Razzetti, USN Ret, email to the author, 22 April 2020. Razzetti was Chief of Staff to Commander, Escort Squadron 8, 1971–73.

28 Razzetti.

29 Razzetti.

30 The Radio Collective Call Sign was 'Argentina' and an individual aircraft call sign would have a number, such as 'Argentina two, three' (23).

31 The Radio Collective Call Sign was 'Neckware' and the individual aircraft call sign would have a number assigned, such as 'Neckware one, two' (12).

32 In 1972, the Commander of COMCORTRON 8, (then) Commander Virgil Snyder, USN, initiated an exchange/liaison programme with CTF 67 for himself and his chief staff officer to fly missions on a P-3, while a P-3 Tactical Officer would sail with one of the tailships. That was usually the squadron's flagship, *Courtney*.

33 Rooney's email to the author.

34 Wikipedia, 'USS Wasp (CV-18) 1968–1970', https://en.wikipedia.org/wiki/USS_Wasp_(CV-18)#1968–1970. Obtained on 26 September 2020.

Chapter 7

1   USS *Threadfin*, October 1970 Deck Log Book, NARA.

2   According to the Sixth Fleet's command history for 1970, a single nuclear fast attack submarine was operating in the Mediterranean at the time, the USS *Tulibee*, SSN-597. It could have been a cooperative target for the tailships.

3   *Threadfin's* log entry 0000-0400, 2 October stated, "underway submerged operating in company with USS *Hammerberg* (DE1015) and USS *Courtney* (DE1021) in accordance with CTF 69 MOVORD 105-70".

4   USS *Threadfin*, October 1970, Deck Log Book, NARA.

5   USS *Threadfin*, October 1970.

6   NHHC, S.P. Lee II (AGS-31), https://www.history.navy.mil/research/histories/ship-histories/danfs/s/s-p-lee-ags-31.html.

7   At night, many of these tiny fishing boats showed a small white light that bobbled about as the boat rolled with the waves. It did not dawn on those on the bridge that the fishermen would see the oncoming warship.

8   The author, as one of the *Courtney's* CIC watch supervisors, experienced passing through the Strait of Messina at night too many times to count.

9   USS *Van Voorhis*, October 1970 Deck Log Book, NARA.

10 USS *Van Voorhis*, October 1970.

11 USS *Van Voorhis*, October 1970.

12 USS *Andrew Jackson*, October 1970 Deck Log Book, NARA.

13 USS *Andrew Jackson*, October 1970.

14 USS *Andrew Jackson*, October 1970.

15 Captain Eugene Razzetti, USN Ret, email to the author on 16 November 2020; his response to my question was that he was aware that SSBNs operated in the Med. He stated: "I was a COMSIXTHFLT Flag Plot Watch Officer [June 1973–June 1975]. But: who they were, where they were, and what they were doing was 'Compartmented'. Only our senior staff officers followed their movements. Our staff submariner kept a separate (folding) Med chart, based on TS back channel traffic. He would brief the

Admiral in his cabin, or in Flag Plot after those of us with no need to know were sent out."

16 John M. Hightower (AP), 'NATO May Get Mediterranean Polaris Subs', *Washington Post*, Sunday, 3 February 1963, P.A10. The author thanks Mr Norman Polmar for a copy of the article.

17 Eliot, George Fielding, 'Polaris in the Mediterranean', *The Army Times*, 23 February 1963, p. 14.

18 Dominic Johnson and Dominic Tierney, *Failing to Win: Perceptions of Victory and Defeat* (Boston: Harvard University Press, 2006), p. 96.

19 United States Sixth Fleet, 'Sixth Fleet Command History', Chronology Section, 1970, NHHC.

20 USS *Van Voorhis*, October 1970.

21 The author's diary expressed frustration that it took several months for his ship to minimize the use of the two unique radars. By July 1971, the ships did practice routine emissions control.

22 As noted in Chapter 4, intelligence assumed Soviet Foxtrots would be operating between Crete and Libya in order to report on Sixth Fleet carrier battle groups transiting to and from the eastern Mediterranean.

23 USS *John F. Kennedy*, CVA-67, October 1970, Deck Log Book, NARA.

24 United States Sixth Fleet, 'Sixth Fleet Command History 1970', Section B, Operations, subsection 3a Surface, NHHC.

25 A MODLOC is an Acronym for Miscellaneous Operational Details, Local Operations limited to established fleet operating areas. Surface Warfare Officers School, 'Depart Head Combat Systems, Newport, Rhode Island, Information Sheet, Movement Reports, 2/96', https://man.fas.org/dod-101/navy/docs/swos/ops/72-7.html. Obtained on 27 August 2022.

26 USS *Courtney*, October 1970, Deck Log Book, NARA.

27 USS *Courtney*, October 1970.

28 USS *Courtney*, October 1970.

29 USS *Clamagore*, SS-343, November 1970, Deck Log, NARA.

30 OT2 Harry Jones email to the author, 15 March 2022. Jones served aboard both the *Van Voorhis* and the *Lester* between 1970 and 1972.

31 USS *Courtney*, November 1970, and USS *Van Voorhis*, November 1970, Deck Log Books, NARA.

32 USS *Clamagore*, November 1970, Deck Log Book, NARA.

33 USS *Clamagore*, November 1970.

34 USS *Clamagore*, November 1970.

35 USS *Van Voorhis*, November 1970, Deck Log Book, NARA.

36 The date was provided in an email by CDR Jack Flanagan, SC USN Ret, former supply officer of the USS *Lester*. It was confirmed by USS *Lester*, November 1970, Deck Log Book, NARA.

37 Master Chief Oceanographic Specialist Technician John Ellis, USN Ret, email to the author, 19 July 2022.

38 USS *Cutlass*, November 1970, Deck Log Book, NARA.

39 *Lester* was operating within a box south of Sardinia. Author's calculations based upon *Lester*'s December 1970 Deck Log Book, NARA.

40 USS *Lapon*, December 1970, Deck Log Book, NARA

Chapter 8

1 Kucherov, interview with COMSIXTHFLT (Vice Admiral Isaac C. Kidd, Jr, USN), *US News and World Report*.

2 US Sixth Fleet, 'Sixth Fleet Command History 1971', Section VI Intelligence, 1972, NHHC.

3 See Soviet Fifth *Eskadra* OOB as composed from the author's diary.

4 US Sixth Fleet, 'Sixth Fleet Command History 1971', Section VI Intelligence.

5 US Sixth Fleet, 'Sixth Fleet Command History 1971', Section VI Intelligence.

6 US Sixth Fleet, 'Sixth Fleet Command History 1971', Section VI, Intelligence.

7 Deep Storm website, www.deepstorm.ru. Obtained 22 October 2022.

8 Deep Storm.

9 "Escort Squadron Eight began ASW tests in the Western Mediterranean." It is safe to assume this was another 'special hydrographic operation'. 'Escort Squadron Eight Command History 1971', NHHC.

10 Harry Jones email to the author, 15 March 2022.

11 USS *Courtney*, January 1971 Deck Log Book, NARA.

12 The Rhone Fan (named after France's Rhone River) "is a large Plio-Pleistocene turbidite deposit … the fan is fed from the broad Rhone River delta … The Rhone Fan is elongated in a rough north–south direction." Normark, William R., Barnes, Neal E. and Coumes, Francis, 'Rhone Fan, Mediterranean', Submarine Fans and Related Turbidite Systems, (ed Arnold H. Bouma, W.R. Normark and N.E. Barnes), *Frontiers in Sedimentary Geology* (New York: Springer-Verlag, 1985), pp. 151–56.

13 US Sixth Fleet, 'Sixth Fleet Command History 1971', Section I, Chronology NHHC.

14 US Sixth Fleet, 'Sixth Fleet Command History 1971', Section III, Operations, NHHC.

15 USS *Courtney*, January 1971 Deck Log Book, NARA.

16 Deep Storm; these were K-147 and K-323.

17 USS *Courtney*, February 1971 Deck Log Book, NARA.

18 US Sixth Fleet, 'Sixth Fleet Command History 1971', Section I, Chronology, NHHC.

19 *Grand Canyon* was replaced by the USS *Cascade*, AD-16. *Cascade* would be the 'Mother Hen' during the rest of the squadron's Mediterranean deployment.

20 USS *Courtney*, March 1971 Deck Log Book, NARA.

21 US Sixth Fleet, 'Sixth Fleet Command History 1971', Section I, Chronology, NHHC.

22 Deep Storm; at this time there were only five Foxtrot submarines and one Juliett.

23 Kucherov, interview with COMSIXTHFLT (Vice Admiral Isaac C. Kidd, Jr, USN), *US News and World Report*.

24 'Command History Escort Squadron Eight 1971', NHHC.

25 Rooney's email to the author.

26 *Courtney* and *Lester* participated in the NATO Exercise Dawn Patrol 71 in the Tyrrhenian Sea 28–30 April. USS *Springfield*, April 1971 Deck Log Book, NARA.

27 Deep Storm.

28 US Sixth Fleet, 'Sixth Fleet Command History 1971', Section I Chronology, p. 8, NHHC.

29 Deep Storm.

30 US Sixth Fleet, 'Sixth Fleet Command History 1971', Section I Chronology, pp. 9–12.

31 Derived from the author's notebook and nautical chart.

32 Derived from the author's notebook and nautical chart.

Chapter 9

1 US Sixth Fleet, 'Sixth Fleet Command History 1972', Section VI Intelligence, p.VI-1.

2 US Sixth Fleet, 'Sixth Fleet Command History 1972', Section VI Intelligence, p.VI-1. 'Inchopping' refers to a ship/sub/aircraft entering a different area of operations and being placed under the operational control of the new command. For example, when a ship under control of the Second Fleet passed into the

Mediterranean, it had Inchopped and would then be under the control of Sixth Fleet. 'Outchopping' is the opposite of this.

3   US Sixth Fleet, 'Sixth Fleet Command History 1972', Section VI Intelligence, p.VI-1.

4   US Sixth Fleet, 'Sixth Fleet Command History 1972', Section III Operations, p.III-4, NHHC.

5   Author's diary, 3–10 February 1972.

6   United States Sixth Fleet, 'Sixth Fleet Command History 1972', Section I, Command History Chronology, 1 January to 31 December 1972, NHHC.

7   The author learned of this after he was assigned to the Office of Naval Intelligence in the late 1970s as a Mediterranean Desk watch officer.

8   Relating that incident during his interview with the author, Captain Spruell said he received a complement from the *Leningrad* on his ship-handling skills.

9   Polmar, *Guide to the Soviet Navy*, Fourth Edition, p. 9.

10 Polmar, *Guide to the Soviet Navy*, Third Edition, p. 363.

11 Norman Polmar, and K.J. Moore, *Cold War Submarines: The Design and Construction of US and Soviet Submarines* (Potomac Books, 2004), p. 113.

12 Author's diary.

13 'Cryptologic Almanac 50th Anniversary Series (U) The Widowmaker: SIGINT and Submarine K-19', Derived from: NSA/CSS Manual 123-2. Dated 24 Feb 1998, DOCID: 4110868.

14 US Sixth Fleet, 'Sixth Fleet Command History 1972', Intelligence, p.VI-3.

15 According to www.deepstorm.ru, these submarines were, Foxtrots B-26, B-31, B-94, B-98, B-409 and B-416. Juliett K-318 also entered the Mediterranean.

16 *Courtney*'s May 1972, Deck Log Book, NARA. It should be noted that in the intelligence section of Sixth Fleet's 1972 history, there is no mention that this transfer of Soviet submarines occurred in May.

17 Not possessing *Hammerberg*'s deck log, one can only assume that she mirrored *Courtney*'s track.

18 *Courtney*'s May 1972 Deck Log Book, NARA. This was probably Juliett K-318.

19 *Courtney*'s May 1972 Deck Log Book, NARA.

20 *Courtney*'s July 1972 Deck Log Book, NARA.

21 *Courtney*, July 1972.

22 *Courtney*, July 1972.

23 Author's diary.

24 Author's diary.

25 Email to the author from CDR Mark D. Tabing, USN Ret, 28 July 2023.

26 Author's diary.

27 The author, who at the time was *Courtney*'s CIC Watch Supervisor, heard over his sound-powered phones, the sonarman yelling 'high speed props bearing 350'. All within the sonar shack panicked, as they though the Russian had fired a torpedo. But they were kept in the compartment by the senior chief sonarman, who kept the door closed, yelling expletives at them to stay at their stations.

28 *Courtney*'s July 1972 Deck Log Book, NARA

29 Solomon, Louis P., *Transparent Oceans: The Defeat of the Soviet Submarine Force* (Bethesda, Maryland: Pearl River Publishing, 2015), pp. 61–62.

30 Solomon, *Transparent Oceans*, p. 61.

31 Solomon, *Transparent Oceans*, pp. 60–61.

32 Solomon, *Transparent Oceans*, p. 63.

33 Solomon, *Transparent Oceans*, p. 63.

34 Solomon, *Transparent Oceans*, p. 63.

35 Solomon, *Transparent Oceans*, p. 63.

36 IUSS Caesar Alumni Association, 'Brawdy American Naval Facility', https://www.iusscaa.org/art26.pdf. Obtained on 22 December 2021.

37 Solomon, *Transparent Oceans*, p. 64.

38 United States Sixth Fleet, 'Sixth Fleet Command History 1972', Section VI, Intelligence, p. VI-3.

39 National Public Radio, 'Munich Olympics Massacre', https://www.npr.org/2022/09/04/1116641214/munich-olympics-massacre-hostage-terrorism-israel-germany.

40 *Courtney*s September 1972 Deck Log Book, NARA. The reason for this test is unknown. It could have been a follow-up to the August test in the Atlantic that validated the technique that ascertained the directionality of the noise field using two towed arrays.

41 *Courtney*'s October 1972 Deck Log Book, NARA.

42 *Courtney*'s October 1972 Deck Log Book.

43 National Public Radio, 'Munich Olympics'.

44 US Sixth Fleet, 'Sixth Fleet Command History 1972', Section VI, Intelligence, p. VI-3.

45 Six Fleet Command History 1972, Section I, Calendar, pp. I-1 through I-14.

46 Sixth Fleet Command History 1972, Section VI, Intelligence, p. VI-3.

47 Haddock, Monograph.

48 '1973 Command History, US Sixth Fleet and Naval Striking and Support Forces Southern Europe', 28 February 1974, Section VI Intelligence, p. VI-1. NHHC.

49 'At Home Abroad – Or Homeporting Overseas', *All Hands*, p. 9.

50 Flanagan, *Recollection*.

51 Haddock, Monograph.

52 Haddock, Monograph.

53 '1973 Command History, US Sixth Fleet and Naval Striking and Support Forces Southern Europe', 28 February 1974, Section III Operations, p. III-10, NHHC.

Chapter 10

1   IUSS *Caesar* Alumni Association, 'An Unofficial History of The Surveillance Towed Array Sensor System (SURTASS) 1972–2015', https://www.iusscaa.org/articles/surtass_history.pdf.

2   Polmar and Moore, *Cold War Submarines*, p. 173.

3   Polmar and Moore, *Cold War Submarines*, p. 185.

4   Owen R. Cote Jr, 'The Third Battle: Innovation in the US Navy's Silent Cold War Struggle with Soviet Submarines', Newport Paper Number 16 (Newport, Rhode Island: Naval War College, 2003).

5   Polmar and Moore, *Cold War Submarines*, p. 286.

6   Bi-static sonar is a sonar configuration in which the sonar transmitter and receiver platforms are separated at a considerable distance.

7   'An Unofficial History of SURTASS'.

8   Japanese Maritime Defense Force acquired a single SURTASS to equip its own purpose-built SWATH ship.

9   Congressional Research Service, TAGOS(X) Ocean Surveillance Shipbuilding Program: Background and Issues for Congress, https://crsreports.congress.gov/product/pdf/IF/IF11838/12. Obtained 1 March 2023.

10 M. Lasky, R.D. Dolittle, B.D. Simmons, and S.G. Lemon, 'Recent progress in towed hydrophone array research', IEEE Journal of Oceanic Engineering, Volume 29, Issue: 2 (April 2004), pp. 374–87.

11 Naval History and Heritage Command, 'Brontstein II *FF-10370', https://www.history.navy.mil/content/history/nhhc/research/histories/ship-histories/danfs/b/bronstein-ii.html.

12 Naval History and Heritage Command, 'Brontstein II *FF-1037'.

13 Edward H.Lundquist, 'Bronstein-class Escorts Introduced New Sensors and Weapons', *Defense Media Network*, 30 November 2016, https://www.defensemedianetwork.com/stories/bronstein-class-escorts-introduced-new-sensors-and-weapons/.

14 Polmar and Moore, *Cold War Submarines*, p. 171.

15 Lundquist, 'Bronstein-class Escorts Introduced New Sensors and Weapons'.

16 Polmar and Moore, *Cold War Submarines*, p. 160.

17 Polmar and Moore, *Cold War Submarines*, p. 159.

18 Lundquist, 'Bronstein-class Escorts Introduced New Sensors and Weapons'.

19 Captain William Steagall, USN Ret, email to the author 2 February 2023: "As an ensign, I reported aboard [*Albert David*] in December 1974. The TASS was already installed. We would operate with the USS *Sample*."

20 America's Navy, 'AN/SQQ-89(V) Undersea Warfare/Anti-Submarine Combat System', https://www.navy.mil/Resources/Fact-Files/Display-FactFiles/Article/2166784/ansqq-89v-undersea-warfare-anti-submarine-warfare-combat-system/. Obtained 15 January 2023.

21 Military Aerospace Electronics, 'Navy Says Lockheed Martin to Build AN/SQQ-89 Shipboard Anti-Submarine Warfare (ASW) and counter-mine systems', https://www.militaryaerospace.com/sensors/article/14169960/shipboard-antisubmarine-warfare-asw-countermine. Obtained 15 January 2023.

22 AN/SQQ-89A(V)15 Integrated Undersea Warfare (USW) Combat System Suite, https://www.dote.osd.mil/Portals/97/pub/reports/FY2013/navy/2013ansqq89a.pdf?ver=2019-08-22-111213-517. Obtained 14 March 2023.

Chapter 11

1 Flanagan recounted the meeting with Admiral Weschler in an email to the author on Saturday, 27 June 2021.

2 Stillwell, Paul, *The Reminiscences of Vice Admiral Thomas R. Weschler, USN (Retired)*, Volume II (Annapolis, Maryland: US Naval Institute Press, 1995), p. 785.

3 Stillwell, *Reminiscences of Vice Admiral Thomas R. Weschler*, p. 665.

4 Stillwell, *Reminiscences of Vice Admiral Thomas R. Weschler*, p. 785.

5 Lasky, Dolittle, Simmons and Lemon.

ABOUT THE AUTHOR

Captain John Rodgaard, USN (Ret.) has 41 years in the US Navy, with 29 years as a naval intelligence officer. His published works are *A Call To The Sea: Captain Charles Stewart of The USS Constitution*; *A Hard Fought Ship: The Story of HMS Venomous*, and *From Across the Sea: North Americans In Nelson's Navy*. He is a recipient of the Naval Institute's History Author of the Year. He has contributed numerous articles/reviews to maritime/naval history periodicals. He co-edits The 1805 Club's The Trafalgar Chronicle. Rodgaard holds an A.B. in History and Political Science; an M.A. in Political Science, and is a 1994 Naval War College graduate.

John Rodgaard has captured a significant episode of the Cold War detailing the complexity of confronting the Soviet Navy at its apex of combat power in a way that brings great credit to those he served with on the pointy end of the spear. *Tailships* truly puts the pieces together on what tools were employed to make the playing field against the 5th Eskadra as uneven as possible. A must read book for operational personnel serving today.

David Winkler, PhD
Editor of *Naval History* book reviews
Author *Cold War at Sea*

Rodgaard offers a fascinating and detailed chronicle of the three little ships that led a revolution in undersea warfare during the Cold War. This book is a technological, operational, and human history of how navies adapt and innovate in a challenging maritime world.

Dr. Benjamin "BJ" Armstrong,
author of *Naval Presence and the Interwar US Navy and Marine Corps:
Forward Deployment, Crisis Response, and the Tyranny of History*

Few today remember the existential nature of the Cold War, when the U.S. and Soviet navies were constantly eyeball-eyeball in a hair-trigger environment where one ill-advised move could result in hostilities leading to potential nuclear war. In "Tailships," the author masterfully tells the story of the see-saw "battle" between stealthy Soviet submarines and American technological advances trying to track them. It is well-worth the read for anyone seeking to better understand that perilous time.

Sam Cox
Rear Admiral, U.S. Navy (Ret.)
Former Commander of the Office of Naval Intelligence